NUCLEAR WAR

Opposing Viewpoints

NUCLEAR WAR

Opposing Viewpoints

David L. Bender & Bruno Leone, *Series Editors*

Bonnie Szumski, *Book Editor*

OPPOSING VIEWPOINTS SERIES ®

Greenhaven Press

577 Shoreview Park Road
St. Paul, Minnesota 55126

Library of Congress Cataloging-in-Publication Data
Main entry under title:

Nuclear war.

  (Opposing viewpoints series)
  Bibliography: p.
  Includes index.
    1. Nuclear   warfare—Addresses,   essays,   lectures.
I. Szumski, Bonnie, 1958-   . II. Series.
U263.N7787 1985   355'.0217   85-14799
  ISBN 0-89908-353-6 (pbk.)
  ISBN 0-89908-378-1 (lib. bdg.)

"Congress shall make no law...
abridging the freedom of speech,
or of the press."

first amendment to the U.S. Constitution

The basic foundation of our democracy is the first amendment
guarantee of freedom of expression. The *Opposing Viewpoints
Series* is dedicated to the concept of this basic freedom and the
idea that it is more important to practice it than to enshrine it.

Contents

Why Consider Opposing Viewpoints?

"It is better to debate a question without settling it than to settle a question without debating it."

Joseph Joubert (1754-1824)

The Importance of Examining Opposing Viewpoints

The purpose of the Opposing Viewpoints Series, and this book in particular, is to present balanced, and often difficult to find, opposing points of view on complex and sensitive issues.

Probably the best way to become informed is to analyze the positions of those who are regarded as experts and well studied on issues. It is important to consider every variety of opinion in an attempt to determine the truth. Opinions from the mainstream of society should be examined. But also important are opinions that are considered radical, reactionary, or minority as well as those stigmatized by some other uncomplimentary label. An important lesson of history is the eventual acceptance of many unpopular and even despised opinions. The ideas of Socrates, Jesus, and Galileo are good examples of this.

Readers will approach this book with their own opinions on the issues debated within it. However, to have a good grasp of one's own viewpoint, it is necessary to understand the arguments of those with whom one disagrees. It can be said that those who do not completely understand their adversary's point of view do not fully understand their own.

A persuasive case for considering opposing viewpoints has been presented by John Stuart Mill in his work *On Liberty*. When examining controversial issues it may be helpful to reflect on his suggestion:

> The only way in which a human being can make some approach to knowing the whole of a subject, is by hearing what can be said about it by persons of every variety of opinion, and studying all modes in which it can be looked at by every character of mind. No wise man ever acquired his wisdom in any mode but this.

Analyzing Sources of Information

The Opposing Viewpoints Series includes diverse materials taken from magazines, journals, books, and newspapers, as well as statements and position papers from a wide range of individuals, organizations and governments. This broad spectrum of sources helps to develop patterns of thinking which are open to the consideration of a variety of opinions.

Pitfalls to Avoid

A pitfall to avoid in considering opposing points of view is that of regarding one's own opinion as being common sense and the most rational stance and the point of view of others as being only opinion and naturally wrong. It may be that another's opinion is correct and one's own is in error.

Another pitfall to avoid is that of closing one's mind to the opinions of those with whom one disagrees. The best way to approach a dialogue is to make one's primary purpose that of understanding the mind and arguments of the other person and not that of enlightening him or her with one's own solutions. More can be learned by listening than speaking.

It is my hope that after reading this book the reader will have a deeper understanding of the issues debated and will appreciate the complexity of even seemingly simple issues on which good and honest people disagree. This awareness is particularly important in a democratic society such as ours where people enter into public debate to determine the common good. Those with whom one disagrees should not necessarily be regarded as enemies, but perhaps simply as people who suggest different paths to a common goal.

Developing Basic Reading and Thinking Skills

In this book carefully edited opposing viewpoints are purposely placed back to back to create a running debate; each viewpoint is preceded by a short quotation that best expresses the author's main argument. This format instantly plunges the reader into the midst of a controversial issue and greatly aids that reader in mastering the basic skill of recognizing an author's point of view.

A number of basic skills for critical thinking are practiced in the activities that appear throughout the books in the series. Some of the skills are:

Evaluating Sources of Information The ability to choose from among alternative sources the most reliable and accurate source in relation to a given subject.

Separating Fact from Opinion The ability to make the basic distinction between factual statements (those that can be demonstrated or verified empirically) and statements of opinion (those that are beliefs or attitudes that cannot be proved).

Identifying Stereotypes The ability to identify oversimplified, exaggerated descriptions (favorable or unfavorable) about people and insulting statements about racial, religious or national groups, based upon misinformation or lack of information.

Recognizing Ethnocentrism The ability to recognize attitudes or opinions that express the view that one's own race, culture, or group is inherently superior, or those attitudes that judge another culture or group in terms of one's own.

It is important to consider opposing viewpoints and equally important to be able to critically analyze those viewpoints. The activities in this book are designed to help the reader master these thinking skills. Statements are taken from the book's viewpoints and the reader is asked to analyze them. This technique aids the reader in developing skills that not only can be applied to the viewpoints in this book, but also to situations where opinionated spokespersons comment on controversial issues. Although the activities are helpful to the solitary reader, they are most useful when the reader can benefit from the interaction of group discussion.

Using this book and others in the series should help readers develop basic reading and thinking skills. These skills should improve the reader's ability to understand what they read. Readers should be better able to separate fact from opinion, substance from rhetoric and become better consumers of information in our media-centered culture.

This volume of the Opposing Viewpoints Series does not advocate a particular point of view. Quite the contrary! The very nature of the book leaves it to the reader to formulate the opinions he or she find most suitable. My purpose as publisher is to see that this is made possible by offering a wide range of viewpoints which are fairly presented.

David L. Bender
Publisher

Introduction

"The unleashed power of the atom bomb has changed everything...and we thus drift toward unparalleled catastrophe."

Albert Einstein

In his book, *Weapons and Hope*, Freeman Dyson suggests that new weapons have traditionally provided nations with hope for winning wars. It was the hope of ending World War II that partially motivated the group of scientists in Los Alamos to develop the most powerful weapon of all, the atom bomb. While the "bomb" did indeed end the war, the victory was shrouded by inexpressible human tragedy and the knowledge that the world would never be the same. For many, the bomb blasts signalled the end of hope. After the devastation of Nagasaki and Hiroshima, no one could doubt that a nuclear war would be an "unparalleled catastrophe." Yet, despite the threat of unlimited destruction, America's national defense priorities have not changed. The dilemma of how the nation can remain safe and prepared for war, when, according to the Defense Department, a war fought with nuclear weapons would mean 100 million casualties, remains a bitter controversy.

Colin S. Gray, president of the National Institute for Public Policy, believes that "the United States must possess the ability to wage war rationally." He and others stress that, in spite of the incalculable destructive power of nuclear weapons, nuclear war is not fundamentally different from other wars. The US must have some type of nuclear war plan, just as it should for conventional weapons. These experts believe that nuclear war calls for a different kind of strategic plan, but that national security makes it imperative that the US have ways of using nuclear weapons effectively. Presently, both America and the Soviet Union have such plans. Their existence, however, does not eliminate the controversy over their necessity.

Critics of plans for the strategic use of nuclear weapons would agree with prominent author Jonathan Schell who believes that such plans are "a vain hope." These critics argue that any use of nuclear weapons would lead to untold destruction, calamitous climate changes, and massive radiation sickness. These people theorize that the only way to preserve our national security is through prevention. Arms control agreements, Soviet/American cooperation to prevent nuclear weapons from reaching Third World nations, and unilateral measures on the part of the US to reduce weapons are the only ways to "use" nuclear weapons.

One thing is certain: an all-out nuclear war between the US and the USSR would wreak untold devastation in both countries, and would probably severely affect the rest of the world as well. In the final scene in the popular film *WarGames*, a computer is asked to imagine the outcome of a nuclear war and determine a "winner." After playing out several fictitious wars on its screen, the computer flashes the words, "There is no winner." While there is a chance that out of the ashes of a nuclear war rudimentary societies in both the Soviet Union and the US might begin again, the pride, joy, and relief normally generated by victory would not occur. A nuclear war would be at best a hollow, Phyrric victory.

In *Nuclear War: Opposing Viewpoints*, experts from many fields debate what may certainly be deemed one of the most important issues of our time. The five topics debated are: How Would a Nuclear War Begin? Would Humanity Survive a Nuclear War? Will Civil Defense Work? Will Nuclear Arms Agreements Work? and Can Space Weapons Eliminate the Risk of Nuclear War? The authors represented include scientists, defense strategists, and representatives of prominent organizations. To a certain extent, all of the viewpoints address themselves to the crucial importance of achieving both national and individual security in a world fraught with the dangers of nuclear weapons. As readers explore these issues, they will participate in a debate that has dominated the national consciousness since the bombings of Hiroshima and Nagasaki.

How Would a Nuclear War Begin?

Chapter Preface

In 1979, *The Progressive* magazine published a Princeton undergraduate's crude but workable plans for the building of an atomic bomb. While a debate ensued over whether or not *The Progressive* should have been allowed to publish the plans, an even more unsettling idea arose from the controversy. If a very bright undergraduate could piece together the mysteries of building an atomic bomb, how much more easily might experienced terrorists make one—terrorists who not only have access to the required materials, but more ominously, hold strong convictions for exploding one.

There is a real fear of nuclear war originating from terrorist action. But the fear is just as great of a nuclear war growing out of a superpower confrontation not unlike the 1963 Cuban Missile Crisis. During that crisis, the Soviet Union's attempt to place missile bases in Cuba provoked a chilling American reaction. President John F. Kennedy threatened the Soviet Union with a nuclear showdown, and for the intervening hours before the Soviets backed down and removed the bases, the world teetered on the brink of World War III. It is possible that in a future crisis neither side would "blink," or that a simple misunderstanding or miscommunication could send the world into a mistaken, but no less devastating, nuclear war.

The incredible destructive power of one nuclear weapon means that any explosion, whether accidental or purposeful, would leave in its wake unlimited human death and misery. Even more frightening than the human cost, a single explosion could not help but involve the superpowers, and any impulsive reaction on the part of the US or USSR could lead to an all-out nuclear war. The viewpoints which follow debate the most plausible possibilities.

"Attempts by the Soviet Union to match US development of a greater strategic counterforce capability might provide the pretext for the Pentagon to launch a preemptive first strike."

The US Could Begin a Nuclear War

Robert C. Aldridge

Robert C. Aldridge is a former design engineer for the Polaris and Trident missile systems at Lockheed. During his work on these systems, he concluded that the US was building weapons not for the purpose of deterrence, but to be able to achieve a disabling first strike against the Soviet Union. This belief prompted him to quit Lockheed. In the following viewpoint, Aldridge traces nuclear strategy since World War II and decides that the Pentagon's strategy for attacking Soviet military targets could only be implemented in a first strike.

As you read, consider the following questions:

1. What is "counterforce," as explained by the author?
2. Why does the author believe that the idea of a Soviet first strike is "preposterous"?
3. What might provoke the Pentagon into launching a first strike, according to the author?

Robert C. Aldridge, *First Strike: The Pentagon's Strategy for Nuclear War*. Boston: South End Press, 1983. Reprinted with permission of the author.

"I have become death, the destroyer of worlds," quoted Dr. Robert Oppenheimer from the Bhagavad Gita as he witnessed the first atomic explosion. Oppenheimer headed the project which culminated in that blaze of light across the New Mexico desert on July 16, 1945. At that instant the United States entered the nuclear age. Three weeks later history's second atomic blast ripped through the Japanese city of Hiroshima. Only three days after that the nuclear specter struck again as Nagasaki disappeared in a fiery massacre. Those first three tests of the United States' newly found power took place in less than a month and left behind misery and mutilation that has lasted for decades.

For at least the first decade of the nuclear age the US monopolized the ability to start and win a nuclear war. It exercised that ability when it escalated World War 2 to atomic weapons, purportedly to bring that war to a quick end. A deeper reason for this escalation, however, appears to have been a warning to Russia not to overrun Europe and Asia during the final days of the war. Had the USSR not stopped its advances more cities might have been incinerated. These events serve as a grim reminder that when the United States had the ability to launch an unanswerable nuclear strike there was no reluctance to do so if it served its purpose. . . .

Destroying Soviet Military Targets

It would seem that 400 deliverable hydrogen bombs would provide an adequate deterrent. More than this number, however, are carried on only two Poseidon submarines. The total US weapons stockpile contains over 30,000 nuclear warheads: approximately 22,000 deployed for tactical use and about 10,000 on strategic carriers. A strategic force of this size does not make sense if the US doctrine is, indeed, to retaliate against cities under a deterrence policy. Such a force is necessary, however, if the United States wants the capability to destroy Soviet strategic military facilities.

This brings us to *counterforce*. As a nuclear strategy, counterforce means aiming attack missiles at military targets. The word means to *counter* the enemy's military *forces* which includes missile silos, command posts, nuclear storage depots, strategic air bases, communications centers, and submarine pens. Many of these targets are called "hard" because they are buried deep in bunkers or silos and are reinforced with steel and concrete. Weapons used to destroy hard targets would have to be extremely precise. Although counterforce weapons are not necessarily first strike weapons (which will be discussed below), counterforce does have offensive connotations because many counterforce targets would have to be destroyed *before* they are used or their destruction would be of no significance. Furthermore, these are the installations which would be targeted if either the US or the USSR were contemplating an unanswerable nuclear first strike.

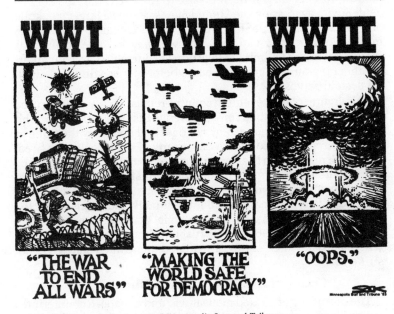

WWI WWII WWIII

"THE WAR TO END ALL WARS" "MAKING THE WORLD SAFE FOR DEMOCRACY" "OOPS."

Reprinted with permission from the Minneapolis Star and Tribune.

First strike is an ambiguous term which has been assigned several meanings. In one sense it is used to describe whatever country initiates nuclear war. It is also associated with a (hoped for) limited use of nuclear weapons to stop a massive attack with conventional armament. This is more often called "first use." . . .

Counterforce is not necessarily equated with first strike because there are degrees of counterforce. The ability to destroy bomber bases, for instance, would require counterforce weapons or counterforce targeting. But destroying a bomber base does not constitute a disarming first strike because silo-based and submarine-based missiles would be certain to retaliate.

A disarming first strike capability can be described as the ultimate in counterforce. That is, it would comprise an arsenal of counterforce weapons capable of destroying the entire strategic force of the other superpower. Although counterforce does not necessarily mean first strike, first strike is counterforce in its maximum sense . . . .

Shooting Missiles Means Striking First

In January 1962 . . . Defense Secretary McNamara made the first official reference to a counterforce capability: "A major mission of the strategic retaliatory forces is to deter war by their capability to destroy the enemy's warmaking capabilities." The following month, on February 17th, McNamara indicated that in order to deter Soviet aggression the United States needed a larger stockpile of weapons than the USSR. "We may have to retaliate with a single massive attack," he claimed, "or we may be able to use our retaliatory forces to limit damage done to ourselves, and our allies, by knocking out the enemy's bases before he has time to launch his second salvos. . . ."

This argument of preventing counter-retaliation is still being used today. But what must be remembered is that the capability to hit missile silos before the second salvo is fired is exactly the same as that required to destroy them before any of the missiles are fired. As one former aide to McNamara pointed out: ". . . there could be no such thing as a primary retaliation against military targets after an enemy attack. If you're going to shoot at missiles you're talking about first strike." President Kennedy didn't clear up the ominous implications of US strategic doctrine when he told reporters in March 1962 that "Krushchev must not be certain that, where our vital interests are threatened, the United States will not strike first." . . .

Counterforce Weapons and Nuclear War

The real utility of limited nuclear war and enhanced counterforce options became apparent on May 30, 1975 when James Schlesinger finally acknowledged publicly that the US would consider "first use" of nuclear weapons to stop a large scale communist advance with *conventional* armaments in Europe. This raised cries of indignation from people who had believed the US was adhering strictly to the deterrent philosophy. Schlesinger's proclamation was later extended to Korea and was quickly supported by then President Ford. Although Schlesinger admitted at that time that first use of nuclear weapons by either NATO or the Warsaw Pact would pose grave risks of escalating into major nuclear war, that threat to fire first still stands today.

Let us look closer at the Nixon-Schlesinger targeting doctrine of selectivity and flexibility. Besides opening the door wider for more overt development of counterforce weapons, it is designed to make limited nuclear war seem to be a more acceptable option. Aiming at military targets sounds like the way a war should be run. It seems more humane than obliterating population areas. And if it is limited that is better yet. . . .

A Handful of Missiles

The whole concept is based on the supposition that the Soviets might launch a handful of missiles at the United States. There was no explanation given as to why they would launch such an attack in the first place, nor did anyone ask for one. The hypothesis was blindly accepted by an unquestioning people. But firing one or two missiles at the United States is a preposterous notion for two reasons.

First, if the Soviets did initiate limited nuclear war they would have no assurance that US response would be equally limited. It could well be massive retaliation. Even if US commanders wanted to keep it limited they might not be able to maintain control of the nuclear forces to prevent massive retaliation.

Kennedy Contemplated Nuclear War

At the time of the 1962 missile crisis, the United States initiated a blockade of Cuba and prepared for invasion, knowing that there were substantial risks of escalation that could lead to nuclear war. "We all agreed in the end," Robert F. Kennedy said afterward, "that if the Russians were ready to go to nuclear war over Cuba, they were ready to go to nuclear war, and that was that. So we might as well have the showdown then as six months later." (One member of the Joint Chiefs of Staff, Kennedy recalled, "argued that we could use nuclear weapons, on the basis that our adversaries would use theirs against us in an attack.") President Kennedy thought the risks of nuclear war were considerable and that such a war would produce "150 million fatalities in the first eighteen hours."

Richard Barnet, *The Bulletin of the Atomic Scientists*, February 1979.

Secondly, a limited Soviet attack on the US is unrealistic because even if US retaliation were also limited it could still be more severe. In that case hostilities would not be likely to end there. If the response inflicted greater damage the Soviets would undoubtedly feel it necessary to even things up. This escalation could develop into total war which would devastate both sides. It is highly improbable that a potential belligerent would discount such a risk and gamble on a limited exchange. The hypothetical set of circumstances used to justify the targeting doctrine of selectivity and flexibility cannot stand close scrutiny....

Despite all the talk about a second strike counterforce capability, *there is no practical difference between such a capability and a first strike counterforce capability.* If the US can destroy a sizeable portion of the Soviet ICBM force after absorbing a Soviet first strike, under the stress of a going war and when atmospheric conditions created by nuclear explosions are far from favorable, then it would have a far greater chance of destroying all Soviet silo-based missiles with a preemptive first strike when the element of surprise and choice of time are in its favor and Soviet missiles are not in a high state of readiness. This is a first strike capability even if the intention is not there to use it. Furthermore, attempts by the Soviet Union to match US development of a greater strategic counterforce capability might provide the pretext for the Pentagon to launch a preemptive first strike.

"We consider nuclear war unfeasible and suicidal for both, and our chief adversary views it as feasible and winnable for himself."

The Soviet Union Could Begin a Nuclear War

Richard Pipes

Richard Pipes is Baird professor of History at Harvard University. In 1981-82 he served as the director of East European and Soviet Affairs for the National Security Council. In 1976 he chaired "Team B," a group of people appointed by the President's Foreign Intelligence Advisory Board to analyze the strategic intentions of the Soviet Union. His books include *The Formation of the Soviet Union*, *Russia Under the Old Regime* and his most recent, *Survival Is Not Enough*. In the following viewpoint, excerpted from one of Mr. Pipes' best known essays, "Why the Soviet Union Thinks it Could Fight and Win a Nuclear War," he argues that the Soviets think differently than we do about nuclear war and that their strategy entails the ability to fight and win such a war.

As you read, consider the following questions:

1. The author believes that Soviet doctrine about nuclear war includes five elements. What are these elements?
2. The author believes that a US goal is a reduction in nuclear weapons. Does he believe that the Soviets have the same goal? Why or why not?

Richard Pipes, "Why the Soviet Union Thinks It Could Fight and Win a Nuclear War," from *US Soviet Relations in the Era of Detente*. Boulder CO: Westview Press, 1981. Reprinted with permission.

American and Soviet nuclear doctrines, it needs stating at the outset, are starkly at odds. The prevalent U.S. doctrine holds that an all-out war between countries in possession of sizable nuclear arsenals would be so destructive as to leave no winner; thus resort to arms has ceased to represent a rational policy option for the leaders of such countries vis-á-vis one another. The classic dictum of [Karl von] Clausewitz, that war is politics pursued by other means, is widely believed in the United States to have lost its validity after Hiroshima and Nagasaki. Soviet doctrine, by contrast, emphatically asserts that while an all-out nuclear war would indeed prove extremely destructive to both parties, its outcome would not be mutual suicide: the country better prepared for it and in possession of a superior strategy could win and emerge a viable society. "There is profound erroneousness and harm in the disorienting claims of bourgeois ideologies that there will be no victor in a thermonuclear world war," thunders an authoritative Soviet publication. The theme is mandatory in the current Soviet military literature. Clausewitz, buried in the United States, seems to be alive and prospering in the Soviet Union. . . .

Novelty of Nuclear Weapons

Soviet military theorists reject the notion that technology (i.e., weapons) decides strategy. They perceive the relationship to be the reverse: strategic objectives determine the procurement and application of weapons. They agree that the introduction of nuclear weapons has profoundly affected warfare, but deny that nuclear weapons have altered its essential quality. The novelty of nuclear weapons consists not in their destructiveness...the innovation consists of the fact that nuclear weapons, coupled with intercontinental missiles, can by themselves carry out strategic missions which previously were accomplished only by means of prolonged tactical operations:

> Nuclear missiles have altered the relationship of tactical, operational, and strategic acts of the armed conflict. If in the past the strategic end-result was secured by a succession of sequential, most often long-term, efforts [and] comprised the sum of tactical and operational successes, strategy being able to realize its intentions only with the assistance of the art of operations and tactics, then today, by means of powerful nuclear strikes, strategy can attain its objectives directly.

In other words, military strategy, rather than a casualty of technology, has, thanks to technology, become more central than ever. By adopting this view, Soviet theorists believe themselves to have adapted modern technological innovations in weaponry to the traditions of military science.

Implicit in all this is the idea that nuclear war is feasible and that the basic function of warfare, as defined by Clausewitz, remains permanently valid, whatever breakthroughs may occur in technology. "It is well known that the essential nature of *war as a continuation of politics does not change with changing technology and armament.*" This code phrase from [V. D.] Sokolovskii's authoritative manual [*Soviet Military Strategy*] was certainly hammered out with all the care that in the United States is lavished on an amendment to the Constitution. It spells the rejection of the whole basis on which U.S. strategy has come to rest: thermonuclear war is not suicidal, it can be fought and won, and thus resort to war must not be ruled out. . . .

Destroying the Enemy

In the Soviet view, a nuclear war would be total and go beyond formal defeat of one side by the other: "War must not simply [be] the defeat of the enemy, it must be his destruction. This condition has become the basis of Soviet military strategy," according to the *Military-Historical Journal.* Limited nuclear war, flexible response, escalation, damage limiting, and all the other numerous refinements of U.S. strategic doctrine find no place in its Soviet counterpart (although, of course, they are taken into consideration in Soviet operational planning). . . .

Soviets' Grand Strategy

The unrelenting desire of Soviet grand strategy—to control the entire planet—has never been fully acknowledged by European nations. And, more pointedly, not credited by American analysts. Even though the Soviets have made no secret of this intention.

It has been the diplomatic policy of the United States to assume that the aggressive and expansionist drives of the Soviets could be mitigated by reason and cooperation (détente).

Diplomats and policy makers do not make mistakes. But in retrospect, errors of judgment as vast as these can hardly be viewed as anything less than a gross betrayal of the American people.

What Will Happen to You When the Soviets Take Over? Ingo Swann, ed., 1980.

The strategic doctrine adopted by the USSR over the past two decades calls for a policy diametrically opposite to that adopted in the United States by the predominant community of civilian strategists: not deterrence but victory, not sufficiency in weapons but superiority, not retaliation but offensive action. The doctrine has five related elements: (1) preemption (first strike), (2) quantitative superiority in arms, (3) counterforce targeting, (4) combined-arms operations, and (5) defense.

The costliest lesson which the Soviet military learned in World War II was the importance of surprise. Because Stalin thought he had an understanding with Hitler, and because he was afraid to provoke his Nazi ally, he forbade the Red Army to mobilize for the Geman attack of which he had had ample warning. As a result of this strategy of "passive defense," Soviet forces suffered frightful losses and were nearly defeated. This experience etched itself very deeply on the minds of the Soviet commanders: in their theoretical writings no point is emphasized more consistently than the need never again to allow themselves to be caught in a surprise attack. Nuclear weapons make this requirement especially urgent because, according to Soviet theorists, the decision in a nuclear conflict in all probability will be arrived at in the initial hours. In a nuclear war the Soviet Union, therefore, would not again have at its disposal the time which it enjoyed in 1941-42 to mobilize reserves for a victorious counteroffensive after absorbing devastating setbacks.

Given the rapidity of modern warfare (an ICBM can traverse the distance between the USSR and the United States in thirty minutes), not to be surprised by the enemy means, in effect, to inflict surprise on him. Once the latter's ICBM's have left their silos, once his bombers have taken to the air and his submarines to sea, a counterattack is greatly reduced in effectiveness. These considerations call for a preemptive strike. Soviet theorists draw an insistent, though to an outside observer very fuzzy, distinction between "preventive" and "preemptive" attacks. They claim that the Soviet Union will never start a war—i.e., it will never launch a preventive attack—but once it had concluded that an attack upon it was imminent, it would not hesitate to preempt. They argue that historical experience indicates outbreaks of hostilities are generally preceded by prolonged diplomatic crises and military preparations which signal to an alert command an imminent threat and the need to act . . . .

Need for Stockpiling Weapons

There is no indication that the Soviet military share the view prevalent in the U.S. that in the nuclear age numbers of weapons do not matter once a certain quantity had been attained. They do like to pile up all sorts of weapons, new on top of old, throwing away nothing that might come in handy. This propensity to accumulate hardware is usually dismissed by Western observers with contemptuous references to a Russian habit dating back to Czarist days. It is not, however, as mindless as it may appear. For although Soviet strategists believe that the ultimate outcome in a nuclear war will be decided in the initial hours of the conflict, they also believe that a nuclear war will be of long duration: to consummate victory—that is, to destroy the enemy—may take months or even longer. Under these conditions, the possession of a large arsenal of nuclear delivery systems, as well as of other types of weapons, may well prove to be of critical importance . . . .

Soviet theorists regard strategic nuclear forces (organized since 1960 into a separate arm, the Strategic Rocket Forces) to be the decisive branch of the armed services, in the sense that the ultimate outcome of modern war would be settled by nuclear exchanges. But since nuclear war, in their view must lead not only to the enemy's defeat but also to his destruction (i.e., his incapacity to offer further resistance), they consider it necessary to make preparations for the follow-up phase, which may entail a prolonged war of attrition. . . .

Soviets Want a Victory

In recent years, scientists have raised serious doubts whether major nuclear war can be waged without causing universal destruction. The validity of this proposition ultimately cannot be tested except under combat conditions, which, one hopes, will never occur. However, the issue at stake is not the objective reality, such as it may be, but the perception of that reality by those who make the political and military decisions. Throughout history, nations have gone to war in pursuit of goals that could have been demonstrated beforehand to be beyond their reach. Alexander the Great had not the means to conquer the world, nor Germany those to defeat its vastly superior neighbors in a *Blitzkrieg*, and yet both chose to try. The unceasing efforts of the USSR to upgrade both its offensive and defensive nuclear forces at all levels, far beyond any conceivable deterrent needs, strongly suggest that its leaders believe in their doctrine that nuclear weapons are the means of quick and decisive victory. In view of this overwhelming evidence, the burden of proof falls on those who are of a different opinion.

Richard Pipes, *Survival Is Not Enough*, 1984.

The notion of an extended nuclear war is deeply embedded in Soviet thinking, despite its being dismissed by Western strategists who think of war as a one-two exchange. As [P.M.S.] Blackett noted sarcastically already in 1948-49: "Some armchair strategists (including some atomic scientists) tend to ignore the inevitable counter-moves of the enemy. More chess playing and less nuclear physics might have instilled a greater sense of the realities." He predicted that a World War III waged with the atomic bombs then available would last longer than either of its predecessors, and require combined-arms operations—which seems to be the current Soviet view of the matter.

Soviet Civil Defense

As noted, the U.S. theory of mutual deterrence postulates that no effective defense can be devised against an all-out nuclear attack: it is this postulate that makes such a war appear totally irrational. In order to make this premise valid, American civilian strategists have argued against a civil-defense program, against the ABM, and against air defenses.

Nothing illustrates better the fundamental differences between the two strategic doctrines than their attitudes to defense against a nuclear attack. . . .

The Soviet Union does not regard civil defense to be exclusively for the protection of ordinary civilians. Its chief function seems to be to protect what in Russia are known as the "cadres," that is, the political and military leaders as well as industrial managers and skilled workers—those who could reestablish the political and economic system once the war was over. Judging by Soviet definitions, civil defense has as much to do with the proper functioning of the country during and immediately after the war as with holding down casualties. . . .

Soviets Winning Strategy

Enough has already been said to indicate the disparities between American and Soviet strategic doctrines of the nuclear age. These differences may be most pithily summarized by stating that whereas we view nuclear weapons as a deterrent, the Russians see them as a "compellant"—with all the consequences that follow. Now it must be granted that the actual, operative differences between the two doctrines may not be quite as sharp as they appear in the public literature: it is true that our deterrence doctrine leaves room for some limited offensive action, just as the Russians include elements of deterrence in their "war-fighting" and "war-winning" doctrine. Admittedly, too, a country's military doctrine never fully reveals how it would behave under actual combat conditions. And yet the differences here are sharp and fundamental enough, and the relationship of Soviet doctrine to Soviet deployments sufficiently close, to suggest that ignoring or not taking seriously Soviet military doctrine may have very detrimental effects on U.S. security. There is something innately destabilizing in the very fact that we consider nuclear war unfeasible and suicidal for both, and our chief adversary views it as feasible and winnable for himself. . . .

Above all looms the question of intent: as long as the Soviets persist in adhering to the Clausewitzian maxim on the function of war, mutual deterrence does not really exist. And unilateral deterrence is feasible only if we understand the Soviet war-winning strategy and make it impossible for them to succeed.

> *"Seemingly inexplicable, inconsistent and unpredictable human 'goofs' account for 50 to 70 percent of all failures of major weapons."*

Human Error Could Lead to Nuclear War

Lloyd J. Dumas

Lloyd J. Dumas is associate professor of political economy at the University of Texas in Dallas, and a former member of the Committee on Science, Arms Control and National Security of the American Association for the Advancement of Science. In the following viewpoint, Mr. Dumas concludes that given the isolation, boredom, and rate of chemical abuse among members of nuclear personnel, World War III could begin through human error.

As you read, consider the following questions:

1. How could monotony, or boredom, affect military personnel, according to the author?
2. According to Mr. Dumas, how could human failure provoke a nuclear exchange?
3. What, if any, are the author's solutions?

Lloyd J. Dumas, "Human Fallibility and Weapons," *The Bulletin of the Atomic Scientists*, November 1980. Reprinted with the permission of the author.

Everything will work the way it is supposed to work.
Nothing will happen until it is supposed to happen.

Virtually all of the public—and much of the private—discussion of the nuclear arms race proceeds under these implicit assumptions. Yet they have no basis in fact: No systems designed, produced, deployed or activated by human beings can ever achieve perfection.

The fallibility inherent in human activity is generally no more than a nuisance. But where weapons of mass destruction are involved, the consequences can be catastrophic. As the military systems in which these weapons are imbedded have become more complex, geographically dispersed and technologically sophisticated, there is increased probability that they will eventually fail.

Given this simple technological fact, two things are clear: First, even small failures involving weapons of mass destruction are an extremely serious matter. Second, the problem of preventing disaster is greatly complicated by the number and variety of these weapons dispersed throughout the world.

Human 'Goofs'

Seemingly inexplicable, inconsistent and unpredictable human goofs' account for 50 to 70 percent of all failures of major weapons and space vehicles. That puts human errors...ahead of mechanical, electrical and structural failures...as a source of system troubles.

The consequences range from minor delays to major disasters. ...[For example,] the loss of the submarine Thresher with its entire crew [was due to] improper installation of a relief valve...of the propulsion subsystem.''

The problem of malfunction in military systems is, of course, multifaceted. But, as the quotation points up, human reliability is a significant factor. Rather than attempting to deal with this one factor as a whole, which would include design and manufacture, I shall focus on the human component in the control and operation of military systems.

Alcoholism and Drugs

Alcoholism, drug addiction, mental illness and other related problems are pervasive in our society. It is not possible to avoid them in the military.

A 1972 study on drug use in the military, commissioned by the Department of Defense, divided drugs into marijuana, other psychedelics, stimulants, depressants, and narcotics. The study then projected that *daily* drug use for each of the armed services was not less than 0.4 percent for any category, and in some was as high as 8 percent. According to an article in the *Air Force Magazine*, however, there may be reason for some skepticism:

''The stories that get into the public prints represent only the top of the iceberg . . . neither the Air Force nor the other services, nor, for that matter, the civilian authorities, are in any position to produce definitive figures on drug abuse in their jurisdiction. What is known is that the use of drugs of all kinds has for the past several years been dramatically on the upswing.

Berserk Guards

Periodically, specific stories emerge about cases of military personnel with mental or drug-abuse problems who are involved with nuclear weapons. For example, in August 1969, an Air Force major was suspended after having allowed three men, described as

"And we've virtually eliminated the possibility of nuclear war through human error."

having "dangerous psychiatric problems," to continue to guard nuclear weapons at a base near San Francisco. One of the guards was accused of going berserk with a loaded carbine while at the base. His lawyer said that the man had pleaded not to be assigned to a job in which he would handle explosives or weapons. Yet he was frequently on duty as senior officer of a two-man team guarding nuclear missiles. This major testified that although he had received unfavorable psychiatric reports on the three guards, he had not removed them because he was short of staff and without them, "people from Haight-Ashbury" would try to get the weapons. . . .

Stress, boredom and isolation are inherent in the modern military scene, particularly in the nuclear forces. Spending endless hours interacting with electronic control consoles, repeating essentially the same lengthy and detailed routines—this is the stuff of life in the strategic forces.

The deleterious effects of monotony on performance are by now well established. During World War II, N.H. Mackworth of England was commissioned by the Royal Air Force to find out why radar operators on anti-submarine patrol sometimes let U-boats escape detection. He set up laboratory experiments in which detection efficiency was shown to decay considerably in less than an hour of screen watching. . . .

Most military activity, of course, is not performed in situations of individual isolation, but in groups. Particularly in the strategic nuclear forces, however, these groups are often isolated from society for varying periods of time. It is therefore relevant to ask how individuals in socially isolated groups are affected in terms of job performance, stress and interpersonal relationships within the group. . . .

The Human Reliability Factor

Even healthy human beings who are not subjected to extraordinary stress or grinding boredom and isolation may contribute to the human reliability problem in the military because of the control difficulties inherent in all bureaucracies of size. In particular, there is a serious problem of transmission of valid information to the upper echelons, especially where such information points out errors, made either by subordinates or by top-level decisionmakers. . . .

There are various ways in which the human reliability problem interacts with the enormous stockpile of weapons of mass destruction in order to produce potentially dangerous or disastrous situations. There have been a number of serious accidents involving both nuclear weapons and major nuclear weapons carriers. More than 60 have been made public since 1950.

Clearly, human failure in the transport or handling of weapons or in the operation of a nuclear weapons carrier could, and most likely has, produced such an accident. And while there have been no publicly reported accidents involving the explosion of a nuclear weapon, there have been incidents in which the conventional material that surrounds the nuclear material has been detonated resulting in the scattering of some of the plutonium in the weapon.

Accidental Nuclear Exchange

Human failure could also play a major role in precipitating an accidental nuclear exchange. Aside from the Strangelovian scenario of a war triggered by a mentally unbalanced, high-ranking military

31

officer, which certainly cannot be dismissed, there are other possibilities. False warnings of a major nuclear attack, false alerts, or even improperly authorized (but properly coded) messages ordering the launching of nuclear weapons could accidentally generate a holocaust, or at least provide the preconditions. Would all the safeguards so painstakingly designed into the military system prevent any such communications?. . . .

While nuclear extermination by accident is demonstrably possible, there is a far more likely prospect that a renegade government, criminal organization or terrorist group could buy or seize one or more weapons of mass destruction. . . .

Perfection Required and Unattainable

We have created a world in which perfection is required if a disaster beyond history is to be permanently avoided. But in the world of human beings perfection is unachievable. The more weapons we deploy, and the greater their geographic dispersion, the more people will be interacting with them. And the greater will be the likelihood of disaster resulting from human error.

How World War III Will Start

One rainy afternoon at a Strategic Air Command base in England during the late 1950s, a scattering of British and American bomber pilots on alert in the barracks-like ''ready room'' began a game of stacking empty coffee cups on the table in front of them. Overhead, nuclear-armed jet bombers on a training exercise struggled into the air, rattling the crockery on the table with the roar of their engines. Unattended and unnoticed by the bored airmen, a single coffee cup near the edge of the table suddenly danced off and shattered on the floor. Surveying the debris, one of the pilots observed casually, almost diffidently: ''You know, that's how World War III is going to start.''

Gregg Herken, *Vital Issues*, 1982.

Nor can we circumvent this dilemma by turning control over to machines, by somehow automating the human element out of the nuclear forces. For who designs the machines and who will build them? If machines had been in control, a counterattack would almost certainly have been launched when the Ballistic Missile Early Warning System station at Thule, Greenland, sent its false warning of attack in 1960. The judgment of human beings intervened and saved the day on that and countless other occasions.

We cannot escape our fallibility, so we must exercise the wisdom and the instinct for survival that are also fundamental parts of our humanity. We must find a way to coexist permanently with our innate imperfection.

Need to Reduce Risk

Not until we have sharply reduced the vast arsenals of weapons of mass destruction will we have even a serious chance of keeping human reliability problems from eventually triggering a catastrophe. Reversal of the arms race must be our highest priority international goal.

Is it not possible, for example, that a perfectly safe and conservative initiative, like the public dismantling of 15 percent of our land-based missiles, would bring so much international political pressure to bear on the Soviet Union that it might dismantle some of its own nuclear arsenal? Is it not even possible that the USSR might choose to reciprocate out of its own self-interest, to relieve its overburdened economy or to step farther away from the nuclear precipice?

By a series of such initiatives, waiting for reciprocation at each step, perhaps we could achieve through our actions what we have not been able to achieve with all our words and diplomacy—moving back to a more rational force structure.

If our treaty or action initiatives fail, what will we have lost by trying? Our deterrent would still be unstoppable, so we would certainly not be jeopardizing our national security. Any action initiatives would, in fact, increase our security by reducing the possibilities of accidents, including accidental war, and nuclear terrorism.

*"The next nuclear bomb to be exploded
in anger is not likely to belong to the
Americans or the Soviets."*

Nuclear War Could Begin in the Third World

Michael Kinsley

Michael Kinsley is the editor of *The New Republic* magazine in
which he also writes a regular column. He is a former editor of
Harper's magazine and is a contributing editor to *The Washington
Monthly*. In the following viewpoint, Mr. Kinsley states that the
most plausible nuclear danger lies with small Third World nations
with nuclear capability.

As you read, consider the following questions:

1. What nation, according to the author, is most responsible for
   nuclear proliferation?
2. What tactic should the superpowers use to eliminate Third
   World nuclear potential, according to the author?
3. Why does the author believe that this tactic will be opposed
   by anti-nuclear activists?

Michael Kinsley, "Anti-Nuke Forces Pick Wrong Target," *The Los Angeles Times*,
November 18, 1983. Also published as the TRB column, "Bombs Away," *The New
Republic*, November 28, 1983. Reprinted by permission of *The New Republic*, © 1983, The
New Republic, Inc.

The most eloquent liberal rallying cry of the past decade, Sen. Edward M. Kennedy's "The Dream Shall Never Die" speech at the 1980 Democratic convention, contained a long list of reasons for passionate dissatisfaction with the status quo, but not one word about the peril of nuclear war. No one at the time thought this an odd omission.

Today, of course, every liberal politician, including Kennedy, avers that there is no more urgent item on the political agenda. The suddenness of this frenzy of alarm, when nothing fundamental has changed, is one of the things that makes me wonder how serious the current anti-nuclear campaign really is.

Another cause for wonder is the way anti-nuclear politics has served as a reentry vehicle into liberal respectability for dubious characters like Robert S. McNamara and McGeorge Bundy. A decade ago they were widely regarded as war criminals; now a couple of high-minded pronunciamentos about how awful a nuclear war would be, and they start winning peace awards.

Superpower War Glamorous, Unrealistic

But the best evidence that the movement against nuclear weapons isn't really serious is its almost exclusive concentration on the glamorous prospect of war between the superpowers. Any politician or citizen truly eager to reduce the risk of nuclear war ought to be worrying instead about the problem of nuclear proliferation and ought to be contemplating solutions that would be anathema to most anti-nuclear activists.

Proliferation is the serious issue for four reasons:

—First, the next nuclear bomb to be exploded in anger is not likely to belong to the Americans or the Soviets. The system of mutual deterrence carries no guarantee, but it has worked for a third of a century. It depends, though, on stability (the game and the players don't change), on symmetry (each side knows that the other side can respond in kind to a nuclear attack) and on rationality (no loonies at the button). None of these comforting conditions that make deterrence work will apply when smaller countries, engaged in intense local disputes and run by zealots or worse, start getting the bomb—which could happen soon. It's widely assumed that Israel already has it. In 1974 India exploded what it called a "peaceful" nuclear device, which looked (and sounded) just like a bomb. Other nations that seem to be beavering toward nuclear weapons include Libya, South Africa, Argentina, Brazil, Pakistan and South Korea.

Nuclear Proliferation Can Be Stopped

—A second reason why energies of the anti-nuclear movement are misdirected is that the superpower nuclear confrontation, however dangerous, is something that we're basically stuck with. Proliferation is not. A negotiated slowdown or even reversal of the

U.S.-Soviet nuclear-arms race might make the world a bit safer, but not much—neither nuclear superpower will abandon that status voluntarily. Superpower arms negotiations, no matter how urgent and sincere on both sides, cannot achieve total, mutual nuclear disarmament. And, short of total nuclear disarmament, the stand-off and the danger of catastrophe remain. The danger of proliferation, on the other hand, is still—barely—prospective. What's more, preventing a nation from getting nuclear weapons doesn't depend on its good will the way getting one to give them up does.

—A third reason why truly serious anti-nuclear energies ought to be directed against proliferation has to do with the limits of politics. The anti-nuclear movement, perforce, has far more influence over the democratic governments of the West than it can ever have over the Soviet Union. Critics therefore charge, with some justification, that whatever the intentions of anti-nuclear activists, the one effect that they have on the contest between the superpowers is to create pressure for unilateral Western disarmament.

Regarding proliferation though, one-sided pressure on the Western nuclear powers (the United States, Britain, France) is

Don Wright, *Miami News*. Reprinted with permission.

perfectly appropriate, since the Western nations deserve the blame. The Soviets haven't given the bomb to anyone. The United States, by contrast, has delivered nuclear information, equipment and fuel to nations around the world, ostensibly for power plants but with laughably inadequate safeguards against weapons manufacture.

One example: India's "peaceful" explosion used "heavy water" supplied by the United States. India has refused to sign the Nuclear Non-Proliferation Treaty, under which 112 nations have pledged (however deceitfully) not to go nuclear. What could be clearer? Under a 1978 U.S. law, nations that won't pledge not to develop nuclear weapons and won't agree to international inspection can't get nuclear fuel from us. (Only the major nuclear powers, so far, can make enriched uranium to fuel nuclear power plants.)

India's Bomb

In 1980 President Jimmy Carter used his authority to waive this rule and gave India more fuel. Earlier this year the Reagan Administration arranged for France to supply the fuel instead—an evasion of the law that also has been used to resupply South Africa and Brazil. India explicitly reserves the right to reprocess this fuel into plutonium for more "peaceful" nuclear explosions.

The reason given for sliding down this slippery slope with India and other countries is that remaining a "reliable supplier" is the best hope of retaining leverage over their nuclear activities. The reason not given usually is a desire to curry favor as part of the geopolitical waltz....

—Thus the final reason for zeroing in on proliferation: Just as unilateral negligence by Western nuclear powers has created this nightmare, unilateral action by the West, or even the United States alone, could end it. The means would be drastic, but certainly not out of proportion with the hysterical rhetoric of the anti-nuclear movement. If the United States wants to stop the spread of nuclear weapons, it does not need treaties or negotiations or a reputation as a reliable supplier to get its way.

Iraqi Bombing Exemplary

Despite a lot of talk, only one nation has actually done anything in recent years to reduce the risk of nuclear war breaking out: Israel, with its 1981 bombing raid on the Iraqi nuclear research reactor. If America really wanted to prevent additions to the nuclear club, we could follow Israel's example and destroy nuclear potential (even Israel's, if necessary) by using conventional force. No one could stop us. The mere threat of using such force, if persuasive, would almost surely be enough to make the most recalcitrant nation sign the non-nuclear pledge and open its facilities to inspection.

What I'm suggesting, only half in jest, is naked, ugly superpower imperialism. It also could turn violent. We are the big guys, you are the little guys. We have the bomb, you cannot. Dismantle your facilities or we will do it for you. Sorry. Imperialism and violence aren't in the spirit of the anti-nuclear movement, which is peace-loving and against the big powers. But what might be called instant disarmament is in keeping with the logic of anti-nuclear rhetoric, which holds that the prospect of nuclear war puts conventional war in the shade.

This popular assertion may or may not be true (recent developments in conventional warfare are pretty horrible) but certainly nothing would make a major outbreak of conventional war between the superpowers more likely than elimination of the fear that it could go nuclear. Why not, then, a little preemptive conventional war, if necessary, to eliminate the greatest realistic prospect of a nuclear one?

But maybe the anti-nuclear movement is not that serious.

"In the past five years...computers have produced more than a hundred false alerts."

Computer Error Could Begin Nuclear War

Norman Cousins

Norman Cousins is an editor emeritus for *Saturday Review* where he was an editor for forty-two years. Mr. Cousins has labored tirelessly for the cause of world peace through world government and is a world-recognized spokesperson for internationalism. A former member of the Commission to Study Organized Peace, he is the founder and president of the United World Federalists and co-chairman of the National Committee for a Sane Nuclear Policy, an anti-nuclear organization. In the following viewpoint, Mr. Cousins' experience with a computer chess game becomes a model for how a nuclear war could begin by computer error.

As you read, consider the following questions:

1. What happened to the author's chess computer that caused him to second-guess the use of sophisticated computers in society?
2. Does the author believe that people can prevent computer error?
3. Does this scenario sound like a likely one to you? Why or why not?

Some time ago in these pages, I wrote about electronic chess. What seemed especially noteworthy at that time was not just that the computer could play a sophisticated game, but that its physical dimensions were so modest. Thirty years or so ago, some specialists believed it would be impossible to construct a chess computer because of size requirements. One computer expert said the first three moves would require a device the size of a cigar box. To get as far as the sixth move would call for a machine the size of a clothes closet. By the twelfth move, the machine would need a structure twice the size of the Pentagon. All this, of course, was before the reign of transistors and, more recently, of silicon chips. Today, a computer chess machine has all its thinking equipment contained under the playing surface of the board in a space less than two inches deep.

Some things are significant about the chess-playing computer. First is the high quality of play. It has a systematic plan of attack. At the same time, it is careful not to expose any of its own pieces to attack without retaliation. In this respect, the machine belies the usual criticism made of computers; namely, that they are incapable of doing and anticipating complex choices. This machine examines its options and has a fairly good idea of what is going on in its opponent's mind. The quality of its play improves noticeably in proportion to the time it takes between moves. It is not just a computering machine but a thinking machine. It understands the process of cause and effect; it can look far down a road and identify factors affecting its decision. It can be an implacable and remorseless opponent. It does not hesitate to pounce upon any oversight. It will not observe the amenities and point out an obvious error. It lacks manners.

Computers Not Infallible

But this thinking machine is not infallible. What is most interesting and perhaps significant about its behavior is that, under certain circumstances, it can become flustered. If it is suddenly confronted by a highly unorthodox and massed attack, for example, it can lose its cool and go stumbling all over the board, adding peril to predicament, self-insult to self-injury. This ludicrous state of affairs doesn't happen very often, but it is a spectacle when it does. It prompts reflections about the use of sophisticated computers in society, and the degree of control they have over our lives. Indeed, the lives of hundreds of millions of people ride on the ability of computers to monitor national security.

Computers and Nuclear War

Because of the danger of a surprise nuclear-missile attack on the United States, with warning time limited not to hours but to minutes, the nation's military planners employ computers as an integral part of our defense strategy. Since there is no way to protect the American people against attacking missiles, our range of action is limited to retaliatory response. It is conceivable that a computer error or errors could touch off a full-scale nuclear war, setting fire to hundreds of cities, killing millions of people, and changing conditions of life on this planet. Are attack-alert mechanisms impervious to error? Is it possible that computers can yield erroneous and dangerous information when confronted with unorthodox moves not anticipated by the programmers? Can computers go berserk, taking with them whole societies?

Computer Error a Grave Concern

Computers, which occasionally tell us we have died, or never existed, or must pay a bill a second time, are also intimately involved in the nuclear arsenals. The record of mistakes is extensive. During an eighteen-month period, the North American Air Defense Command had 151 false alarms. Four resulted in orders that increased the state of alert of B-52 bomber crews and intercontinental-ballistic-missile units. A major false alert, lasting a full six minutes, occurred when a technician mistakenly mounted on an American military computer a training tape of a Soviet attack. Mechanical malfunction and human errors have also led to a number of accidents with nuclear weapons.

James E. Muller, "On Accidental Nuclear War," 1982.

The answer is that errors have already occurred in the computerized military warning systems. In the past five years, according to some defense-watchers, computers have produced more than a hundred false alerts. Fortunately for most of the people living in the U.S. and U.S.S.R., and for a great many others, these errors were spotted early enough to prevent the release of our own nuclear-tipped missiles. A (1984) motion picture, *WarGames*, has as its theme the capability of an ingenious youngster to penetrate the Pentagon's computer codes and touch off a nuclear alert. There are many far-fetched aspects of the film, which U.S. military officials have been quick to point out, but what is basically relevant is the computer's central role in the decision-making process that can lead to nuclear war, and the demonstrated fact of computer fallibility. It is not inconceivable that a computer error would not be caught in time.

Stumbling Toward the Brink

Is there no way to educate the American people to the reality that present methods of protecting the national security are unworkable? How can we gain attention for the truth that control of force, and not the pursuit of force, should be at the heart of national policy? How long will we stumble toward the nuclear brink before

41

we recognize that unfettered national sovereignty in a nuclear age is producing the most costly madness known to history? What must be done to construct new approaches to peace based on definable and enforceable codes of behavior in the world arena? The most serious question of all: when will thinking people think seriously about the things that count?

These questions are beyond the ken of computers. Only people can answer them.

*"Human judgment will always be there
to insure that we provide reliable, timely,
unambiguous warning."*

Computer Error Could Not Provoke Nuclear War

James Hartinger, interviewed in *US News & World Report*

General James Hartinger is chief of the North American Aerospace
Defense Command as well as the Air Force Space Command. He
is responsible for detecting evidence of an impending attack on the
US. In the following viewpoint, General Hartinger explains advances made in computer technology and concludes that it would
be virtually impossible for a computer to precipitate nuclear war.

As you read, consider the following questions:

1. How many false warnings of a nuclear attack has the US
   received, according to General Hartinger?
2. In the first incident, how did he determine that it was a false
   alarm?
3. Do you believe that computer error could precipitate nuclear
   war? Why or why not?

Question: General Hartinger, how many false warnings have you had of a possible missile attack on the U.S.?

Answer: We've had two in the past four years or so. The first occurred on Nov. 9, 1979, when a technician inadvertently loaded an exercise-scenario tape into the operational system. So the displays at the Strategic Air Command and National Military Command Center showed possible missiles that were being tracked.

It took a few minutes to determine that this was a human error.

Question: How were you able to determine that it was an error and not a real attack?

Answer: We have an instantaneous conferencing capability with all the sensor sites—all of our tracking stations. We went to them and ascertained that none were tracking any missiles. So we knew it had to be a computer error or, in this case, a personnel error.

As a result of that incident, we took steps that guarantee that it could never recur. We developed an off-site test facility in 1980 here in Colorado Springs where we test all the software and all the hardware before we install it in the computer system in our combat operations center in Cheyenne Mountain. So none of our testing is done any longer on the operational system.

Second False Warning

Question: How did the second false attack warning occur?

Answer: It was on June 3, 1980. Again, our automatic computer-generated displays appeared to show missiles being tracked.

Our missile-warning center again conferenced all the sensor sites and determined that no missiles actually were being tracked. So it had to be a computer error. It took less than a minute and a half to determine that.

We spent many hours investigating, and, finally, after we managed to duplicate the fault, we isolated the problem to a little chip on the circuit board that had been in the system for some time.

Once we determined the cause, we went off that major computer system, and we did many things to see that an incident like that would not recur.

Question: What did you do to prevent this from happening again?

Answer: Well, one of the things we did was to increase each computer-message word length to 32 bits so there would be more redundancy in checking whether these were valid messages. About five months after that second incident, we went back on the major computer string after we had incorporated these fixes. In the three years since then, we have sent out over 175 million messages, and we have not sent one false message.

Question: In those incidents involving false warnings of attack, how close was the United States to stumbling into a nuclear war by mistake?

Answer: We didn't come close at all. By going to all the sensor sites, we determined in less than a minute and a half that there was a computer fault and no one was tracking any missiles.

Human Judgment Insures Reliability

Question: Are you saying that it would be impossible to have a nuclear war triggered by a false attack warning—for example, a computer error in your headquarters?

Answer: Obviously, there can be computer faults—hardware and software errors; there can be personnel errors; there can be solar activity—solar blanking that affects sensors; there can be auroral effects. Also, a decaying satellite can look like an incoming warhead to a sensor. That is the reason we have a man in the loop. On every space or missile launch, that is why I assess whether it's a threat to North America. Human judgment will always be there to insure that we provide reliable, timely, unambiguous warning.

Accidental War Unrealistic

Today, the chance that a flock of Canada geese crossing a radar screen or a failed computer chip could start a nuclear war is effectively nonexistent. Scare stories to the contrary, in peacetime there is no danger of an accidental nuclear war, a conclusion reached by all serious investigators of the problem. The current situation was not automatic, for in the early days of nuclear weapons the danger of accidental war was considerable. Yet through large investments in hardware and careful organization of our nuclear forces we have managed this problem well.

Paul Bracken, *The Washington Post National Weekly Edition*, January 21, 1985.

Question: How can you be sure that someone at the command headquarters in Cheyenne Mountain won't push the button and fire off missiles in response to a false alarm?

Answer: There are no buttons to push. Our mission is to provide early warning and attack assessment to the national command authorities through the National Military Command Center in the Pentagon. So there are no buttons to push, as in the *WarGames* movie.

Question: Do you think it is possible for a computer hacker to get into your system and trick your computers, as happened in *WarGames*?

Answer: A person like a student could not gain access to the computer system in Cheyenne Mountain, because we are not on the commercial telephone network. No one can dial up our computer system.

45

All the data that comes from the sensor sites to Cheyenne Mountain is scrambled—that is, it's encrypted. When it arrives at Cheyenne Mountain, it is unscrambled. And then it has to face a most trying, taxing protocol interface to be able to enter the computer system. So it would be impossible for somebody to get into our computer system in Cheyenne Mountain.

Question: Since all this publicity about computer hackers breaking into secure computers, have you taken any additional measures to protect the integrity of the system here?

Answer: Well, we have looked at our system, and we feel that we were taking every precaution possible before the movie *WarGames* was made.

"Nuclear war is not only unthinkable psychologically, it is unfeasible and untenable technically."

Nuclear War Will Not Occur

Edward A. Walsh

A retired lieutenant colonel, Edward A. Walsh served twenty-five years in the Air Force, ten of that in Intelligence. In the following viewpoint, Mr. Walsh discusses and rejects the most likely scenarios which could lead to a nuclear war.

As you read, consider the following questions:

1. Why does the author believe that the Russians would not be willing to fight a nuclear war?
2. What does the author think of civil defense?
3. The author refutes several nuclear war scenarios. What are they?

Humanity is at the crossroads of destiny, and very few recognize the subtle turning point in the history of the world. Certainly, no one in a responsible position of government—ours and all others— seems aware of what is taking place in the progression of materials, peoples, philosophy, and international relations. Barely audible whispers of protest out of a wilderness of conflict are lost in the maelstrom of power politics.

The most difficult keynote of this new day for the diehard traditionalists to digest is the maxim that *all-out nuclear war will never happen!* Nor will there be a limited nuclear confrontation, since basic logic rejects containment; escalation would be as night follows day. Those who consider the latter a practical strategy have lost sight of what has happened to such concepts down through the centuries of man's all-out hostility toward his fellow man. The side about to lose a limited nuclear exchange would certainly raise the ante until the game reached the no-limit stage. Starting a nuclear war would be like a man setting fire to a house in which he is chained to the floor. The very nature, mutuality, and magnitude of nuclear devastation has made nuclear war obsolete as an instrument of national policy, except as a deterrent force, which cancels it out as a weapon of offense. Nuclear war is not only unthinkable psychologically, it is unfeasible and untenable technically.

Man Is Not Suicidal

Man is selfish, cantankerous, provocative, and belligerent, but he is also extremely intelligent and certainly not suicidal as a species. He has not reached his current state of environmental mastery just to destroy himself in a fit of technological summitry. It would violate any purpose of existence for him to terminate his tenure on Earth with his ongoing escalation of enlightenment and accomplishment still intact, in spite of his bellicosity. Rather, think of him as on his way to a longevity of refinement in a universe of infinite resources—in a dictated, enforced peace if necessary.

The facts of current events unveil a gradual change in the mosaic of international strife, the last gasps of primitive conflict in the Middle East (Afghanistan included), Central America, and Southeast Asia notwithstanding. Unfortunately, the neurotic fear of nuclear holocaust has generated near hysteria in some elements of the world's population, a debilitating emotion that erupts in irrational controversy. That fear, of course, is based on the probability of nuclear war between the superpowers, a probability that evaluates to nearly *zero*. In any discussion of such a probability, it would seem incumbent upon us to know more about the Russians than most Americans do. The vague presentation of chronological history does little to establish any degree of empathy with the Russian mind and spirit.

For centuries, Russia was largely a peasant country ruled by a close-knit autocracy of royal aristocrats. There was practically no

48

Reprinted with permission of Mike Shelton.

middle class of free and independent farmers, settlers, builders, and shrewd entrepreneurs. Except for the royalty and peasantry labels, it is still very much the same. It wasn't until after World War II that Russia reached the barebones stage of a modern nation by Western standards, and they still are struggling to attain a comparable standard of living. Much can be said to support the contention that the Russian government's obsession with war-making potential has been responsible for much, if not all, of the deprivations to which the Russian masses are still subjected.

The Russians resorted to a scorched-earth policy when confronted by Hitler's irresistible legions. However, the towns, roads, bridges, etc., they destroyed were obsolete facilities of an outworn age. Those areas have since been rebuilt in more modern form. These former peasants have worked very hard during the past 40 years in achieving a civilization roughly comparable to our own, although falling far short of our conveniences and affluence. They are justifiably proud of their high-rise office and apartment buildings, factories, transportation networks, agricultural complexes, and universities. They are making impressive strides in hydroelectric and nuclear power, as well as in medical and surgical science. No one in his right mind discredits their space program—which is militarily oriented, as is our own.

Russians Would Not Risk War

Slavic nature is not the kind to risk destruction of even part of these accomplishments in this ever more sophisticated world. They definitely want no part in having to do it all over again. Why should they? They have developed and are exploiting a very effective apparatus of subversion and terrorism to undermine capitalistic competition and international opposition. *That* is where our greatest concern should be focused, along with the insidious threat of chemical and/or biological aggression. It should be a red-flagged footnote that Communist Russia has never attacked an outside force that could hurt them in return, although tiny Finland did give the big bear a bloody nose. Their vast military build-up is more a matter of blackmail potential and bargaining strength than one of outright assault. It is warranted in the eyes of the Russian people as a shield against the "evil-minded capitalistic aggressors," an image that has brainwashed the Soviet man in the street into a state of paranoia about the West. (Americans also have been infected with the same disease.)

The Impossibility of War

It is that same unprecedented military escalation on the part of the Russians that is trotted out in support of our own military establishment's determination to match the Russians plane for plane, ship for ship, tank for tank, gun for gun, and man for man. The truth of the matter is that not only is nuclear war unmanageable, but conventional war against the Russians is impossible! *Where* would it take place, Alaska? The Russians are not going to extend their supply lines into Africa, North or South America, or even Japan. They can't. Neither can the U.S. ever reach Europe, the Middle East, or Asia with sufficient manpower and arms to match their forces. Convoys are extinct. Not only can the most modern of warships be destroyed by one missile, as was demonstrated in the Falkland Islands war, but either side has the capability of wiping out an entire fleet of ships with one blast.

We will never meet the Russians in an all-out conventional war for an even more deductive rationale. No such confrontation could be visualized without the gradual introduction of nuclear weapons, tactical at first, then strategic. The heads of government are conscious of this. Nevertheless, our generals and admirals are so taken up by their computerized games of war, which play with the attrition of millions of human beings as so many chess pieces, that they have lost touch with the soul of humanity. War on a worldwide scale is a thing of the past, relegated to the scrap heap of human relations by man's basic instinct for survival—the most powerful motivation of mortal existence. . . .

Accidental War

What about an accidental or madman-initiated nuclear war? A massive launch of nuclear missiles is out of the realm of accidental probability. It is certainly possible, although extremely unlikely, for a single missile to leave its launching pad by accident. In such a case, there should be plenty of time to send it a signal to deactivate and/or destroy itself. Just in case a maverick missile did approach its target, the receiving country would probably have been notified by hot line before the disaster struck. The victim would also have detected and tracked the incoming warhead as a single blip and would probably have the capability of intercepting and destroying it. Whatever happened certainly would not uncork the nuclear bottle. Intense controversy and delicate negotiations would instigate apologies and/or compensation, as applicable. The accidental incident might just create an atmosphere for serious consideration of weapons reduction and eventual disarmament.

No president or dictator, madman or otherwise, would take it upon himself to launch an all-out nuclear attack without due consultation with his staff. It is a natural human phenomenon that there would be certain members of that staff with an invincible sense of survival who would resort to assassination before allowing themselves and their nation to be subjected to retaliatory holocaust.

Superpower Monopoly on Nuclear Weapons

As for an Idi Amin or a Muammar alQaddafi—as power-hungry and unstable as he might be—it is quite within reason that he would not touch a nuclear device with a pole as long as the Suez Canal. He must realize that a dormant contrivance of such threatening proportions in his cellar would be an invitation for a live one in his attic, and it would not necessarily have to come from Israel. The destruction of the feeder-type reactor being built by the French in Iraq is not a tactic peculiar to the Israelis. That is a well-established and actively considered concept of preemptive defense against attack, and it is a lesson not lost on the belligerent factions among the smaller powers. It would seem the better part of wisdom for all those warring contestants around the world to avoid at all costs the slightest indication of a nuclear missile or bombing capability.

Nuclear War Unimaginable

It is difficult to imagine getting into a conventional war with the Soviet Union that wouldn't immediately raise the spectre of nuclear conflict. And I think the superpowers will go to almost unimaginable lengths to avoid that possibility. I cannot imagine either the United States or the Soviet Union contemplating the use of nuclear weapons.

Robert W. Tucker, *Policy Review*, Winter 1985.

It so happens that each of them is allied formally or in spirit with one or the other of the superpowers. Neither Russia nor the U.S. would allow one of its clients to be attacked or threatened by nuclear weapons without severe retribution in kind. In any scenario of logic, the superpowers have a monopoly on any decision to initiate the use of any type of nuclear weapon.

The glaring exception would be the time when terrorists will have attained a nuclear capacity, and the world had better prepare itself for that eventuality. Rather than a nuclear war between the superpowers, the next great confrontation of worldwide significance might well creep up on us in the form of an all-out campaign, including military, by the free world to crush terrorism by whatever means available, including the invasion of any country providing refuge. That could, of course, generate a sticky situation between the Western powers and Russia, where much support for terrorism originates. However, even that contingency would not be sufficient cause for a nuclear outburst. It is reasonably conceivable that the Russians themselves would find it expedient to join the battle as the parasitic disease of terrorism infects their own vital organs with nuclear fever. . . .

Saving Money

It is not enough to elect our officials in Washington and then leave such matters exclusively up to them while attending to our personal affairs. Many of them are more concerned with their political fortunes than with the fate of mankind. The proposals submitted are not only for allocating our finances and resources more effectively, but also offer the possibility of saving enough money to balance the budget as well. Only by raising a crescendo of protest against the business-as-usual attitude prevailing among many of our representatives can we hope to shove our ponderous bureaucracy off its soft seat and onto a course into the Space Age.

We must insist on continued technological superiority over the forces of impending conquest and rid ourselves of the overburdening trappings of yesteryear, when musketry and cannonballs carried the day. We must assume that our free society is endowed with the motivation and perseverance for unfettered creativity that will prevail over the regimentation of those whose initiative is subject to ideological expedience. If *that* is not the case, then we in the Western world are in for a rough time no matter what we do.

"History must never forget that we worked hard for a nuclear war, we paid for it, and we deserve it."

Nuclear War?
We Deserve It!

Gary Macy

Gary Macy teaches in the department of Religious Studies at the University of San Diego. Mr. Macy's satire on the merits of a major nuclear exchange provides a compelling and unusual opinion on the issue as a whole. By employing extreme irony, Mr. Macy attempts to expose the absurdities in many of the current debates on nuclear war.

As you read, consider the following questions:

1. What liberal goals does the author satirically suggest would be met by a nuclear war? What conservative goals would be met?
2. What do you think is Mr. Macy's real attitude toward nuclear war?
3. Why did he choose to present his ideas in a satire?

Gary Macy, "Every Cloud Has a Silver Lining," *Christianity & Crisis*, March 5, 1984. Reprinted with permission. Copyright 1984, Christianity & Crisis, 537 West 121st Street, New York, New York 10027.

One hears a great deal these days about an alleged debate over nuclear war. In fact, there is no such debate. Reviewing the literature, I have found all sides equally vehement in proclaiming their distaste for nuclear war, and no person or faction pointing out its potential advantages.

There are of course differences of opinion. Liberals contend that a nuclear freeze or a comprehensive test ban or abolition of all nuclear weapons is the best tactic. Conservatives argue for building up our nuclear armory to get ahead of the Soviets and preserve deterrence. (Soviet conservatives presumably make the same argument, with suitable adjustments.) But all sides agree that nuclear war must be avoided at all costs, even unto the trillions. Since everyone so far has avoided the really basic question, this essay, by addressing the neglected arguments in favor of nuclear war, will provide a tentative probe into virgin territory. It will also be unique in its detachment from ideology, for it will point out the need for a new approach, fresh thinking, etc., to the hard Right and the far Left, to conservatives and liberals and even to people who don't much care about these matters.

Nuclear Fuel for Everyone

Consider, first, the liberal perspective. Surely one of the liberals' most cherished goals is a more equal distribution of the world's resources. But nuclear war would clearly be the swiftest and most effective means to achieve this end. First of all, an inexpensive source of nuclear fuel would be immediately available to everyone. The simple brick, in theory, could heat an entire village. Furthermore, this material would be widely distributed simply by the action of the war itself, thus eliminating costs of transportation and the endless red tape of other aid programs.

Second, and here lies the charm of the argument, the entire third world would almost instantaneously become the first world, thus bringing about in a matter of days or weeks what even centuries of development might never achieve. With the first and second worlds more or less eliminated, the third world would become, for all practical purposes, the *only* world.

If this dream comes to pass, transnational corporations will no longer drain the resources of the multitudinous poor to line the pockets of the few: The few and their pockets will be gone. Instead of providing pools of cheap labor and stocks of underpriced resources, the underdeveloped countries will be the *only* sources of labor and the only markets for materials, raw or manufactured. No other imaginable program could as effectively spur their peoples on to self-sufficiency. With lending institutions effectively, and, in some cases, literally, liquidated, all third world debts would be canceled; unencumbered by the need to pay off these debts, underdeveloped economies would blossom swiftly. "Alternative" world economic and social movements would cease to be alternatives as both late capitalism and state socialism would fade, with a slight afterglow, into history.

Race Relations Improved

At least two other major liberal goals will also be achieved if the measures suggested here are adopted. Soviet oppression of intellectuals and religious minorities will smolder, and everyone who can leave the workers' paradise will almost certainly be free to do so. In the U.S., race relations will almost certainly be improved, without any need (or capacity) for busing. Whatever facilities exist for whoever survives will probably be equal. Many forms of prejudice will fade because of difficulties in determining the previous

"Nobody drops a nuclear bomb on me and gets away with it!"

© Ross/Rothco

ethnic, racial, or genetic origins of survivors and their offspring. In a final argument, perhaps the most convincing of all to liberal esthetes, the coming nuclear war will eliminate the "ugly American" (except perhaps in the quite literal sense). A world rid of cheap trinkets and shadowy slides of Macchu Picchu (no, that's the Sistine Chapel) is a world worth fighting for.

The View from the Right

If liberals have many reasons to welcome a nuclear holocaust, conservatives should be dismayed at the prospect of *not* having one. It is they who demand strict governmental fiscal responsibility; and yet, after having been promised "more bang for their bucks" for decades, taxpayers have received little more than a fizzle. Pity the hard-pressed, middle-class worker, slaving for months every year to provide tax money for weapons he or she may never live to see used. What kind of cost-effectiveness is this? Once these docile tax-

55

payers waken to reality, a nuclear thaw movement will erupt in both superpowers, demanding that the U.S. and U.S.S.R., as a matter of simple justice, end the arms race once and for all by the most responsible means: nuclear war.

The results of that war will appeal to other strongly felt conservative instincts. Such a streamlining would definitively get the government off the backs of the people. The entire liberal program of government waste and giveaways should be reduced to more or less natural waste; with government regulations abolished from above, pure capitalism would flourish. The laws of the marketplace would govern all exchange; the private sector would be wholly free to take over hospitals, social relief, the administration of justice, and emergency disaster aid.

Going deeper still, observe that with the elimination of the Soviet Union, the strongest wish of the American conservative movement would be granted and the world would be once again safe for political democracy (i.e., state capitalism). Fortunately, and almost miraculously, the same act of warfare will also meet the dearest hopes of Soviet conservatives, for the destruction of the United States will make the world safe for economic democracy (i.e., state socialism). As always, elegance is found in simplicity.

There are lesser but still worthy conservative gains to be made. As survivors attempt to rebuild, abortion would become less desirable. The debate over artificial contraception would end, for any birth control would be natural (i.e., caused by radiation). Prayer would be not only allowed but encouraged in whatever public schools remained—and elsewhere as well, for we may safely predict a religious revival. And, of course, the phrase "nuclear family" would take on a new intensity. Finally, no one any longer would be able to think of the U.S. as weak-willed; history would remember us as a people who kept their word and were not afraid to bite the bullet. Or, in contemporary terms, to swallow the warhead.

The Silenced Majority

A word should be said about the advantages of a nuclear war for those numerous Americans who, as voting records indicate, are apathetic about this debate as about all others. One or more of the following arguments may have appeal to these passive ones. After the exchange, there would be no more taxes. There would be no more liberals and conservatives heckling one another on media time better spent on "General Hospital," "Battle of the Superstars," and football. (Of course, there would be no more football or media, but there would be real-life, hard-fought scrimmages over such desirables as food and shelter.) There would be no more rush-hour traffic, no more waiting in line for popcorn at the movies, no more digital watches that start beeping in the middle of classes, arias, and lovemaking. There would be no more smokers (in the usual sense).

Despite the multi-faceted appeal of nuclear war, one must anticipate objections. The one that is most passionately voiced is that millions upon millions of people will die. This seems at first a most compelling argument, but on closer inspection its force disappears, as it were, in a cloud of smoke. Most people, after all, don't know millions of other people and in their hearts don't really care if millions die; after all, millions have died in the past, millions will die in the future; let's forget it and have a beer.

Readily Accept Genocide

But, you say, people really do care about their own dying, and about the deaths of friends. Again, the objection only appears to be serious. First, we're all going to die anyway, so why object to this way of going? Second, a syllogism: Most of us profess ourselves ready to die for a good cause; this has already been demonstrated to be a good cause; *ergo*, the objection is held to be invalid. People simply must stop viewing nuclear disaster in emotional terms, and let reason prevail. It is true that this particular line of reasoning may not appeal to the apathetic majority, but then they have decided not to count anyway, in contrast to us nobler souls who will readily accept our inclusion in genocide for the sake of the great liberal/conservative future that has been projected here.

Kill People Only Five Times

Instead of negotiating the reduction of offensive and defensive nuclear weapons, we should negotiate limits on how many times each superpower may kill a person in the event of an all-out war.

The United States and the Soviets have stockpiled enough weapons to destroy each other's citizens 10 times over. The first step, then, is to produce an agreement that would reduce the nuclear arsenals in both countries to the point where they could only kill every American and Soviet citizen *five* times.

Art Buchwald, *St. Paul Pioneer Press*, January 16, 1985.

So much for objections. No self-respecting author can conclude an argument, however, without sharing awareness of the historical background from which the argument arose, and without demonstrating also that the author has read a book. I therefore offer the following observations of the late Alexander Woollcott, the American critic, journalist, wit, and raconteur. His comments were made upon his return from Japan in the late '30s:

[This] leaves only one topic that I have not touched upon—to wit: our future war with Japan about which, from time to time, I have heard wiseacres talking ever since I can remember. More often of late, than for some years past. Heaven knows, I heard enough about it over there, not from the Japanese, of course, but in the bar at the Peking Club, or in the veranda cafe of some Pacific liner, or aboard some small craft fog-bound in the Yellow Sea....I heard how many years a really satisfactory war would take, how we would have to begin by frankly yielding up the Philippines and then spend two years gathering forces for recapturing them....Oh, I heard much of the kind of thinking which made the last war come true.

Most of the talk was ever so cheerful, but war is not my trade and I am afraid I kept foreseeing this one in terms of youngsters now oblivious at school and of homes on midland farms waiting every day for letters that will never come. I only hope that if there is such a war and we win it, we shall remember that we won it because we were larger, richer, and more numerous, and therefore not feel too proud about it.

How strange are the quirks of history! How sad should posterity (if any) believe the coming nuclear disaster to be some unplanned mishap, accident, or surprise of history. This would be the greatest injustice. Never before in the history of humankind have so much money, so much time, and so much genius been concentrated on a single concerted project. The pyramids, even the Roman Empire itself, pales in comparison. No! History must never forget that we worked hard for a nuclear war, we paid for it, and we deserve it.

When Should the US Use Nuclear Weapons?

In this chapter, the authors discuss many possible ways in which a nuclear war could begin. Implied, but not discussed, is the question of at what point, if any, the US should become involved in a nuclear confrontation. This activity will give you a chance to explore the possible incidents that could trigger the outbreak of nuclear war and under what conditions the US may be persuaded to use nuclear weapons.

While many believe it is unlikely that the US would be the first to use nuclear weapons, you should recall that in 1962, John F. Kennedy announced publicly that the US would contemplate using them if the Soviet Union refused to remove its missile bases from Cuba.

The cartoon below, while a comical exaggeration, nevertheless illustrates one view of when the US should contemplate getting involved in a military confrontation. The list below suggests other, more significant reasons.

Reprinted with permission from the Minneapolis Star and Tribune.

Part I

Examine the list of incidents which could provoke the US to use nuclear weapons. Rank them from 1-10 according to which you believe would most likely cause the US to use nuclear weapons. (1 for most likely, 10 for least likely.)

Incidents

_____ the Soviet Union places nuclear missiles in Nicaragua

_____ the US moves military troops into Nicargauga

_____ the US, relying on its military superiority, launches a first strike against the Soviet Union

_____ the Soviet Union, relying on its military superiority, launches a nuclear first strike against the US

_____ computer error provokes an accidental missile launch

_____ Iraq, a Soviet ally, develops the bomb and uses it to attack Israel, a US ally; Israel bombs Iraq and involves both the US and the Soviet Union in a major confrontation

_____ one person in a missile silo becomes convinced a nuclear war is necessary and launches an attack

_____ Japan becomes a major world power and provokes a nuclear war

_____ The Soviet Union invades Western Europe

_____ Terrorists gain possession of nuclear weapons and initiate a situation that leads to superpower involvement

Part II

Working in either small groups or all together, the class should discuss the following questions:

1. What conditions must exist before the US uses nuclear weapons?
2. Would the US ever be justified in attacking enemy population centers with nuclear weapons?
3. Would the US ever be justified in launching a nuclear first strike?

Finally, reflect on the viewpoints in this book and your other knowledge about American government and discuss whether or not you believe the US is likely to use its nuclear weapons.

Periodical Bibliography

The following list of periodical articles deals with the subject matter of this chapter.

Jack Anderson	"Can We Have a Missile Accident?" *Parade Magazine*, August 14, 1983.
William M. Arkin	"Why SIOP-6?," *Bulletin of the Atomic Scientists*, April 1983.
William J. Broad	"Computer Security Worries Military Experts," *New York Times*, September 25, 1983.
Ashton B. Carter	"The Command and Control of Nuclear War," *Scientific American*, January 1985.
Christianity and Crisis	"Deterrence Is Crazy. Preemption Is Criminal," April 29, 1985.
Lloyd J. Dumas	"Real Nuclear War for Less than $1," *New York Times*, July 2, 1983.
Daniel Ford	"US War Plans: Nuclear First Strike from a Failure to Communicate," *Los Angeles Times*, May 12, 1985.
Daniel Ford	"The Button," *New Yorker*, April 8, 1985.
Brian Michael Jenkins	"Nuclear Terrorism and Its Consequences," *Society*, July 1980.
Josh Martin	"WarGames," *Multinational Monitor*, December/January 1985.
Howard Morland	"Are We Readying a First Strike?" *Nation*, March 16, 1985.
Newsweek	"Nuclear War: Can We Reduce the Risk?" December 5, 1983.
Personal Computing	"Could 'WarGames' Happen?" October 1983.
Daniel Poneman	"Risky Nuclear Trade," *New York Times*, November 26, 1983.
Stephen Shenfield	"Soviet Thinking About the Unthinkable," *Bulletin of the Atomic Scientists*, February 1985.
Time	"The Nuclear Threat Is Spreading as More Countries Try to Get the Bomb," June 3, 1985.

Would Humanity Survive a Nuclear War?

Chapter Preface

In 1983 a group of scientists developed a study on the climatic effects of both limited and all-out nuclear wars. The study, known as TTAPS (an acronym based on the last names of the scientists involved) came to the forbidding conclusion that the human species might not survive a nuclear confrontation. The study continues to be hotly debated both for its scientific accuracy and its political ramifications, and many questions remain as to the survivability of humanity in the event of an all-out nuclear exchange.

While it is doubtful that every man, woman, and child would perish, the question remains as to whether civilization would continue as we know it. Would the survivors possess enough knowledge to reconstruct the technological and scientific advances of the past? Or would a new stone age begin, with the charred remnants of a once progressive era providing only an incongruous landscape for the human survivors as they struggle to relearn the rudiments of civilization?

"The argument that a nuclear war could eliminate the human species or bring an end to civilization as we know it has not stood up to the light of objective and scientific examination."

Humanity Can Survive a Nuclear War

Jack C. Greene

Jack C. Greene, now retired, served as director of post-attack research (1963-1973) and as deputy assistant director of research (1973-1974) for the US Defense Civil Preparedness Agency. In the following viewpoint, Mr. Greene expresses his belief that while a nuclear war would be a horrendous experience, the United States could still survive and ultimately recover.

As you read, consider the following questions:

1. What would the US be like two weeks after a nuclear war, according to the author?
2. How long does the author believe it will take for the agricultural industry to recover after a nuclear attack?
3. How does Mr. Green's view of the post-nuclear world differ from that of Dr. Ehrlich's? Name three specific examples.

Jack C. Greene, "Recovery from Nuclear Attack," reprinted with permission from *The Apocalyptic Premise: Nuclear Arms Debated,* edited by Ernest W. Lefever and E. Stephen Hunt, published by the Ethics and Public Policy Center, 1030 15th Street NW, Washington DC 20005.

On December 5, 1945, just four months after the news burst on the world that an atomic bomb had been developed by the United States and had been dropped on Japan, Dr. Hans Bethe, one of the designers of the bomb, was asked to appear before the Special Committee on Atomic Energy of the U.S. Senate. The committee was concerned that an atomic explosion might "ignite" the earth's atmosphere or start some sort of chain reaction in the air or in the ocean.

Although these fears are no longer taken seriously, fears of other almost equally catastrophic occurrences have arisen to take their place. These include:

—triggering a new ice age;

—upsetting the delicate balance of nature, leading to disastrous changes in the ecology;

—creation of vast radioactive wastelands that would be uninhabitable for generations;

—great increases in the incidence of leukemia and other malignancies among the survivors;

—vast increases in the number of congenital defects due to gene mutations, lasting for many generations;

—depletion of the ozone layer in the stratosphere, thus decreasing the protection from ultraviolet radiation and causing proliferation of skin cancers, killing wild and domestic animals, and making it difficult, if not impossible, to grow many of the crops that provide our food and fiber.

Total Destruction Comforting

The underlying motive behind these negative hypotheses may be psychological. If everyone "knew" that nuclear war either directly or indirectly would trigger a mechanism for annihilating the human species, somehow the world would appear more secure. No sane person would initiate a series of events that would lead to everyone's death, including his own. Thus to many people the idea of assured destruction contains elements of reassurance. . . .

The chances of surviving the immediate effects of the bombs caused by high overpressures and thermal radiation—effects that killed most of the victims of the atomic bombs in Japan—are about two in three. There is about one chance in two of surviving the fallout radiation effects as well. In all, the chances are about one in three of *not* receiving a radiation, blast, or burn injury.

In short, the prospects are:

—one in three of being killed outright by blast or thermal effects;

—one in six of being killed by fallout-radiation;

—one in six of being injured, but non-fatally, by blast, thermal, or fallout radiation;

—one in three of being uninjured. . . .

Now picture the United States one or two weeks after a full-scale attack against major military targets and population centers.

66

Approximately 50 percent of the population would have survived. Certain assumptions, based on years of research, can be made about the composition of the surviving population:

1. The next census will show a United States population of a little over 100 million—approximately the same as in 1921.

2. The population is no longer predominantly urban, for a considerably higher percentage of the rural population survived.

3. The male-female ratio remains about the same, but the age distribution is different. There are considerably fewer of the very old or very young.

4. The life expectancy of the average person is shortened, perhaps by as much as four to five years.

5. Proportionally there are fewer doctors and hospitals, corporate headquarters and executives, petroleum-refining and pharmaceutical-production plants, and public administrators.

There Will Be Survivors

No one wants a nuclear war, but . . . if one does occur, there will be survivors. The earth and its living organisms have survived scores, perhaps hundreds, of collisions with celestial objects releasing manyfold the amount of energy now stored in our arsenals. It is the energy release and not the radioactive fallout that accounts for the majority of the deaths occurring immediately after a nuclear bombing.

John R. Totter, *Society*, September/October 1983.

---

6. Many of the males in the surviving population are or will soon be temporarily sterile.

7. There is an increase in the percentage of orphans and other dependents as well as an increase in broken families.

8. There are other changes in the composition of the labor force, both geographically and in terms of skills.

9. About 50 per cent of the manufacturing capacity of the nation has been destroyed and an additional 20 per cent damaged. Of the remaining 30 per cent, some will not be accessible until radiation levels decay or decontamination has been performed.

10. Many domestic and wild animals and crops have been killed or severely damaged; compared to people, a higher percentage have survived.

11. People are learning how to avoid or minimize the consumption of contaminated food and water and how to ration carefully their exposure to external sources of radiation.

12. The general behavior pattern among the survivors is adaptive rather than maladaptive. By and large, people can be counted

on to participate constructively in future efforts to achieve national recovery as long as there appears to be a leadership that has a plan and knows what it is doing.

Survivors of the direct blast and early fallout effects still face an uncertain future. Serious additional hazards and obstacles must be overcome before the society to which they now belong returns to a semblance of its pre-attack status. Some of the hazards will have to be faced immediately, while others will not become important until months or even years later . . . .

Life-Support Inadequacies

People who have to remain in fallout shelters because of continuing high fallout-radiation levels in the outside environment may run out of food and water. Unless adequate supplies of water for drinking are maintained, severe consequences will be experienced within a very short time. People either will leave the shelter in search of water, thereby exposing themselves to excessive radiation, or will become ill from dehydration. If water is completely denied, deaths will begin to occur in a few days . . . .

The food and water problem is one of distribution, not of insufficient resources. Although water distribution systems could be damaged and water service interrupted, analysis has shown that in most cases enough water for drinking would be available—trapped in the plumbing, in hot water heaters, in the flush tanks of toilets, and the like. Proportionally far more food would survive than people to consume it. The problem is getting the food to the people who need it . . . .

Radiological contamination of food and water would not be a serious complicating factor. With simple precautions people could avoid use of food and water with excessive contamination levels. Most people would not be affected to any significant extent.

In summary: there is no intrinsic reason why life-support requirements for the survivors of a nuclear attack should not be met. The basic problem is one of distributing the surviving supplies.

Epidemics and Diseases

Among the potential contributors to an increase of epidemics and diseases in a post-nuclear-war society are these factors:

a. Many sanitation facilities and waterworks could be either destroyed, damaged, or disrupted.

b. Public health organizations could be disrupted and lose personnel.

c. There could be inadequate supplies of prophylactic and therapeutic chemicals—vaccines, anti-toxins, antibiotics, and other necessities for disease control.

d. The higher-than-normal radiation exposures to which the survivors of nuclear war have been subjected may increase susceptibility to infection and disease . . . .

Knowledge is the single most important factor that would serve to mitigate the effects of epidemics and diseases. Knowledge cannot be destroyed by a nuclear attack. The great discoveries of Pasteur and Lister do not need to be repeated.

No Danger of Devastation

Even under the worst circumstances imaginable, there is no danger of a repetition of the bubonic plague that devastated Europe in the mid-fourteenth century, or other types of catastrophic epidemics.

Modest expenditures, primarily for developing detailed plans to augment supplies of broad-spectrum antibiotics quickly, could have a significant payoff in the event of a nuclear attack upon the United States.

Radiation Effects

Contrary to what . . . others seem to believe, radiation would not be sufficient to extinguish all life on earth. A realistic appraisal, based upon existing knowledge, suggests that 20 percent of the population in their present residences would not need to spend any time in shelters; 33 percent would need to spend two to three days in shelters, while 45 percent might have to spend from three days to two weeks. . . . With adequate planning and with dispersal, losses could be reduced to about 20 percent of the population.

Henry C. Huntley, *Society*, September/October 1983.

In sum, the specter of pestilence and disease stalking the land in the aftermath of nuclear war is probably just that—a specter, not a realistic probability. It need not, and probably would not, occur.

Economic Breakdown

The post-attack economic problem may be thought of in two parts—the physical component and the need for management. Would the physical constituents of the economy—land with acceptably low radiation levels, seeds, fertilizers and pesticides, industrial plants, energy, raw materials, transportation, a skilled labor force—be available where needed in sufficient amounts so that, if used in an optimal way, the goods and services required by the survivors could be produced? If not, economic recovery could not occur, and the question of management becomes academic.

Do we have confidence in our ability to forecast the kinds and degrees of damage that could result to U.S. industry and its production capacity in the event of nuclear war?

The answer is yes. But it is a qualified yes.

Limitations in the ability to predict levels of damage to the various industrial sectors probably lie mostly in the uncertainties about the type of attack (targeting) an enemy would undertake, and the number and explosive power of the weapons that would be used. . . .

Common sense indicates that this country could continue to grow the food and fiber necessary to sustain its citizens after nuclear attack. The United States has a highly efficient agricultural industry. Less than 4 per cent of the total population is all that is required not only to meet the needs of the nation but also to provide huge surpluses for export. This industry is almost immune to significant damage in a nuclear attack. Farm machinery would be scarcely affected at all, and the farm workers themselves are not very vulnerable providing they take simple precautions against fallout. Priority allocation of fuel for the farm machinery and of fertilizers and other farm inputs is all that is necessary to bring the agricultural industry substantially back to its pre-attack rate. . . .

Late Radiation Effects

Longer-term radiation effects would include thyroid damage, bone cancer, leukemia, and other forms of cancer of the types that occur today. Radiation does not induce new forms of cancer; it increases the frequency of occurrence of those that result from other causes. A physician examining cancer patients in the post-war world would not be able to discriminate between cancers caused by the fallout radiation and those that would have occurred anyway. Radiation exposure would increase the incidence of various types of cancer so that the net effect would be observable on a statistical basis. There is no danger that the increased incidence would be great enough to pose a threat to the survival of the society. . . .

Perspective is provided by a comparison of the death expectancy from late radiation effects among the survivors with the death expectancy from various causes in today's society. In the comparison, it is assumed all the fallout-radiation-induced leukemia and other cancers among the survivors will result in death, which of course is extreme and not to be expected. . . .

Perhaps it is more meaningful to compare post-attack radiation effects with the dangers of cigarette smoking, since both take their toll over time. According to the U.S. Public Health Service, 340,000 people die annually from causes attributed to cigarette smoking. If the smoking habits of the surviving population were to be similar to those of our existing population, the chance of dying from smoking would be seven times greater than that of dying from post-attack radiation effects.

This estimate assumes 100 million survivors with an average exposure of 100 roentgens—a realistic possibility. . . .

70

The various ecological catastrophes postulated to follow a nuclear war—fire, erosion, flooding, pest outbreaks, epidemic diseases, and balance-of-nature disturbances—have been individually examined in terms of their probable importance. The objective of the scientist who conducted this research, Dr. Robert Ayres, formerly of the Hudson Institute, was to "take seriously and examine in their own terms all of the supposed mechanisms leading to catastrophe which have been subjects of speculation in recent years." He summarized by saying, "We have not found any of these mechanisms to be plausible in terms of any reasonable definition of catastrophe." . . .

Forty Million Survivors

About 40 million Americans are likely to survive a worst-case large-scale nuclear attack, even without any protective measures. The total absence of civil defense preparations, the public's all but complete ignorance of the realities of nuclear war and the consequent potential for an exacerbation of a nuclear tragedy are among the most dangerous characteristics of our present defense effort.

Edward Teller, *The New York Times*, January 3, 1984.

In thinking about post-attack ecology, it is useful to keep in mind that nature may not be so delicately balanced after all. No logical weight of nuclear attack could induce gross changes in the balance of nature that approach in type or degree the ones that human civilization has already produced. This includes cutting most of the original forests, tilling the prairies, irrigating the deserts, damming and polluting the streams, eliminating certain species and introducing others, overgrazing hillsides, flooding valleys, and even preventing forest fires. Man has radically changed the face of this continent, but should he leave the scene it seems overwhelmingly probable that the continent would gradually return to a state very like its original one, rather than fluctuate violently or continue to change to a new state of equilibrium. . . .

Genetic Damage

In common with late-radiation and ecological effects of nuclear war, the genetic effects of radiation are widely misunderstood and, consequently, feared. The specter of a vast increase in the incidence of congenital defects among our descendants is awesome. Perspective is hard to develop, partly because any threat to our children is laden with emotion.

But a great deal is now known about the genetic effects of radiation. Dr. H. J. Muller, Nobel Prize-winning American geneticist, established that gene mutations produced by ionizing radiation are not different in their effect from the mutations produced by other agents. Therefore, any nuclear-war-produced genetic damage would not be manifested in unfamiliar ways, such as the birth of two-headed monsters. Rather, there would be a statistical increase in cases of the various types of genetic-related diseases and disabilities that occur in today's world. . . .

Whether the expected genetic consequences of nuclear war are currently overstated or understated, the discrepancy probably is small. Even though the radiation-induced genetic consequences of a nuclear war may add some degree of suffering to the attack survivors and their offspring, these consequences will not be of sufficient magnitude to threaten the survival of the society or seriously impede recovery.

Jury Is Still Out

On the question of whether the United States would recover following a massive nuclear attack, the jury is still out—and most probably always will be. Everyone hopes and most people believe the question will always remain in the abstract. The probability of nuclear war seems very remote, and we will never know for sure whether recovery is possible unless nuclear war actually occurs.

No nation can realistically hope to be better off after a nuclear exchange than it was before. One might inflict more damage on the other than it itself sustained, but any such "victory" would be a Pyrrhic one.

The argument that a nuclear war could eliminate the human species or bring an end to civilization as we know it has not stood up to the light of objective and scientific examination. New hypotheses for doom and disaster will arise, and they must be examined and evaluated. But no prudent society will allow unproved hypotheses to exert a paralyzing influence on its preparedness programs.

"We could not exclude the possibility of a full-scale nuclear war entraining the extinction of Homo sapiens.*"*

Humanity Cannot Survive a Nuclear War

Paul R. Ehrlich

Paul R. Ehrlich is the Bing Professor of Population Studies at Stanford University, where he has taught since 1959. A Fellow of the American Association for the Advancement of Science and of the American Academy of Arts and Sciences, Dr. Ehrlich has served as president of Zero Population Growth and has received the John Muir Award of the Sierra Club. In the following viewpoint, Dr. Ehrlich documents the unprecedented disaster that a nuclear war would wreak. He and his colleagues conclude that a nuclear war may mean the end of the human species.

As you read, consider the following questions:

1. According to the author, would biological catastrophe occur in all nuclear war scenarios?
2. How many people would be killed during a nuclear war, according to Dr. Ehrlich?
3. Does Dr. Ehrlich believe that plants and animals would fare better than humans?

Reprinted from THE COLD AND THE DARK, The World after Nuclear War, by Paul R. Ehrlich, Carl Sagan, Donald Kennedy, and Walter Orr Roberts, by permission of W. W. Norton & Company, Inc. Copyright © 1984 by Open Space Institute, Inc.: The Center on the Consequences of Nuclear War.

The environment that will confront most human beings and other organisms after a thermonuclear holocaust will be so altered, and so malign, that extreme and widespread damage to living systems is inevitable. It is, for example, entirely possible that the biological impacts of a war, *apart* from those resulting directly from a blast, fire, and prompt radiation, could result in the end of civilization in the Northern Hemisphere. Biologists can agree to that as easily as we all could agree that accidentally using cyanide instead of salt in the gravy could spoil a dinner party.

My primary task here today is to give you some technical background to explain *why* numerous biologists—especially ecologists—are convinced that decision-makers in many nations vastly underrate the potential risks of nuclear war . . . .

It would be extremely difficult to design a major nuclear war that would not lead to a biological catastrophe of unprecedented dimensions . . . .

750 Million Deaths

Blast alone, according to one estimate, would be expected to cause 750 million deaths. As many people *as existed on the planet when our nation was founded* would be vaporized, disintegrated, mashed, pulped, and smeared over the landscape by the explosive force of the bombs. Another study predicts that 1.1 *billion* people would be killed and a like number injured immediately by blast, heat, and radiation. In other words, almost *half* of the current global population—including most of the residents of the rich nations of the Northern Hemisphere—could become casualties within a few hours.

It is also crystal clear that the very fabric of industrial society would be destroyed by such a war. Virtually all cities—which are the political, industrial, transport, financial, communications, and cultural centers of societies—would simply cease to eixst. Much of humanity's know-how would disappear along with them. Medical care and other disaster-relief services would be essentially nonexistent—there would be no place for help to come from. Survivors in the once-rich nations would not only face the crushing psychological burdens of having witnessed the greatest catastrophe in human history, they would also know there was no hope of succor.

Such a situation is so mind-boggling that many take it to be a worst-case estimate of the potential damage to *Homo sapiens* in World War III. Instead, as we shall now see, I have only described the obvious tip of the iceberg. The fates of the 2-3 billion people who were not killed immediately—including those in nations far removed from targets—might in many ways be worse. They, of course, would suffer directly from the freezing temperatures, darkness, and midterm fallout . . . . But the most significant long-term effects would be produced indirectly by the impact of these

74

and other factors on the environmental systems of the planet. . . .

Reduced temperatures would have dramatic direct effects on animal populations, many of which would be wiped out by the unaccustomed cold. Nevertheless, the key to ecosystem effects is the impact of the war on green plants. Their activities provide what is known as *primary production*—the binding of energy (through photosynthesis) and the accumulation of nutrients that are necessary for the functioning of all biological components of natural and agricultural ecosystems. Without the photosynthetic activities of plants, virtually all animals, including human beings, would cease to exist. All flesh is truly "grass."

Both cold and darkness are inimical to green plants and to photosynthesis. . . .

No Safety from Nuclear War

There are no sanctuaries from nuclear war. The interconnecting web of systems that sustain life on the planet would be shattered. A nuclear attack would be suicide for the nation that launched it, even if there was no retaliatory strike. "Now," said one of the many Russian physicists who contributed to the [nuclear winter] study, "the whole of the earth and human civilization itself are held hostage." Can a nuclear war be won? As Dr. Sagan has said, "The ashes of communism and capitalism will be indistinguishable."

Physicians for Social Responsibility, *The Final Epidemic for all Living Things.*

The impacts of such low temperatures on plants would depend, among other things, on the time of year that they occurred, their duration, and the tolerances of different plant species to chilling. An abrupt onset of cold is particularly damaging. After a nuclear war, temperatures are expected to fall precipitously over a short time; thus it is unlikely that normally cold-tolerant plants could acclimate before they were exposed to lethal temperatures. . . .

What all this boils down to is that virtually all land plants in the Northern Hemisphere would be damaged or killed in a war that occurred just prior to or during the growing season. Most annual crops would likely be killed outright, and there would also be severe damage to many perennials if the war were to occur when they were growing actively. Damage might, of course, be less if it happened during the season when they were dormant. . . .

Sunlight and Plants

Cold, remember, is just *one* of the stresses to which green plants would be subjected. The blockage of sunlight that caused the cold would also reduce or terminate photosynthetic activities. This would have innumerable consequences that would cascade through food chains including those supporting human beings.

Primary productivity would be reduced roughly in proportion to the amount of light reduction, even if the vegetation were not otherwise damaged. If the light level declined to 5 percent or less of normal levels—which is likely to be the case for months in the middle latitudes of the Northern Hemisphere—most plants would be unable to maintain any net growth. Thus, even if temperatures remained normal, the productivity of crops and natural ecosystems would be enormously reduced by the blocking of sunlight following a war. In combination, the cold and darkness would constitute an unprecedented catastrophe for those systems. . . .

Radioactive Fallout

Ecosystems of the Northern Hemisphere would also be subjected to much higher levels of ionizing radiation from radioactive fallout than has been previously thought. One estimate suggests that a total of about 2 million square miles downwind of the detonations would be exposed to 1,000 rems or more of radiation, mostly within 48 hours. Such levels of radiation would be lethal to all exposed people and to many other sensitive animal and plant species.

As much as 30 percent of the midlatitude land area of the Northern Hemisphere might be exposed to more than 500 rems of radiation within a day. Such a dose would result in death for about half of the *healthy* adult human beings exposed. Because of other stresses, however, few of the adults in those areas would be healthy, so radiation might finish off many millions of wounded, sick, cold, hungry, and thirsty survivors. Those that did not die would be ill for weeks and prone to cancer for the remainder of their lives. The total number of people afflicted would certainly exceed one billion and might include everyone in the Northern Hemisphere—depending on the details of the nuclear exchange. . . .

Effects on Animals

The disaster that would befall many or most of the plants of the Northern Hemisphere from the effects of a nuclear exchange would contribute to an equal or greater disaster for the higher animals. Wild herbivores and carnivores and domestic animals either would be killed outright by the cold or would starve or die of thirst because surface waters were frozen. Following a fall or winter war, many dormant animals in colder regions might survive, only to face extremely difficult conditions in a cold, dark spring and summer.

Scavengers that could withstand the projected extreme cold would likely flourish in the postwar period because of the billions of unburied human and animal bodies. Their characteristically rapid population growth rates could, after the thaw, quickly make rats, roaches, and flies the most prominent animals shortly after World War III.

Soil organisms are not directly dependent on photosynthesis and

Reprinted by permission: Tribune Media Services.

can often remain dormant for long periods. They would be relatively unaffected by the cold and the dark. But in many areas the loss of above-ground vegetation would expose the soil to severe erosion by wind and water. Soil organisms may not be terribly susceptible to the atmospheric aftereffects of nuclear war, but entire soil ecosystems are likely to be destroyed anyway....

Starvation for Many

There is little storage of staple foods in human population centers, and most meat and produce are supplied by current production. Only cereal grains are stored in any significant quantities, but the storage sites are usually located in relatively remote areas. Thus, after a nuclear war, supplies of food in the Northern Hemisphere would be destroyed or contaminated, located in inaccessible areas, or quickly depleted. People who survived the other effects of the war would soon be starving. Furthermore, countries that now depend on large imports of foods, including those untouched by nuclear detonations, would suffer immediate and complete cessation of incoming food supplies. They would have to fall back on local agricultural and natural ecosystems. For many developing countries, this could mean starvation for large fractions of their populations....

Plausible nuclear war scenarios can be constructed that would result in the dominant atmospheric effects of darkness and cold spreading over virtually the entire planet. Under those circumstances, human survival would be largely restricted to islands and coastal areas of the Southern Hemisphere, and the human population might be reduced to prehistoric levels.

The Fate of the Earth

When many of us read Jonathan Schell's book, *The Fate of the Earth*, we were very much impressed by the moving way in which he presented the case, but I suspect that most biologists, like myself, thought it was a little extreme to imagine that our species might actually disappear from the face of the planet. It did not seem plausible from what we knew then.

Now, the biologists have had to consider the possibility of the spread of darkness and cold over the entire planet and throughout the Southern Hemisphere. It still seemed unlikely to them that that would immediately result in the deaths of all the people in the Southern Hemisphere. We would assume that on islands, for instance, far from sources of radioactivity and where the temperatures would be moderated by the oceans, some people would survive. Indeed, there probably would be survivors scattered throughout the Southern Hemisphere and, perhaps, even in a few places in the Northern Hemisphere.

But one has to ask about the long-term persistence of these small groups of people, or of isolated individuals. Human beings are very social animals. They are very dependent upon the social structures that they have built. They are going to face a very highly modified environment, one not only strange to them but also in some ways much more malign than people have ever faced before. The survivors will be back in a kind of hunter and gatherer stage. But hunters and gatherers in the past have always had an enormous cultural knowledge of their environments; they knew how to live off the land. But after a nuclear holocaust, people without that kind of cultural background will suddenly be trying to live in an environment that has never been experienced by people anywhere. In all likelihood, they will face a completely novel environment, unprecedented weather, and high levels of radiation. If the groups are very small, there is a possibility of inbreeding. And, of course, social and economic systems and value systems will be utterly shattered. The psychological state of the survivors is difficult to imagine.

Facing Possible Extinction

It was the consensus of our group that, under those conditions, we could not exclude the possibility that the scattered survivors simply would not be able to rebuild their populations, that they would, over a period of decades or even centuries, fade away. In other words, we could not exclude the possibility of a full-scale nuclear war entraining the extinction of *Homo sapiens*.

Let me briefly recap. A large-scale nuclear war, as far as we can see, would leave, at most, scattered survivors in the Northern Hemisphere, and those survivors would be facing extreme cold, hunger, water shortages, heavy smog, and so on, and they would be facing it all in twilight or darkness and without the support of an organized society.

The ecosystems upon which they would be extremely dependent would be severely stressed, changing in ways that we can hardly predict. Their functioning would be badly impaired. Ecologists do not know enough about these complicated systems to be able to predict their exact state after they had "recovered." Whether the biosphere would ever be restored to anything resembling that of today is entirely problematical.

Society in the Northern Hemisphere would be highly unlikely to persist. In the Southern Hemisphere tropics, events would depend in large part on the degree of propagation of the atmospheric effects from North to South. But we can be certain that, even if there were not a spread of atmospheric effects, people living in those areas would be very, very strongly impacted by the effects of the war—just by being cut off from the Northern Hemisphere.

And, I repeat, if the atmospheric effects did spread over the entire planet, then we cannot be sure that *Homo sapiens* would survive.

"If we are to deal intelligently, wisely, with the nuclear arms race, then we must steel ourselves to contemplate the horrors of nuclear war."

Nuclear Winter Is a Real Danger

Carl Sagan

Carl Sagan is David Duncan Professor of Astronomy and Space Sciences and director of the Laboratory for Planetary Studies at Cornell University. Dr. Sagan first became well-known for popularizing astronomy and planetary science with his television series *Cosmos*. He is also the author of the popular bestseller on evolution, *Dragons of Eden*. Along with four other scientists, Sagan produced a report detailing the effects of a nuclear winter, the atmospheric phenomenon which may follow a prolonged nuclear war. In the following viewpoint, Dr. Sagan reviews this research, and concludes that steps must be taken toward disarmament in order to ensure the future of the human species.

As you read, consider the following questions:

1. What model did Dr. Sagan and his colleagues use when detailing the effects of dust and soot following a nuclear exchange?
2. According to the author, what would be the impact of a small nuclear exchange?
3. Why can Dr. Sagan's conclusions only remain theoretical?

Except for fools and madmen, everyone knows that nuclear war would be an unprecedented human catastrophe. A more or less typical strategic warhead has a yield of 2 megatons, the explosive equivalent of 2 million tons of TNT. But 2 million tons of TNT is about the same as all the bombs exploded in World War II—a single bomb with the explosive power of the entire Second World War but compressed into a few seconds of time and an area of 30 or 40 miles across. . . .

In a 2-megaton explosion over a fairly large city, buildings would be vaporized, people reduced to atoms and shadows, outlying structures blown down like matchsticks and raging fires ignited. And if the bomb were exploded on the ground, an enormous crater, like those that can be seen through a telescope on the surface of the Moon, would be all that remained where midtown once had been. There are now more than 50,000 nuclear weapons, more than 13,000 megatons of yield, deployed in the arsenals of the United States and the Soviet Union—enough to obliterate a million Hiroshimas.

But there are fewer than 3000 cities on the Earth with populations of 100,000 or more. You cannot find anything like a million Hiroshimas to obliterate. Prime military and industrial targets that are far from cities are comparatively rare. Thus, there are vastly more nuclear weapons than are needed for any plausible deterrence of a potential adversary. . . .

1.1 Billion Killed

The World Health Organization, in a recent detailed study chaired by Sune K. Bergstrom (the 1982 Nobel laureate in physiology and medicine), concludes that 1.1 billion people would be killed outright in such a nuclear war, mainly in the United States, the Soviet Union, Europe, China and Japan. An additional 1.1 billion people would suffer serious injuries and radiation sickness, for which medical help would be unavailable. It thus seems possible that more than 2 billion people—almost half of all the humans on Earth—would be destroyed in the immediate aftermath of a global thermonuclear war. This would represent by far the greatest disaster in the history of the human species and, with no other adverse effects would probably be enough to reduce at least the Northern Hemisphere to a state of prolonged agony and barbarism. Unfortunately, the real situation would be much worse. . . .

Determined by Chance

The U.S. Mariner 9 spacecraft, the first vehicle to orbit another planet, arrived at Mars in late 1971. The planet was enveloped in a global dust storm. As the fine particles slowly fell out, we were able to measure temperature changes in the atmosphere and on the surface. Soon it became clear what had happened:

The dust, lofted by high winds off the desert into the upper Martian atmosphere, had absorbed the incoming sunlight and prevented much of it from reaching the ground. Heated by the sunlight, the dust warmed the adjacent air. But the surface, enveloped in partial darkness, became much chillier than usual. Months later, after the dust fell out of the atmosphere, the upper air cooled and the surface warmed, both returning to their normal conditions. We were able to calculate accurately, from how much dust there was in the atmosphere, how cool the Martian surface ought to have been.

Scientists' Responsibility

It is. . . a direct responsibility of scientists in the Soviet Union and in the United States to make known to all people what great dangers would be posed by the starting of any kind of a nuclear conflict, in order to preclude the very possibility of a nuclear war which undoubtedly would result in not just the dying out of the present civilization, but the threatening of life as such on this beloved planet of ours.

Alexander Kuzin, *The Cold and the Dark*, 1985.

Afterwards, I and my colleagues, James B. Pollack and Brian Toon of NASA's Ames Research Center, were eager to apply these insights to the Earth. In a volcanic explosion, dust aerosols are lofted into the high atmosphere. We calculated by how much the Earth's global temperature should decline after a major volcanic explosion and found that our results (generally a fraction of a degree) were in good accord with actual measurements. Joining forces with Richard Turco, who has studied the effects of nuclear weapons for many years, we then began to turn our attention to the climatic effects of nuclear war. [The scientific paper, "Global Atmospheric Consequences of Nuclear War," is written by R.P. Turco, O.B. Toon, T.P. Ackerman, J.B. Pollack and Carl Sagan. From the last names of the authors, this work is generally referred to as "TTAPS."] . . .

Horrifying Consequences

Some of what I am about to describe is horrifying. I know, because it horrifies me. There is a tendency—psychiatrists call it "denial"—to put it out of our minds, not to think about it. But if we are to deal intelligently, wisely, with the nuclear arms race, then we must steel ourselves to contemplate the horrors of nuclear war.

The results of our calculations astonished us. In the baseline case, the amount of sunlight at the ground was reduced to a few percent of normal—much darker, in daylight, than in a heavy overcast and too dark for plants to make a living from photosynthesis. At least in the Northern Hemisphere, where the great preponderance of strategic targets lies, an unbroken and deadly gloom would persist for weeks.

Even more unexpected were the temperatures calculated. In the baseline case, land temperatures, except for narrow strips of coastline, dropped to minus 25° Celsius (minus 13° Fahrenheit) and stayed below freezing for months—even for a summer war. (Because the atmospheric structure becomes much more stable as the upper atmosphere is heated and the lower air is cooled, we may have severely *under*estimated how long the cold and the dark would last.) The oceans, a significant heat reservoir, would not freeze, however, and a major ice age would probably not be triggered. But because the temperatures would drop so catastrophically, virtually all crops and farm animals, at least in the Northern Hemisphere, would be destroyed, as would most varieties of uncultivated or undomesticated food supplies. Most of the human survivors would starve.

In addition, the amount of radioactive fallout is much more than expected. Many previous calculations simply ignored the intermediate time-scale fallout. That is, calculations were made for the prompt fallout—the plumes of radioactive debris blown downwind from each target—and for the long-term fallout, the fine radioactive particles lofted into the stratosphere that would descend about a year later, after most of the radioactivity had decayed. However, the radioactivity carried into the upper atmosphere (but not as high as the stratosphere) seems to have been largely forgotten. We found for the baseline case that roughly 30 percent of the land at northern midlatitudes could receive a radioactive dose greater than 250 rads, and that about 50 percent of northern midlatitudes could receive a dose greater than 100 rads. A 100-rad dose is the equivalent of about 1000 medical X-rays. A 400-rad dose will, more likely than not, kill you.

Assault on Civilization

The cold, the dark and the intense radioactivity, together lasting for months, represent a severe assault on our civilization and our species. Civil and sanitary services would be wiped out. Medical facilities, drugs, the most rudimentary means for relieving the vast human suffering, would be unavailable. Any but the most elaborate shelters would be useless, quite apart from the question of what good it might be to emerge a few months later. Synthetics burned in the destruction of the cities would produce a wide variety of toxic gases, including carbon monoxide, cyanides, dioxins and furans. After the dust and soot settled out, the solar ultraviolet flux would be much larger than its present value. Immunity to disease would decline. Epidemics and pandemics would be rampant, especially after the billion or so unburied bodies began to thaw. Moreover, the combined influence of these severe and simultaneous stresses

on life are likely to produce even more adverse consequences—
biologists call them synergisms—that we are not yet wise enough
to foresee.

Even Small Nuclear Wars

But what if nuclear wars *can* be contained, and much less than
5000 megatons is detonated? Perhaps the greatest surprise in our
work was that even small nuclear wars can have devastating
climatic effects. We considered a war in which a mere 100 megatons were exploded, less than one percent of the world arsenals,
and only in low-yield airbursts over cities. This scenario, we found,
would ignite thousands of fires, and the smoke from these fires
alone would be enough to generate an epoch of cold and dark
almost as severe as in the 5000-megaton case. The threshold for
what Richard Turco has called The Nuclear Winter is very low.

The Victorious Will Perish Too

While the effects of nuclear winter would be most severe in the
Northern Hemisphere, the Southern Hemisphere would also be
affected. Without actually having a nuclear war, it is impossible to
establish with certainty how severe these effects would be. But it
is possible that the human race could be wiped out.

The concept of nuclear winter clearly demonstrates that a nuclear
war cannot be won and must never be fought. Even a preemptive
first strike so "successfully" carried out that retaliation would be impossible would most likely trigger nuclear winter, destroying the
"victorious" aggressor by cold and darkness.

The People, January 19, 1985.

Could we have overlooked some important effect? The carrying
of dust and soot from the Northern to the Southern Hemisphere (as
well as more local atmospheric circulation) will certainly thin the
clouds out over the Northern Hemisphere. But, in many cases, this
thinning would be insufficient to render the climatic consequences
tolerable—and every time it got better in the Northern Hemisphere,
it would get worse in the Southern.

Our results have been carefully scrutinized by more than 100
scientists in the United States, Europe and the Soviet Union. There
are still arguments on points of detail. But the overall conclusion
seems to be agreed upon: There are severe and previously unan-
ticipated global consequences of nuclear war—subfreezing temperatures in a twilit radioactive gloom lasting for months or longer.

Scientists initially underestimated the effects of fallout, were
amazed that nuclear explosions in space disabled distant satellites,
had no idea that the fireballs from high-yield thermonuclear explo-

sions could deplete the ozone layer and missed altogether the possible climatic effects of nuclear dust and smoke. What else have we overlooked?

Nuclear war is a problem that can be treated only theoretically. It is not amenable to experimentation. Conceivably, we have left something important out of our analysis, and the effects are more modest than we calculate. On the other hand, it is also possible— and, from previous experience, even likely—that there are further adverse effects that no one has yet been wise enough to recognize. With billions of lives at stake, where does conservatism lie—in assuming that the results will be better than we calculate, or worse?

Many biologists, considering the nuclear winter that these calculations describe, believe they carry somber implications for life on Earth. Many species of plants and animals would become extinct. Vast numbers of surviving humans would starve to death. The delicate ecological relations that bind together organisms on Earth in a fabric of mutual dependency would be torn, perhaps irreparably. There is little question that our global civilization would be destroyed. The human population would be reduced to prehistoric levels, or less. Life for any survivors would be extremely hard. And there seems to be a real possibility of the extinction of the human species.

It is now almost 40 years since the invention of nuclear weapons. We have not yet experienced a global thermonuclear war— although on more than one occasion we have come tremulously close. I do not think our luck can hold forever. Men and machines are fallible, as recent events remind us. Fools and madmen do exist, and sometimes rise to power. Concentrating always on the near future, we have ignored the long-term consequences of our actions. We have placed our civilization and our species in jeopardy.

Fortunately, it is not yet too late. We can safeguard the planetary civilization and the human family if we so choose. There is no more important or more urgent issue.

"The Sagan Report. . . . is a scare tactic, a way to destroy national resolve by suggesting that our enemy is nuclear weapons, not the Soviet Union."

Nuclear Winter Is a Scare Tactic

Herbert I. London

Dr. Herbert I. London is dean of the Gallatin Division, New York University, and director of Visions of the Future, a division of the Hudson Institute. In the following viewpoint, Dr. London expresses the belief that reports depicting the possibilty of nuclear winter are exaggerated, based on somewhat dubious evidence, and, most importantly, spread fear and frustration. This fear can lead the American people to believe that the only way to avoid a nuclear war is to disarm the nation, thereby leaving the United States hopelessly vulnerable to Soviet attack.

As you read, consider the following questions:

1. What, according to the author, is "entirely overlooked" in the nuclear winter reports?
2. Why does the author believe that doomsday messages are harmful? How can they provoke, rather than end, war?
3. Does the author see an alternative to the nuclear winter scenario? What is it?

The prophets of doom have found a new target. Instead of concentrating on a Malthusian libretto that projects dwindling food supplies and overpopulation—a scenario made less credible every day there are grain surpluses—they have produced a moral play of nuclear war. Led by Carl Sagan, professor of astronomy and space science at Cornell University, a group of American and Soviet researchers have written a report in which it is predicted that long-term atmospheric effects on a scale greater than heretofore conceived will result from a nuclear weapons exchange. These effects include subfreezing temperatures, protracted darkness, and exposure to radioactivity more severe than previously projected; in fact, these effects will lead inevitably to what I predict will be the activist's calling card of the future—"nuclear winter." No one will escape the cold, inexorable movement of nuclear winter as it spreads its deadly spell over every inch of the globe, even that last beachhead of radioactive freedom in Australia.

Sagan and his colleagues, including Paul Ehrlich, the father of the population explosion that never exploded, ran computer models of nuclear war exchanges ranging from 100 to 100,000 megatons. They calculated how much dust and smoke would result from a nuclear blast and how this cloud cover would absorb light and create an unbroken pass of darkness inadequate to sustain photosynthesis. The lack of sunlight would presumably cause freezing that destroys crops and animals, thus challenging the very existence of life itself. This is indeed nuclear winter, or, more accurately, nuclear freeze (no pun intended).

Uncountable Exaggerations

There are so many things wrong with the Sagan report that one scarcely knows where to begin criticizing it. For one thing, most people, with the exception of fools and fiends, realize that a nuclear exchange would have horrendous effects on life and ecology. Every scientist who has worked with radioactive weapons is aware of that. Second, the scenario for nuclear war developed by Sagan *et al.* accounts only for a major nuclear exchange. However, it is plausible to consider a nuclear war that is limited. Moreover, while no one should argue for a limited nuclear war, or any nuclear war for that matter, it is also fair to say that a limited war is better than an all-out war. Third, the collateral damage that the report emphasizes is related to an air burst of huge megatonnage. At no point do the authors point out that, while this nation has been reducing its total megatonnage, the Soviets have been increasing theirs. The SS-18 is the largest weapon in the Soviet arsenal, about twice the size of the proposed MX. Therefore, the potential for global damage in a nuclear exchange is not equivalent on both sides. Yet, this report will be distributed here, not where it would do the most good.

nuclear winter \ n(y)ü-klē-ər wint-ər \ *noun:*
see, SNOW JOB

What is entirely overlooked by this report is the extreme difficulty associated with predicting the environmental effects of a nuclear exchange. According to the most responsible physicists, the range of uncertainty is so great—because of the set of assumptions and imponderables—that one can discuss a nuclear summer that is dark and hot as easily as the nuclear winter that is dismal and cold. If, for example, the Earth is covered in soot and smoke, heat radiation from the Earth's surface will not easily escape into space. The eventual surface temperature will depend on the competition between the inflow and outflow of radiation. Clearly, this prospect is as uninviting as nuclear winter. However, what this equally plausible scenario introduces are the inconsistencies in the report submitted by Sagan and his colleagues.

Ultimately, what one must consider are the motives in distributing the Sagan report. If it is the intent to apprise people of the danger nuclear war holds, this report can only reinforce beliefs already well established. If it is designed to produce disarmament by pointing out the horrendous consequences of nuclear exchange, one can be sure our "true believers" will act on that premise, while our enemy will emphasize the need to be vigilant in the face of Western threats. Our concern about global catastrophe and their concern about a potential enemy will not result in similar strategies. Of that, one can be quite sure.

The Sagan report is the scientific equivalent of the film, *Testament*, and the television program, *The Day After*. It is a scare tactic, a way to destroy national resolve by suggesting that our enemy is nuclear weapons, not the Soviet Union. No one wants to fight a nuclear war, but the question of how you prevent it still remains. Our disarmament in the face of Soviet continuing armament can insure peace, but only under the yoke of Pax Sovietica. Is this what these apostles of doom really want?

Good !!!

If every person in the world were to light a match at the same instant, we could increase the global temperature by 10 degrees, melt the polar ice caps, flood every coastal city the world, kill millions of people, destroy the food chain, and influence global ecology for centuries—but that is entirely in the realm of speculation. The event *can* occur, but is quite unlikely. So, too, the Sagan report is in the realm of speculation. So long as we maintain a credible deterrent, the chance of nuclear exchange is remote. This doesn't mean it can't happen or won't happen; it only means that a deterrent is our best chance of preventing nuclear war.

Inviting Nuclear War

Those fear-mongers who believe they perform a public service in promoting visions of apocalypse either know not what they do or confuse a contingency with actuality. The way to invite nuclear war or nuclear blackmail is through unilateral disarmament. That can only bring on the very disaster any sane person wants to avert. Every leader already knows what horrors lie in the wake of nuclear war. The question is still one of prophylactics. Perhaps Sagan and his scientific colleagues should do a computer analysis of how to avoid war, albeit that result is readily predictable. In fact, I could guess its conclusion would undoubtedly be accepted in both the U.S. and the Soviet Union: Americans should rid themselves of these terrible weapons of destruction.

Like the prophets of doom from yesteryear, these contemporary doomsayers seem to be obsessed by the very tragedy they claim to abhor. Have these apostles of anti-nuclear positions reached a stage of philosophical nihilism? Is Orwellian thought to be found in claims of life by those who secretly welcome death? Is necromancy the fashionable fascination, the latest addiction of the privileged classes?

Making War Bearable

At a recent meeting of the American-Soviet scientific forum sponsored by the Nuclear Freeze Foundation, there was consensus in criticizing the Federal Emergency Management Agency (FEMA) for suggesting that food supplies might survive a nuclear attack. The FEMA study was excoriated not only for its contingent conclusions, but for its attitude. Sen. Edward M. Kennedy (D.-Mass.) argued: "This kind of thinking makes nuclear war seem more bearable."

In the present climate of opinion, any expression of hope regarding nuclear war is regarded as Pollyannish. There is either Armaggeddon or conciliation. What Sagan *et al.* seem to be saying is that mutually assured destruction is a desirable policy. The moral consequences of holding a civilian population hostage seem to have eluded them.

It might also be asked whether a prediction of global holocaust is really a detterent. In an open society, this logic can affect public opinion, but in a closed society, there is no reason to believe this view—or any other view—can have an impact on government policymakers. After all, in a crisis, they may believe their system's demise is a form of death anyway.

Nuclear Winter Calculations Inaccurate

It should be realized that the predictability of nuclear-winter effects is extremely poor. Not only is there a lack of reliable scientific data, but there are physical and environmental imponderables that cannot be accurately gauged. In this respect, it would have been more responsible for Mr. Sagan and his colleagues to have waited until these uncertainties were significantly reduced before reporting their Doomsday story.

However, their greatest irresponsibility was in fabricating nuclear-war scenarios that did not reflect the realities of the situation, the most important of which is that neither the United States nor the U.S.S.R. wants to put the world into a nuclear deep freeze. Even if the nuclear winter calculations were of great accuracy, why would either of these nations want to wage war so insanely?

Sam Cohen, *Washington Times*, June 28, 1984.

It should also be noted that the orthodoxy reflected in this report makes it difficult for scientists to withstand the pressure that accompanies less onerous predictions. And Edward Teller has taken so much heat for so long, it hardly matters to him, but what about his not so self-assured global outcomes from a nuclear war? Can they be dispassionate and still find acceptance in the scientific community?

Sacrificing National Defense

I can't speculate, but I am not pleased when a report buttressed by "scientific verities" enters the arena of political discourse in order to score points in a national debate. If it were up to our doomsday prophets, national defense would be the sacrificial lamb for their new social order. Of course, it should be asked what this new social order might resemble. For one thing, it would make a mockery of our national defense. Sagan may believe Soviet scientists share his gloomy forecasts, but whether or not they do is inconsequential; Soviet leaders do not. A reduction in American arms or a freeze—a position Sagan proposes—will not make the world more safe than at present if the result is a decided Soviet nuclear edge. Everyone is aware of the dangers to which the report alludes. Yet, that in itself has little meaning unless there are realistic proposals for neutralizing this analysis of doom.

It is my contention that these new prophets have only one prediction up their sleeve—the nightmare of total annihilation. However, that view standing alone is like tossing oil on a fire. Fear begets fear, and fear can trigger extreme reactions. If one of those extreme reactions is reduced defense vigilance, then God help us all.

Fortunately, most prophets have been Cassandras and most have been wrong. There is no reason to believe that Sagan and his friends are any different from their predecessors. The problem with these prophets is not really their vision of the future, but their influence on the present. That is something we have to counteract with good sense, courage, and the bright light of hope and reason.

Preventing Nuclear War

Reason in this context is the realization that nuclear war is prevented through deterrence, not fear. Moreover, if deterrence fails, as Jonathan Schell argues, then we must have a war-fighting strategy to limit damage, compress the period of bombing, and reduce casualties to the extent this is possible. In fact, a war-fighting strategy potentiates the effectiveness of one's deterrent. It makes it perfectly clear to our adversary that, if we must fight, we can fight.

"A war fought with nuclear weapons would put an end to civilization as we know it."

Nuclear War Would Cause Total Destruction

Helen Caldicott

Dr. Helen Caldicott practices pediatrics at Boston's Children's Hospital Medical Center. A leading critic of the nuclear power and armaments industries, she is president of Physicians for Social Responsibility, an anti-nuclear group of physicians. In the following viewpoint, Dr. Caldicott urges all to become better informed about the nuclear hazards humanity faces and challenges the reader to take action to ensure human survival on Earth.

As you read, consider the following questions:

1. According to Dr. Caldicott, what level of radiation is safe for humans?
2. How long does the author believe a nuclear war would last?
3. What is the only way to ensure survival of the human race, according to the author?

Helen Caldicott, *Nuclear Madness: What You Can Do!* New York: Bantam Books, 1980. Reprinted with the permission of the author.

I am a child of the Atomic Age. I was six years old when American atomic bombs were deployed against the Japanese, and I have grown up with the fear of imminent annihilation by nuclear holocaust. Over the years my fear has increased. . . .

As a physician, I contend that the power and weapons industry's nuclear technology threatens life on our planet with extinction. If present trends continue, the air we breathe, the food we eat, and the water we drink will soon be contaminated with enough radio-active pollutants to pose a potential health hazard far greater than any plague humanity has ever experienced. Unknowingly exposed to these radioactive poisons, some of us may be developing cancer right now. Others may be passing damaged genes, the basic chemical units which transmit hereditary characteristics, to future generations. And more of us will inevitably be affected unless we bring about a drastic reversal of our government's pronuclear policies. . . .

Reversing the Nuclear Age

It is of the utmost urgency that we refocus our attention on the problems posed by nuclear technology, for we have entered and are rapidly passing through a new phase of the Atomic Age. . . . Because of the proliferation of nuclear weapons, the likelihood of nuclear war, the most ominous threat to public health imaginable, becomes greater every day.

In view of the threat that nuclear technology poses to the ecosphere, we must acknowledge that Homo sapiens has reached an evolutionary turning point. Thousands of tons of radioactive materials, released by nuclear explosions and reactor spills, are now dispersing through the environment. Nonbiodegradable, and some potent virtually forever, these toxic nuclear materials will continue to accumulate, and eventually their effects on the biosphere and on human beings will be grave: many people will begin to develop and die of cancer; or their reproductive genes will mutate, resulting in an increased incidence of congenitally deformed and diseased offspring—not just in the next generation, but for the rest of time. An all-out nuclear war would kill millions of people and accelerate these biological hazards among the sur-vivors: the earth would be poisoned and laid waste, rendered uninhabitable for aeons. . . .

Watching my patients die of respiratory failure, and seeing other children in the wards die of leukemia and cancer, has motivated me to speak publicly and write this. Knowing that the incidence of congenital diseases and malignancies will increase in direct ratio to the radioactive contaminants polluting our planet, I cannot remain silent. . . .

Whether natural or human-made, all radiation is dangerous. There is no ''safe'' amount of radioactive material or dose of radia-tion. Why? Because by virtue of the nature of the biological damage done by radiation, it takes only one radioactive atom, one cell, and one gene to initiate the cancer or mutation cycle. Any exposure at all therefore constitutes a serious gamble with the mechanisms of life.

Today almost all geneticists agree that there is no dose of radiation so low that it produces no mutations at all. Thus, even small amounts of background radiation are believed to have genetic effects.

Similarly, there is no disagreement among scientists that large doses of ionizing radiation cause a variety of different forms of cancer. Starting fifteen years after the explosions, the incidence of cancers of the stomach, ovary, breast, bowel, lung, bone, and thyroid doubled among Japan's bomb survivors. Approximately five years after the nuclear attack on Hiroshima, an epidemic of leukemia occurred that within ten years reached a level of incidence forty times higher among the survivors than among the nonexposed population....

Humanity's Fate at Stake

Brownell: Do you think, after what you've seen, that nuclear war and nuclear bombs can be survived?

Sussan: No. I absolutely do not believe that at all. I think that what we are dealing with now is not a political issue. The life and death of the human race is *not* a political issue. The continuation of man on earth is *not* a political issue. *And that's absolutely what we are dealing with here.*

Herbert Sussan and Will Brownell, *Survive*, March/April 1983.

The truth is that we are courting catastrophe. The permissive radiation policy supported by the American government in effect turns us into guinea pigs in an experiment to determine how much radioactive material can be released into the environment before major epidemics of cancer, leukemia, and genetic abnormalities take their toll....

Albert Einstein's Nightmare Transcended

In 1946 Albert Einstein, apprehensive about humanity's misuse of the power of the atom, expressed great concern for the future of mankind. Today's nuclear arsenal must exceed his worst nightmare: Between them, the United States and the Soviet Union, alone, have deployed some 50,000 nuclear bombs which stand ready to exterminate virtually all life on earth.

When compared to the threat of nuclear war, the nuclear power controversy shrinks to paltry dimensions. A reactor meltdown might kill as many as 50,000 people; a war fought with nuclear weapons would put an end to civilization as we know it . . . .

What would happen if the world's nuclear arsenals were put to use?

Erupting with great suddenness, a nuclear war would probably be over within hours. Several hundred to several thousand nuclear bombs would explode over civilian and military targets in the United States (every American city with a population of 25,000 or more is targeted), and an equal or greater number of bombs would strike the principal targets in Europe, the Soviet Union, and China. Both major and minor population centers would be smashed flat. Each weapon's powerful shock wave would be accompanied by a searing fireball with a surface temperature greater than the sun's that would set firestorms raging over millions of acres. (Every 20-megaton bomb can set a firestorm raging over 3,000 acres. Theoretically a 1,000-megaton device, which has never been built, exploded in outer space could devastate an area the size of six western states.) The fires would sear the earth, consuming most plant and wild life. Some experts believe that the heat released might melt the polar ice caps, flooding much of the planet. Destruction of the earth's atmospheric ozone layer by the rapid production of nitrous oxide would result in increased exposure to cosmic and ultraviolet radiation.

Blast Shelter Ineffective

People caught in shelters near the center of a blast would die immediately of concussive effects or asphyxiation brought on as a result of oxygen depletion during the firestorms. Exposure to immense amounts of high-energy gamma radiation, anyone who survived near the epicenter would likely die within two weeks of acute radiation illness.

Those who survived, in shelters or in remote rural areas, would reenter a totally devastated world, lacking the life-support systems on which the human species depends. Food, air, and water would be poisonously radioactive. Physical suffering would be compounded by psychological stress: For many, the loss of family, friends, and the accustomed environment would bring on severe shock and mental breakdown.

In the aftermath, bacteria, viruses, and disease-bearing insects— which tend to be thousands of times more radio-resistant than human beings—would mutate, adapt, and multiply in extremely virulent forms. Human beings, their immune mechanisms severely depleted by exposure to excessive radiation, would be rendered susceptible to the infectious diseases that such organisms cause: plagues of typhoid, dysentery, polio, and other disorders would wipe out large numbers of people.

The long-term fallout effects in the countries bombed would give rise to other epidemics. Within five years, leukemia would be rampant. Within 15 to 50 years, solid cancers of the lung, breast, bowel, stomach, and thyroid would strike down survivors.

Exposure of the reproductive organs to the immense quantities of radiation released in the explosions would result in reproductive sterility in many. An increased incidence of spontaneous abortions and deformed offspring, and a massive increase of both dominant and recessive mutations, would also result. Rendered intensely radioactive, the planet Earth would eventually become inhabited by bands of deformed humans scrounging for existence like troglodytes.

What wolud be left? Experts have projected two possible scenarios. According to one, hundreds of millions of people in the targeted countries would die, but some might survive. According to the second, the synergistic ecological effects of thermal and nuclear radiation, long-term fallout, and exposure to increased cosmic radiation would make it doubtful that anyone could live for very long. Destruction would most likely be absolute. There will be no sanctuary.

Is it not remarkable how we manage to live our lives in apparent normality, while, at every moment, human civilization and the existence of all forms of life on our planet are threatened with sudden annihilation? We seem to accept this situation calmly, as if it were to be expected. Clearly, nuclear warfare presents us with the specter of a disaster so terrible that many of us would simply prefer not to think about it. But soothing our anxiety by ignoring

© 1985 Los Angeles Times Syndicate. Reprinted with permission.

the constant danger of annihilation will not lessen that danger. On the contrary, such an approach improves the chances that eventually our worst fears will be realized. . . .

Abolishing Nuclear Weapons

Only if we abolish nuclear weapons and permanently halt the nuclear power industry can we hope to survive. To achieve these ends, it is vital that people be presented with the facts. Today more than ever, we need what Einstein referred to as a "chain reaction of awareness": "To the village square," he wrote in 1946, "we must carry the facts of atomic energy." Once presented, the facts will speak for themselves.

Out of the growing number of organizations opposed to nuclear power and nuclear arms must come a grassroots movement of unprecedented size and determination. Its momentum, alone, will determine whether we and our children—and all future generations of humankind—will survive.

This may seem somewhat far afield from Sagan's nuclear winter, but it isn't. The idea of a war in which "the survivors will envy the dead" or the globe can not sustain life is "a doomsday machine." Believing in doomsday can either immobilize all efforts at defense or lead to a spasmodic last-grasp attempt to "decapitate" the other side. Either of these notions is dangerous. If we have a doomsday scenario not shared by the other side, we put ourselves in the perilous position of beseeching them for peace on *their* terms. If we believe doom is on the horizon and wish to preempt this prospect, there may be a strong and unjustified desire to launch first in the hope that our enemy will not risk doom through retaliation. Both of these ideas fall into the realm of fearful responses that jeopardize freedom and stability.

A Way Out

There is a way out of the impasse that Sagan and his colleagues do not discuss. That is the maintenance of a credible deterrent that discourages any thought of nuclear use by the other side. This should be accompanied by research into and development of accurate, less fearsome missiles that serve the same role as large destructive warheads. Additionally, efforts must be taken to develop a defensive system that can make nuclear weapons obsolete. Although the technology doesn't exist at the moment, the prospects for it are hopeful. A layered system using conventional, laser, particle beam, and missile components could neutralize up to 95% of the Soviet strike force. While some detractors see this step as destabilizing—mutual assured destruction rears it ugly head again—a modest step toward destabilization could bring the long-term assurance of security. Last, while vigilance is maintained, we should do everything in our power to discuss mutual reduction of force levels with the Soviet leadership. In this case, our willingness to deploy gives our willingness to reduce credibility. However, our side must ask, arms reduction for what? A treaty is only as good as its ability to ensure security. So far, SALT I and SALT II have had the opposite of their intended effect.

In the long term, my impressions are the exact reverse of the doomsayers. We may live with the Damoclean sword over our heads now, but there is a different and brighter prospect ahead. That time will inexorably come if we can put the jeremiads in perspective, maintain our resolve, and take Sagan and company with a grain of salt. Here, the pun is intended.

"*The overwhelming and inaccurate rumors which anti-nuke activitists spread greatly hamper efforts to prepare the nation. . . to meet the challenges of the postwar period.*"

Nuclear War Would Not Cause Total Destruction

Bruce Clayton

Dr. Bruce Clayton holds a Ph.D. in ecology and is a federally-certified Radiological Defense Officer. A nuclear war survival expert, he is the author of *Life After Doomsday* and a frequent contributor to survivalist publications. Dr. Clayton is a member of the Physicians for Social Responsibility, an anti-nuclear group, but disagrees with other members of the group on the issue of survival: While most members believe nuclear war survival is futile, Dr. Clayton believes the destruction would be less than total, and therefore survivable. In the following viewpoint, Dr. Clayton takes the author of the previous viewpoint, Dr. Helen Caldicott, to task, arguing that her facts and ideas on nuclear war are inaccurate, exaggerated, and worst of all, dangerous.

As you read, consider the following questions:

1. Why does Dr. Clayton believe that nuclear war would not be an "unprecedented disaster"?
2. How do the ideas of Dr. Clayton and Dr. Caldicott differ in relation to radiation's genetic effects?
3. What, in Dr. Clayton's opinion, is the worst myth of all?

Bruce Clayton, "Nuclear Nonsense: Dispelling 'Doomie' Myths" Parts I & II, *Survive*, Fall and Winter 1981. Reprinted with permission.

Do you believe that a nuclear war between the United States and the Soviet Union would destroy all life on earth? That the world would be seared to a crisp, and the air, water and land radioactively poisoned forever? Do you believe that we now have bombs that can incinerate half a continent at a time, and that the survivors of a nuclear war would become unrecognizable mutants, doomed to roam forever in a totally devastated world? Do you think the war would be over in a matter of minutes, or hours at the most? Have you heard that any survivors would be doomed anyway by massive outbreaks of leukemia and cancer after the war? Is it obvious to you that there is no point in preparing to survive World War III?

If you said "yes" to any of these questions, you'd better sit down and read this article. Otherwise the things you *think* you know about nuclear war may one day kill you . . . .

I have made a very disturbing discovery. *The stories I had always believed about a nuclear war exterminating the human race were not true!* They weren't even nearly true. A nuclear war would be survivable, I learned. In fact, an informed and prepared family could come very close to achieving a 100 percent probability of long-term survival . . . .

Anti-Nuke Rumors

The overwhelming and inaccurate rumors which anti-nuke activists spread greatly hamper efforts to prepare the nation, or even individual families, to meet the challenges of the postwar period. Doomie myths convince people that survival is impossible . . . and people who are taken in by them simply won't make survival preparations. Because of the myths, these misled believers may very well die in the war or its aftermath even though they could have been saved . . . .

One of the central figures is Dr. Helen Caldicott, M.D. an Australian pediatrician who wrote a popular anti-nuke book called *Nuclear Madness.* Usually when I discuss the myths of nuclear war I take the impersonal approach, citing general rumors which the public erroneously believes to be the truth about nuclear conflict. Having just read Dr. Caldicott's book, however, I think it may be fun to show you some of these misleading stories in actual use.

Let's take a look at some of these Doomie fantasies, shall we? . . .

Nuclear War and Civilization

Myths about the effect on civilizaton: How many times have you read or heard something like this? "A war fought with nuclear weapons would put an end to civilization as we know it."

I think it is probably true that a nuclear war would severely disrupt, perhaps destroy, the economic and social structure of the United States and western Europe. It is possible that it would also destroy the national structure of the Soviet Union, but that is less likely. (In rural areas of Russia, for instance, a typical peasant's standard of living is so low that there is little which a nuclear war could do to make it worse.)

It is very egotistical of us, however, to state so blatantly our belief that the destruction of America (or even just Boston) would be the end of *civilization*. . . .

Assuring Survival After Nuclear War

Survival means understanding that one-third to two-thirds of any population can survive a nuclear war, provided they refuse to be demoralized by myths such as those which have grown out of most descriptions of Hiroshima and Nagasaki. What happened in these two cities, in their fashion, was the world's first nuclear war. Whether there will be a second is open to question. What is certain is that myths from the first nuclear war will cause casualties in the second, unless more people study the facts closely and take steps to assure their own survival.

Will Brownell, *Survive*, March/April 1983.

In reality, even a very severe nuclear war which would kill half or more of the population of the warring countries would be expected to have little direct impact on the population of the rest of world. The nations of the southern hemisphere and many northern hemisphere countries as well would emerge essentially untouched by direct weapons effects. There would be some rather substantial economic and social readjustments to be made, of course, especially if the Soviets were to succeed in launching their projected war of conquest following the nuclear exchange.

Nuclear War and Destruction

The myth of unprecedented destruction: One of my favorite myths is this one, because it shows such dramatic historical myopia:

The detonation of a single weapon of this nature over any of the world's major cities would constitute a disaster unprecedented in human history.

On a qualitative basis, one recalls that the Black Death of the 15th century killed 25 percent of the population of the then-known world, but even a very severe nuclear war threatens only about 5 percent of today's world population. And this passage refers to only *one bomb*! On the quantitative side, I think the 25 million Russians who starved to death in the early 1920s deserve at least a nod. Then there were the volcanic eruptions at Pompeii and St. Pierre which killed almost everyone in these cities. The Romans, and later the Crusaders, were not above leveling conquered cities (so that no two stones remained together) and putting *all* of the defeated inhabitants to death. Neither a nuclear bomb nor a volcano can deal out death and destruction that thoroughly, Let's pause, too and remember 11 million innocent people who made a fatal error or judgment about Hitler and the Nazis. "Unprecedented" isn't really the right word. . . .

Radiation and Cancer

Myths about cancer: Some of the more pernicious myths are those which state that even if survival of the war itself were possible, the survivors would eventually be wiped out by radiation-induced cancers. This story attains its greatest credibility when spread by physicians, who ought to know better.

> The long-term fallout effects in the countries bombed would give rise to other epidemics. Within five years, leukemia would be rampant. Within 15 to 20 years, solid cancers of the lung, breast, bowel, stomach, and thyroid would strike down survivors.

According to Glasstone in *The Effects of Nuclear War*, the experience of the Japanese indicated that there would be a surge of leukemia cases 5 to 10 years after the war, but only among those people who had received large doses of radiation and had been fortunate enough not to die of radiation sickness. The predicted incidence of leukemia among adults who had been exposed to 100 and 200 rems would be *between two and four cases per thousand* former radiation patients. Surviving severely irradiated children who had been under 10 years old at the time of the war would be twice as susceptible, which means four to eight cases of leukemia per thousand. Now I admit that a leukemia rate approaching 1 percent of the radiation patients would be a terrible tragedy, but it wouldn't exactly mean the end of our species, would it? . . .

Nuclear War and Genetics

Myths about radiation and genetics: The next few doomsday stories try to hit us where it really hurts, in our concern for our children. These myths typically take one of two forms. They either assert that a nuclear war will make human reproduction impossible, or they tell us the even more disturbing news that our children will be severely deformed by the radiation. Here are some examples:

> Exposure of the reproductive organs to the immense quantities of radiation in the explosions would result in reproductive sterility in many. An increased incidence of spontaneous abortions and deformed offspring, and a massive increase in both dominant and recessive mutations, would also result. Rendered intensely radioactive, the planet Earth would eventually become inhabited by bands of roving humanoids—mutants barely recognizable as members of our species. . . .
> Reproductive genes will mutate, resulting in an increased incidence of congenitally deformed and diseased offspring—not just for the next generation, but for the rest of time.

102

If you look closely at that first passage you may discover, as I did, the paradoxical notion that sterile parents would give birth to roving bands of unrecognizable mutants through spontaneous abortions...but perhaps I am being too critical. Dr. Caldicott is a specialist in the genetic diseases of children, and her compassion for her patients undoubtedly dominates her thoughts when writing about them....

What about those unrecognizable mutants roaming the earth? (One envisions them gnawing on bleached bones for nourishment and eyeing one another hungrily.) Would this really happen? Would there really be genetic damage to the human race? Would the damage be permanent as Dr. Caldicott indicates? There are several interesting lines of evidence to examine here.

Nuclear War May Be Limited

There is no reason to assume that a nuclear war will lead to the extinction of all, or almost all, humanity. In fact, those who have worked hardest at analyzing scenarios involving nuclear weapons believe that nuclear wars may well be limited; that they can come in many shapes and sizes; that even in unlimited wars a wide variety of outcomes are possible, but that the side with more and better weapons would have a clear advantage; that civil-defense measures can significantly reduce casualties; and that deterrence is most apt to work when it is backed by solid war-fighting capabilities in both the conventional and the nuclear sphere.

Herman Kahn, *Fortune*, June 28, 1982.

First is the universal observation of all biologists, geneticists, and physicians that a fetus which is so deformed as to be *unrecognizable* virtually always dies. (There are exceptions in plant genetics, but they do not concern us here.) An equally universal observation is that if a severely deformed (but recognizable) individual manages to reach sexual maturity it usually has a terrible time acquiring a mate, and eventually dies without offspring. The establishment of a race of unrecognizable mutants would be quite a trick....

[A publication of the National Academy of Sciences] estimated that a 10,000 megaton war would result in significant but temporary damage to the gene pool of our species. The report forecast that damaged genes would increase the birth-defect rate, and that natural selection would weed out these damaged genes over a period of about a thousand years (which is quite a while but not "the rest of time")...

Here's another example of mutations running riot:

In the aftermath, bacteria, viruses, and disease-carrying insects— which tend to be thousands of times more radio-resistant than human beings—would mutate, adapt and multiply in extremely virulent forms.

There has been some scientific concern that increased background radiation would produce an increased mutation rate among insects, bacteria, fungi and viruses, but the concern is more often expressed in terms of our agricultural crops. The rate of mutation and evolution of crop pests is staggeringly high even under normal conditions. Insecticides rarely work for more than a few years before the target insects develop genetic immunity to them, and micro-organisms can become resistant to antibiotics even faster . . . sometimes in a matter of hours. There is no need to invoke radiation, and probably no point.

A less obvious comment is that the natural evolution of infectious diseases tends to be from more virulent to less virulent forms. Disease organisms are parasites, after all, and it is poor practice for a parasite to kill its host. The residual radiation from a nuclear war could produce new and "extremely virulent" diseases, but it could just as easily result in dangerous disease organisms mutating to *benign* forms, and from an evolutionary standpoint it would be more likely. . . .

Myths about the ozone layer: The "ozone layer" is the popular term for a portion of the atmosphere which absorbs most of the ultraviolet light in sunlight. . . .

If the UV threat did in fact materialize, its effects on terrestrial life would be manageable and temporary. Remember that the high UV levels would be present only during the daylight hours. Nights would be normal. Humans would wear protective clothing and would stay out of the sun during the middle of the day. Wild animals already confine their activities to the night, early morning and early evening when UV levels would not be a problem. Even animals as stupid as cows have a history of sleeping in the shade during the day and grazing at night when suffering from sunburn (brought on by eating sensitizing poisonous plants). . . .

It is not uncommon for seeds to lie dormant in the forest floor for decades, waiting for a forest fire to remove the overstory before they sprout. These seeds, too, would be unaffected by high UV levels. If the ozone layer were depleted by a nuclear attack it would be a wild ride, but things would eventually return more or less to normal.

Myths about food and water: Try this one on for size:

> Those who survived, in shelters or in remote rural areas, would reenter a totally devastated world, lacking the life-support systems on which the human species depends. Food, air and water would be poisonously radioactive.

I will state for the record, as have countless civil-defense writers before me, that radiation passes harmlessly through air, food and water without making them radioactive. In fact, many of the canned goods on our supermarket shelves were sterilized with radiation. The only danger is eating food that has fallout particles on it. Wrapped food will not be contaminated even if there is fallout dust on the wrapper. Just be careful about how you open it.

Water from deep wells and surface water from fallout-free areas will be as potable as ever. (Careful, some of it isn't safe to drink even now.) Fallout cannot make water radioactive, but fallout dust in the water does have to be removed before drinking. . . .

Instant Death Unlikely

The worst myth of all: How many times have you heard somebody say something like this?

"I don't have to worry about my family surviving the war. Where we live we'll be vaporized instantly."

Another version goes like this:

"I just hope the first bomb drops on me. I don't want to be around to see the aftermath."

Preparing to Deter, Fight, Survive

If we knew for certain that no one would survive, we could spare ourselves the costs of arming. But we know no such thing. Under the circumstances, I believe it is immoral—an abdication of our responsibility to generations as yet unborn, not to mention our own—and dangerous not to take reasonable precautions to (a) deter, (b) fight, and (c) survive and recuperate from a nuclear war.

Without doubt, even a very limited attack on the United States—one that concentrated more or less exclusively on our strategic forces—would involve catastrophic human and material losses. Yet these would still be considerably less than those associated with strikes on a wide range of civilian and military targets.

Herman Kahn, *Fortune*, June 28, 1982.

The painless, instantaneous death these people long for is another of the myths, and in my opinion, the worst of all. Thermonuclear explosions kill by inflicting injuries similar to those of a serious automobile accident—impact injuries and severe burns. Although it is true that there is a zone around the bomb within which we can expect 100 percent casualties, in an air burst over a city, there is no zone of guaranteed instantaneous death. (Ground bursts with their craters do offer a very small zone of guaranteed instant death, however.)

As an example, at Hiroshima there was a group of Japanese army anti-aircraft gunners who were tracking the bomber when the atom bomb exploded almost literally in their faces. It killed them. . . yet they walked around pleading for help, faceless, blinded and in agony for more than a day before finally dying.

If you have been taking refuge in the "instant death" myth, consider this: It is true that you might get lucky; a building might fall on you, and your worries would be over. But there is no guarantee that the same building would also instantly kill your spouse, children or other relatives. When you decide to let the "first bomb" fall on you, you may be condemning them to experience the terror and pain of a reality which you could not face even in imagination. And they might have to face it without our help and protection. You got "lucky," remember?

You are making that decision even as you read this line. Don't kid yourself. Even putting the decision off until later . . . if ever . . . is a decision.

There are many more nuclear-war doomsday myths ranging from minor misunderstandings to outright lies, but time and space do not allow me to go on. The main thing to remember is that people like myself who are vitally interested in nuclear survivalism and in civil defense have actively investigated every doomsday rumor we have encountered, and they have all turned out to be false or blown far out of proportion to reality.

Recognizing Statements That Are Provable

From various sources of information we are constantly confronted with statements and generalizations about social and moral problems. In order to think clearly about these problems, it is useful to be able to make a basic distinction between statements for which evidence can be found and other statements which cannot be verified or proved because evidence is not available or the issue is too controversial.

Readers should constantly be aware that magazines, newspapers and other sources often contain statements of a controversial or questionable nature. The following activity is designed to allow experimentation with statements that are provable and those that are not.

Most of the following statements are taken from the viewpoints in this chapter. Consider each statement carefully. *Mark P for any statement you believe is provable. Mark U for any statement you feel is unprovable because of the lack of evidence. Mark C for statements you think are too controversial to be proved to everyone's satisfaction.*

If you are doing this activity as a member of a class or group, compare your answers with those of other class or group members. Be able to defend your answers. You may discover that others will come to different conclusions than you. Listening to the reasons others present for their answers may give you valuable insights in recognizing statements that are provable.

If you are reading this book alone, ask others if they agree with your answers. You too will find this interaction very valuable.

> P = provable
> U = unprovable
> C = too controversial

1. No sane person would initiate a series of events that would lead to everyone's death, including his own.

2. The specter of pestilence and disease stalking the land in the aftermath of a nuclear war is not a realistic possibility.

3. Common sense indicates that this country could continue to grow the food and fiber necessary to sustain its citizens after nuclear attack.

4. The post nuclear war environment will be so altered that widespread death and disease is inevitable.

5. Cancer will not be more widespread after a nuclear war than before.

6. Man has greatly altered the ecological balance of the Earth.

7. Industrial society will be destroyed by a nuclear war.

8. Low temperatures and decreased sunlight after a war would have a dramatic effect on plants.

9. Some people are bound to survive a nuclear war.

10. Virtually all land plants in the Northern Hemisphere would be damaged or killed in a nuclear war.

11. Scattered survivors may not be able to recover and rebuild cities after a nuclear war.

12. The only way to survive a nuclear war is to prevent it from happening.

13. Most people realize that a nuclear exchange would have horrendous effects on life and ecology.

14. A limited war is better than an all-out war.

15. The way to invite nuclear war is through unilateral disarmament.

16. No one would argue that the bombs dropped on Hiroshima and Nagasaki were tragedies.

Periodical Bibliography

The following list of periodical articles deals with the subject matter of this chapter.

Herbert L. Abrams and William E. Von Kaenel — "Medical Problems of Survivors of Nuclear War," *New England Journal of Medicine*, November 12, 1981.

Natalie Angier — "Debate Over a Frozen Planet," *Time*, December 24, 1984.

Yorick Blumenfeld — "Armageddon? Ho-Hum," *New York Times*, July 30, 1984.

William F. Buckley — "Nuclear Nonthink," *National Review*, February 4, 1983.

Anne Ehrlich — "Nuclear Winter," *Bulletin of the Atomic Scientists*, April 1984.

Anne Ehrlich & Paul Ehrlich — "After Nuclear War," *Mother Earth News*, November/December, 1983.

Frank von Hippel — "The Myths of Edward Teller," *Bulletin of the Atomic Scientists*, March 1983.

Orr Kelly — "Nuclear War's Horrors: Reality vs. Fiction," *U.S. News & World Report*, November 28, 1983.

Henry Kissinger — "A Need for Defense Short of Apocalypse," *Los Angeles Times*, March 3, 1985.

Edward N. Luttwak — "How to Think About Nuclear War," *Commentary*, August 1982.

Howard Maccabee — "Nuclear Winter: How Much Do We Really Know?" *Reason*, May 1985.

Michael M. May — "Nuclear Winter: Strategic Significance," *Issues in Science and Technology*, Winter 1985.

Thomas Powers — "Nuclear Winter and Nuclear Strategy," *The Atlantic Monthly*, November 1984.

Frank Rose — "Gimme Shelter," *Esquire*, October 1983.

Stephen Schneider — "Nuclear Winter: The Storm Builds," *Science Digest*, January 1985.

Time — "A Cold, Dark Apocalypse," November 14, 1983.

U.S. News & World Report — "Nuclear Arms Make Chance of War Far More Remote," April 9, 1984.

Will Civil Defense Work?

NUCLEAR WAR

Chapter Preface

To many, the implementation of a national civil defense plan and the possibility of nuclear war seem a contradiction in terms. "How," it is asked, "can a nation defend itself against the indefensible?" Yet proponents of civil defense persist. The most common arguments for civil defense seem to fall into two categories: 1) While millions will perish, millions will also be spared, and it is immoral and inhumane not to provide for those who survive. And 2) as long as the Soviet Union continues to formulate and implement civil defense plans, thereby revealing its expectations of survival, it seems imprudent at best, and suicidal at worst, for the United States not to plan for the same possibility.

Thus, while some argue that the lack of a civil defense program could provoke a nuclear war, others believe the opposite to be true, that pursuing a civil defense program could provoke one. Critics of civil defense believe it indicates a national resolve to win a nuclear war. With the knowledge (valid or not) that large numbers of the nation's citizens could survive, a president might be more apt to enter into a nuclear confrontation—or even worse—to initiate one. Others believe that an organized civil defense program is a protection against the Soviet Union starting a nuclear war. An American civil defense program would prevent the Soviets from believing that they could defeat the population, or worse, blackmail the United States into surrender. The viewpoints in this chapter debate these issues.

"The dangers from nuclear weapons have been distorted and exaggerated. . . . These exaggerations have become demoralizing myths, believed by millions of Americans."

Civil Defense Should Be Mandatory

Cresson H. Kearney

Cresson H. Kearney is among a handful of those considered to be survival "experts." He graduated from Princeton University with a degree in civil engineering in 1937 and earned advanced degrees in geology from Oxford University, England. As an infantry reserve lieutenant in Panama during World War II, Kearney improved and invented survival equipment for jungle troops. In 1961 he was offered work as a research analyst at the Hudson Institute, a war research think tank. From 1964 to the present Mr. Kearney has worked at the Oak Ridge National Laboratory on their civil defense project. He is the author of *Nuclear War Survival Skills* in which he expresses his frustration with commonly held notions about the effects of nuclear weapons. In the following viewpoint, excerpted from this book, Mr. Kearney exposes these myths so that the US can begin the necessary task of a mandatory civil defense program.

As you read, consider the following questions:

1. According to the author, why is the danger of nuclear fallout considerably less than what many believe?
2. How are the effects of Hiroshima and Nagasaki exaggerated, according to the author?

Cresson H. Kearny, *Nuclear War Survival Skills*, Coos Bay, OR: Nuclear War Survival Research Bureau, 1982.

An all-out nuclear war between Russia and the United States would be the worst catastrophe in history, a tragedy so huge it is difficult to comprehend. Even so, it would be far from the end of human life on earth. The dangers from nuclear weapons have been distorted and exaggerated, for varied reasons. These exaggerations have become demoralizing myths, believed by millions of Americans.

While working with hundreds of Americans building expedient shelters and life-support equipment, I have found that many people at first see no sense in talking about details of survival skills. Those who hold exaggerated beliefs about the dangers from nuclear weapons must first be convinced that nuclear war would not inevitably be the end of them and everything worthwhile. Only after they have begun to question the truth of these myths do they become interested, under normal peacetime conditions, in acquiring nuclear war survival skills. We will examine the most harmful of the myths about nuclear war dangers, along with some of the grim facts.

Fallout Radiation Myths

Myth: Fallout radiation from a nuclear war would poison the air and all parts of the environment. It would kill everyone. (This is the demoralizing message of *On the Beach* and many similar pseudoscientific books and articles.)

Facts: When a nuclear weapon explodes near enough to the ground for its fireball to touch the ground, it forms a crater. Many thousands of tons of earth from the crater of a large explosion are pulverized into trillions of particles. These particles are contaminated by radioactive atoms produced by the nuclear explosion. Thousands of tons of the particles are carried up into a mushroom-shaped cloud, miles above the earth. These radioactive particles then fall out of the mushroom cloud, or out of the dispersing cloud of particles blown by the winds—thus becoming fallout. . . .

The smallest fallout particles—those tiny enough to be inhaled into a person's lungs—are invisible to the naked eye. These tiny particles fall so slowly, from heights miles above the earth, that the winds carry them thousands of miles away from the site of the explosion before they reach the ground.

The air in properly designed fallout shelters, even those without air filters, is free of radioactive particles and safe to breathe except in a few rare environments. . . .

Need for Shelters Lessens

Within two weeks after an attack the occupants of most shelters could safely stop using them, or could work outside the shelters for an increasing number of hours each day. Exceptions would be in areas of extremely heavy fallout such as might occur downwind from important targets attacked with many weapons, especially missile sites and very large cities. To know when to come out safely, occupants either would need a reliable fallout meter to measure the changing radiation dangers, or must receive information based on measurements made nearby with a reliable instrument.

The radiation dose that will kill a person varies considerably with different people. A dose of 450 R resulting from exposure of the whole body to fallout radiation is often said to be the dose that will kill about half the persons receiving it, although most studies indicate that it would take somewhat less . . . .

Fortunately, the human body can repair most radiation damage if the daily radiation doses are not too large . . . .

Radiation Cannot Penetrate

Myth: Fallout radiation penetrates everything; there is no escaping its deadly effects.

Civil Defense as Insurance

Civil defense is the most humanitarian of all forms of defense because it is solely designed to save human lives. It poses no moral or environmental problems. Without it, we are always at risk; with it, we are always protected.

Civil defense should be looked upon like the expense of fire insurance on your home. None of us begrudges the cost of the premiums, even if we never collect on a burned-down house.

Phyllis Schlafly, *Washington Inquirer*, November 23, 1984.

Facts: Some gamma radiation from fallout will penetrate the shielding materials of even an excellent shelter and reach its occupants. However, the radiation dose that the occupants of an excellent shelter would receive while inside this shelter can be reduced to a dose smaller than the average American receives during his lifetime from X rays and other radiation exposures normal in America today. The design features of such a shelter include the use of a sufficient thickness of earth or other heavy shielding material. Gamma rays are like X rays, but more penetrating . . . .

Firestorm Myths

Myth: A heavy nuclear attack would set practically everything on fire, causing "firestorms" in cities that would exhaust the oxygen in the air. All shelter occupants would be killed by the intense heat.

Facts: On a clear day, thermal pulses (heat radiation that travels at the speed of light) from an air burst can set fire to easily ignitable materials (such as window curtains, upholstery, dry newspaper, and dry grass) over about as large an area as is damaged by the blast. It can cause second-degree skin burns to exposed people who are as far as ten miles from a one-megaton (1 MT) explosion. (A 1-MT nuclear explosion is one that produces the same amount of energy as does one million tons of TNT.) If the weather is very clear and dry, the area of fire danger could be considerably larger. On a cloudy or smoggy day, however, particles in the air would absorb and scatter much of the heat radiation, and the area endangered by heat radiation from the fireball would be less than the area of severe blast damage.

"Firestorms" could occur only when the concentration of combustible structures is very high, as in the very dense centers of a few old American cities. At rural and suburban building densities, most people in earth-covered fallout shelters would have nothing to fear from fire. . . .

Food and Water Myths

Myth: So much food and water will be poisoned by fallout that people will starve and die even in fallout areas where there is enough food and water.

Facts: If the fallout particles do not become mixed with the parts of food that are eaten, no harm is done. Food and water in dust-tight containers are not contaminated by fallout radiation. Peeling fruits and vegetables removes essentially all fallout, as does removing the uppermost several inches of stored grain onto which fallout particles have fallen. Water from many sources—such as deep wells and covered reservoirs, tanks, and containers—would not be contaminated. Even water containing dissolved radioactive elements and compounds can be made safe for drinking by simply filtering it through earth.

Genetic Abnormalities

Myth: Most of the unborn children and grandchildren of people who have been exposed to radiation from nuclear explosions will be genetically damaged—will be malformed, delayed victims of nuclear war.

Facts: The authoritative study of the National Academy of Sciences, *A Thirty Year Study of the Survivors of Hiroshima and Nagasaki*, was published in 1977. It concludes that the incidence of abnormalities is no higher among children later conceived by parents who were exposed to radiation during the attacks on Hiroshima and Nagasaki than is the incidence of abnormalities among Japanese children born to unexposed parents.

This is not to say that there would be no genetic damage, nor that some fetuses subjected to large radiation doses would not be damaged. But the overwhelming evidence does show that the exaggerated fears of radiation damage to future generations are not supported by scientific findings.

115

Myth: Overkill would result if all the U.S. and U.S.S.R. nuclear weapons were used—meaning not only that the two superpowers have more than enough weapons to kill all of each other's people, but also that they have enough weapons to exterminate the human race.

Civil Defense Myth

A popular misconception is that civil preparedness is futile. In fact, many scientific studies over the past 30 years have demonstrated that a modest fallout shelter and evacuation effort could save millions of Americans who would otherwise perish. The Soviet Union, Switzerland, and Sweden have each invested heavily in comprehensive civil defense programs.

Persistent myths that sponsor unreasoning fear and utopian illusions poison public discourse. They can be exorcized only when those held in their spell are willing to accept hard facts. Politicians, preachers, and the press have been grossly negligent in presenting these facts.

Ernest LeFever, *Washington Times*, April 26, 1984.

Facts: Statements that the U.S. and the Soviet Union have the power to kill the world's population several times over are based on misleading calculations. One such calculation is to multiply the deaths produced per kiloton exploded over Hiroshima or Nagasaki by an estimate of the number of kilotons in either side's arsenal. (A kiloton explosion is one that produces the same amount of energy as does 1000 tons of TNT.) The unstated assumption is that somehow the world's population could be gathered into circular crowds, each a few miles in diameter with a population density equal to downtown Hiroshima or Nagasaki, and then a small (Hiroshima-sized) weapon would be exploded over the center of each crowd. Other misleading calculations are based on exaggerations of the dangers from long-lasting radiation and other harmful effects of a nuclear war.

===
"Evacuation and shelters are a vain hope."
===

Civil Defense Is Futile

Jonathan Schell

Jonathan Schell is currently a staff writer for the *New Yorker*. The following viewpoint is selected from his popular work, *The Fate of the Earth*. Originally published as a series of articles in the *New Yorker*, the book quickly became a national bestseller, and started millions of people thinking about the consequences of a nuclear war. *The Abolition*, Schell's latest book, is a sequel which focuses primarily on ways to prevent a modern holocaust. In this viewpoint, Mr. Schell argues that the effects of a nuclear war would be so total and so horrible that plans to survive are a vain hope.

As you read, consider the following questions:

1. What would survive a nuclear attack, according to the author?
2. What percentage of the population does the author maintain would be killed in a nuclear attack?
3. What does the author believe would happen to those who have hidden in shelters?

The statistics on the initial nuclear radiation, the thermal pulses, and the blast waves in a nuclear holocaust can be presented in any number of ways, but all of them would be only variations on a simple theme—the annihilation of the United States and its people. Yet while the immediate nuclear effects are great enough in a ten-thousand-megaton attack to destroy the country many times over, they are not the most powerfully lethal of the local effects of nuclear weapons. The killing power of the local fallout is far greater. Therefore, if the Soviet Union was bent on producing the maximum overkill—if, that is, its surviving leaders, whether out of calculation, rage, or madness, decided to eliminate the United States not merely as a political and social entity but as a biological one—they would burst their bombs on the ground rather than in the air. Although the scope of severe blast damage would then be reduced, the blast waves, fireballs, and thermal pulses would still be far more than enough to destroy the country, and, in addition, provided only that the bombs were dispersed widely enough, lethal fallout would spread throughout the nation. . . . Calculations on the basis of figures for a one-megaton ground burst which are given in the Office of Technology Assessment's report show that ten thousand megatons would yield one-week doses around the country averaging more than ten thousand rems. . . .

These figures provide a context for judging the question of civil defense. With overwhelming immediate local effects striking the vast majority of the population, and with one-week doses of radiation then rising into the tens of thousands of rems, evacuation and shelters are a vain hope. Needless to say, in these circumstances evacuation before an attack would be an exercise in transporting people from one death to another. In some depictions of a holocaust, various rescue operations are described, with unafflicted survivors bringing food, clothes, and medical care to the afflicted, and the afflicted making their way to thriving, untouched communities, where churches, school auditoriums, and the like would have been set up for their care—as often happens after a bad snowstorm, say. Obviously, none of this could come about. In the first place, in a full-scale attack there would in all likelihood *be* no surviving communities, and, in the second place, everyone who failed to seal himself off from the outside environment for as long as several months would soon die of radiation sickness. Hence, in the months after a holocaust there would be no activity of any sort, as, in a reversal of the normal state of things, the dead would lie on the surface and the living, if there were any, would be buried underground. . . .

No Hole Big Enough

If, in a nuclear holocaust, anyone hid himself deep enough under the earth and stayed there long enough to survive, he would emerge into a dying natural environment. The vulnerability of the environ-

"HOW SILLY CAN YOU GET? ... AFTER I SPENT ALL DAY DIGGING AN A-BOMB SHELTER SHE WANTED ME TO SIGN AN ANTI-NUKE PETITION!"

ment is the last word in the argument against the usefulness of shelters: there is no hole big enough to hide all of nature in. Radioactivity penetrates the environment in many ways. The two most important components of radiation from fallout are gamma rays, which are electromagnetic radiation of the highest intensity, and beta particles, which are electrons fired at high speed from decaying nuclei. Gamma rays subject organisms to penetrating whole-body doses, and are responsible for most of the ill effects of radiation from fallout. Beta particles, which are less penetrating than gamma rays, act at short range, doing harm when they collect on the skin, or on the surface of a leaf. They are harmful to plants on whose foliage the fallout descends—producing "beta burn"—and to grazing animals, which can suffer burns as well as gastrointestinal damage from eating the foliage....

Devastate the Environment

A full-scale nuclear attack on the United States would devastate the natural environment on a scale unknown since early geological times, when, in response to natural catastrophes whose nature has not been determined, sudden mass extinctions of species and whole ecosystems occurred all over the earth. How far this "gross simplification" of the environment would go once virtually all animal life and the greater part of plant life had been destroyed and what patterns the surviving remnants of life would arrange themselves into

119

over the long run are imponderables; but it appears that at the outset the United States would be a republic of insects and grass....

The Doom of the US

It has sometimes been claimed that the United States could survive a nuclear attack by the Soviet Union, but the bare figures on the extent of the blast waves, the thermal pulses, and the accumulated local fallout dash this hope irrevocably. They spell the doom of the United States. And if one imagines the reverse attack on the Soviet Union, its doom is spelled out in similar figures. (The great land mass of the Soviet Union and the lower megatonnage of the American forces might reduce the factor of overkill somewhat.) Likewise, any country subjected to an attack of more than a few hundred megatons would be doomed. Japan, China, and the countries of Europe, where population densities are high, are especially vulnerable to damage, even at "low" levels of attack. There is no country in Europe in which survival of the population would be appreciable after the detonation of several hundred megatons; most European countries would be annihilated by tens of megatons. And these conclusions emerge even before one takes into account the global ecological consequences of a holocaust, which would be superimposed on the local consequences. As human life and the structure of human existence are seen in the light of each person's daily life and experience, they look impressively extensive and solid, but when human things are seen in the light of the universal power unleashed onto the earth by nuclear weapons they prove to be limited and fragile, as though they were nothing more than a mold or a lichen that appears in certain crevices of the landscape and can be burned off with relative ease by nuclear fire....

Our knowledge of nuclear effects is too imprecise to permit us to know at exactly what level of attack a given percentage of the population would survive, but the fact that sixty per cent of the population lives in eighteen thousand square miles and could be eliminated by the thermal pulses, blast waves, and mass fires produced by about three hundred one-megaton bombs suggests some rough magnitudes. The fallout that would be produced by the bombs if they were ground-burst would very likely kill ten or fifteen per cent of the remaining population (it could lethally contaminate some three hundred thousand square miles), and if several hundred additional megatons were used the percentage of the entire population killed in the short term might rise to something like eighty-five.... (Yet even one megaton, which contains the explosive yield of eighty Hiroshimas, would, if it should be dropped in the United States in the form of a number of small bombs, be an unimaginable catastrophe. Ten megatons—eight hundred Hiroshimas—would leave any nation on earth devastated beyond anything in our historical experience. A hundred megatons—eight thousand Hiroshimas—is already outside comprehension.)

As soon as one assumes that many tens of millions of people might survive the early stages of an attack, what are often called the long-term effects of a holocaust come into view; in fact, it is only when the imagined attack is reduced to this level that it begins to make sense to talk about many of the long-term effects, because only then will there be people left living to suffer them. The most obvious of these is injury. In an attack that killed from fifty to seventy per cent of the population outright, the great majority of the survivors would be injured. In a limited attack, some people might try to make their way to shelters to escape the fallout, which would be less intense than in the larger attack but still lethal in most populated areas....People who reached shelters and sealed themselves in in time might have a chance of survival in some areas, but a large number of people would have received lethal doses of radiation without knowing it (since exposure to radiation

---

Roasted In a Hole

What kind of civil defense program is going to defend you against 6,000 nuclear warheads? It depends upon whether you want to die in the field or die in a hole. Would you rather be roasted or boiled? It doesn't make any real difference. There *is* no civil defense against the number of warheads that we and the Soviet Union have deployed against one another. And you're just kidding yourself if you think there is. If you take a look at any of the intelligence analysis, it will demonstrate that a civil defense program would *not* protect the Soviet Union from unacceptable damage.

Paul Warnke, *With Enough Shovels*, 1982.

---

is painless) and would enter the shelters and die there, making life in the shelters unbearable for the others. With many people seeking to get into the shelters, attempts to decide who was to be allowed to enter and who was to be kept out would begin in bitterness and end in chaos.... Also, the withdrawal into shelters of the uninjured or lightly injured portion of the population would be more consequential for the survivors as a body, because in a limited attack there might be a considerable number of people on the surface who would have had a chance of surviving if they had not been abandoned. The widespread use of shelters would therefore mean additional deaths; the injured or sick people would die unattended on the surface while the uninjured and healthy people hid underground....

If enough people do live, the economy wil revive in one form or another, but in the meantime people will die: they will starve, because the supply of food has been cut off; they will freeze, because they have no fuel or shelter; they will perish of illness, because they have no medical care....

Future Generations Affected

Lastly, over the decades not only would the survivors of a limited attack face a contaminated and degraded environment but they themselves—their flesh, bones, and genetic endowment—would be contaminated: the generations that would be trying to rebuild a human life would be sick and possibly deformed generations....

I have mentioned the limitless complexity of its effects on human society and on the ecosphere—a complexity that sometimes seems to be as great as that of life itself. But if these effects should lead to human extinction, then all the complexity will give way to the utmost simplicity—the simplicity of nothingness. We—the human race—shall cease to be.

3

"Attempting to save lives and to prevent suffering is more than just a way of earning a living for us. It is a moral imperative."

Physicians Should Prepare for Nuclear Disaster

Howard D. Maccabee

Howard D. Maccabee is currently medical director of the Radiation Oncology Center located in Walnut Creek, California. He is the president of Doctors for Disaster Preparedness (DDP), a national organization of physicians and scientists who believe that it is morally imperative to prepare to save lives and prevent suffering in any type of disaster including nuclear war. In the following viewpoint, Dr. Maccabee elaborates on this position, insisting that physicians must take an active role in the civil defense of the United States.

As you read, consider the following questions:

1. The author makes comparisons of America's civil defense programs and those of other nations. What do these comparisons reveal?
2. What are the five advantages to civil defense, according to the author?
3. Why does the author believe that civil defense is not provocative?

Dr. Howard D. Maccabee, "A Medical and Ethical Argument for Civil Defense," *Emergency Management Review*, Vol. 1, No. 2, 1984.

There are ethical codes in virtually all professions. The helping professions are especially bound, on moral grounds, to give aid in time of need, whether a crisis be of individual or widespread nature. Physicians have traditionally interpreted the Oath of Hippocrates and the Code of Maimonides to mean that we are morally obligated to prevent illness if possible, as well as to treat it if necessary, even at personal risk, such as in epidemics. Attempting to save lives and to prevent suffering is more than just a way of earning a living for us. It is a moral imperative, and as such, it has been embodied in many other forms.

The Principles of Medical Ethics of the American Medical Association states in Section 5:

> A physician may choose whom he will serve. In an emergency, however, he should render service to the best of his ability.

The Internal Code of Medical Ethics, adopted by the Third General Assembly of the World Medical Association in 1949, states that

> A doctor must give emergency care as a humanitarian duty unless he is assured that others are willing and able to give such care.

Need to Prepare

Obviously, it is not possible to give emergency medical care to the victims of any disaster unless some preparations have been made, including education and training, availability of emergency facilities, medicines, supplies and equipment, as well as contingency plans, communication channels, and organizational structures to carry them out. Toward this end, the California Medical Association resolved through its House of Delegates in March, 1983, to "work toward development of a statewide contingency plan to deal with the medical consequences of nuclear war, and asked the California Delegation to the AMA to seek similar efforts at the national level."

As is well known, the American Red Cross and the International Red Cross are committed to aiding the victims of civil disaster as well as those of war. Their outstanding record in this respect is appreciated around the world, and we can be sure that they will do their best in case of a nuclear catastrophe.

It is not well known, however, that the Geneva Convention of 1977, (Sections 51 and 58) called for all nations to make preparations for protection of their populations from the effects of nuclear weapons, including attempts at prevention of war, as well as civil defense measures such as sanctuary for victims and evacuees, and preparations for medical response.

No matter what the official stance of the U.S. Government toward the Geneva Convention, we believe that there is a strong moral responsibility of Federal agencies to help to protect our population through effective civil defense and medical preparations.

Physicians and other health professionals are trained to respond to many types of illnesses; the principles of prevention, diagnosis and treatment are often applicable to problems which appear to be different from the situations by which they were derived. Hospitals, too, are efficient at caring for patients with many different kinds of diseases, even including normal conditions such as pregnancy and childbirth.

In the same sense, civil defense measures can be useful in many different kinds of emergencies. A shelter for blast or radioactive fallout can also be an excellent shelter for a hurricane, tornado, earthquake or fire. An evacuation plan for a nuclear reactor accident can also be useful in case of flood or accidental release of a toxic chemical. Communications networks, early warning systems and organizational structures should serve for any type of emergency. Experiences gained from different situations can be synergistic.

Many Would Survive

No nation other than the United States has advocated or adopted a strategy that purposely leaves its citizens unprotected hostages to its enemies. The rulers of the Soviet Union continue to prepare the Russians to fight, survive, and win a nuclear war. In contrast, influential Americans continue to demoralize us with exaggerated descriptions of nuclear war. Beginning with President Kennedy, all our Presidents have described nuclear war as "the end of mankind," or the like. This notwithstanding the fact that researchers on the effects of nuclear weapons know that although an all-out nuclear war between Russia and the United States would be the worst catastrophe in history, it would not be the end of mankind or of civilization. Today an all-out Soviet attack would result in only about 3% of the area of our country suffering blast and fire damage severe enough to destroy homes and kill most of the occupants!

Cresson H. Kearney, *Nuclear War Survival Skills*, 1982.

My personal observations as a practicing physician in radiation oncology, and my previous experience as a university educator and researcher in biomedical applications of nuclear radiation, have led me to several uncomfortable conclusions. Our people, even the most informed university graduates (and including most of my fellow physicians outside DDP) are generally unprepared for civil disaster, and grossly unable to understand or act rationally in case of nuclear disaster. There are multiple reasons for this, some of which stem from the blind fear resulting from ignorance of facts, and some of which are related to purposeful and accidental misinformation by quasi-political groups, including some physicians, who believe that fear-mongering is desirable in the effort to prevent nuclear war.

Much of the ignorance and misinformation, however, results simply from naive innocence. In this area particularly, efforts in public education, as well as training selected individuals in the community and in government, are to be encouraged, hopefully by increased financial support. It would be desirable to stimulate cooperation with schools and universities, health professional groups, and other volunteer organizations for these purposes.

Comparisons with Other Nations

In 1962, the government of Switzerland began a $3 billion civil defense program aimed at providing underground nuclear shelters for their entire population by the year 2000. They have largely succeeded in this already. Their civil defense budget this year was approximately $200 million (equivalent); this is probably a low estimate because it does not account for spending by individuals building private shelters as required by building codes or, by personal initiative. The population of Switzerland is less than 6½ million, and thus their per-capita expenditure is more than forty (40) times greater than the 70 cents we spent per American citizen.

Switzerland is not a nuclear power and is not considered a threat to the countries surrounding it. The presence of an adequate civil defense system is (properly) not perceived as evidence of aggressive intentions.

US Risk Greater

The sad irony is that we are a nuclear power, and we are involved in international conflicts with nations that are also armed with nuclear weapons. Our risk is greater than that of the Swiss, and yet our program is pitiful by comparison. This, I submit, is an injustice to the American people.

The Soviet Union is in a situation similar to ours in the sense of being a nuclear power and being involved in international conflicts. Their civil defense spending is estimated currently as more than $3 billion (equivalent), which is twenty (20) times our current level. Our relative unpreparedness, I submit, may be an invitation to disaster.

The concept of parity in nuclear weapons is central to strategic thinking for purposes of prevention of aggression. Obviously, if one side in a struggle is overwhelmingly stronger, this causes instability and increases the liklihood of attack on the weaker side.

Critics of Civil Defense

In the past three years, the concept of civil defense has come under heavy attack, with two basic arguments. First, that shelters and evacuation plans and medical preparations are useless and ineffective, and therefore laughable. Ridicule has been a particularly powerful tool in the media. For example, the journalist Robert

Scheer has been able to take quotations by President Reagan and other officials out of context, and with his interpretations, convert them into the briskly selling book *With Enough Shovels*. In this book as in the other parodies, there has been no serious attempt to refute the facts which emerge from Soviet, Swedish, Swiss, Chinese and American studies, i.e. that shelters can save lives. Why did they not laugh when the area around Three Mile Island was successfully evacuated?

Refusing to Plan Is Sinful

Nuclear war would no doubt be the most tragic disaster ever to befall mankind. There is no need to make it any worse by ignoring its consequences. There are, of course, some problems with civil defense as it exists today: crisis relocation is far from perfect, shelters are not invulnerable, panic and confusion may still occur. Yet to refuse to plan for these contingencies is as sinful as launching a nuclear weapon in the first place.

Richard B. Sincere, *Catholicism in Crisis*, January 1983.

The second argument is that of moral opprobrium built around the idea that civil defense plans are provocative, in that they may increase the risk of war by making our opponents think that we are preparing to attack them. If this idea is true, we are already in a very sad and dangerous situation because the Soviet Union already has a much larger civil defense program than ours, and by the previous logic, they must be preparing to attack us. Following out this (poor) line of reasoning would lead to the conclusion that we should attack first, or start on a "crash program" of our own, or surrender. I trust that none of these alternatives would be acceptable to the opponents of civil defense.

Civil Defense Is Not Provocative

Civil defense is not intrinsically provocative. Preparing to give aid to the victims of nuclear war can be entirely consistent with simultaneous efforts at prevention of war. The events of history show that no matter how hard we try to prevent catastrophe, we sometimes fail, and then we are sorry for not having "hedged" a bit, by not having the foresight to save some resources to ameliorate the results. The urge to shelter our people from all types of "storms" comes from basic humanitarian instincts, not from crass calculations of bodycounts and megatonnage. I will point out, in passing, the contradiction that civil defense cannot be ridiculously worthless and dangerously provocative at the same time. In our view, it is neither.

The most effective voice in the criticism of civil defense has been

127

that of a group called "Physicians for Social Responsibility" (PSR) which has produced several symposia on medical consequences of nuclear war, and circulated a film and a book called *The Last Epidemic*, based on the San Francisco symposium that I attended. The central theme of the symposia, the book and the film is that in case of an all-out nuclear war, assuming attacks on centers of populations without warning, the medical consequences would be so horrible and overwhelming, that there is little that the remaining physicians and medical centers could do to help. Their conclusion is that the only response to "the last epidemic" is prevention. There is not time or space for me to point out all the falsehoods and mistakes in the presentations, but it is important to understand the basic flaws in the logic. They are related to drawing conclusions based on "worst-case" assumptions. It is possible that the PSR scenario could occur, but it is also possible, and quite probable that events could take a far different course.

There are many other scenarios for conflict than all-out nuclear attack on population centers without warning, including limited war, phased escalation, attack by a government with limited weapons, terrorist attack, accidental launch and detonation, and "demonstration explosions" as was proposed in order to end the war with Japan in 1945, without harming a large civilian population in Hiroshima and Nagasaki. In all of these scenarios, civil defense could play a vital role in prevention of death and suffering.

Furthermore, even if there were an all-out nuclear "exchange," it is not likely that population centers would be high on the priority list. Obviously the highest priority targets would be nuclear weapon delivery systems (missile silos, submarines, bombers and airbases) in order to prevent further retaliation, with second priority most likely other types of military installations, and third priority the industrial base needed to make war. Population centers, per se, should be lowest on a target priority list, unless the motive is revenge instead of survival. Clearly an attack on military facilities would have horrible indirect effects on many of our cities, but again, in such a case, civil defense and similar measures could prevent tens of millions of casualties.

In a chilling final portion of the PSR presentation, Dr. Jack Geiger charges that it is immoral for physicians to plan to care for the victims of nuclear war, because this may decrease the fear of war and make it more likely. This logic is also faulty. Consider its application to cigarette smoking and lung cancer. Is it immoral for us to plan to treat lung cancer because it may decrease the fear of the disease and thereby encourage cigarette smoking? Absurd.

Advantages of Civil Defense

1) Civil defense measures, unlike offensive weapon systems of deterrence, can not directly threaten the lives of Russians or any other nation. They cannot be accidentally discharged or stolen by

terrorists.

2) Properly designed shelter systems of various types can serve multiple purposes, including storage, parking, community meeting space, etc., and are intrinsically energy-efficient.

3) Construction of shelters is likely to be labor-intensive by comparison with weapons systems, and would probably result in more jobs in portions of the economy that have been distressed.

4) If arms control and reduction negotiations are successful, there may be a transition period of fear and instability while methods of verification are being checked and accepted. An adequate civil defense system could help to bridge these gaps of insecurity.

5) The extension of the above argument would be to replace the doctrine of "mutually assured destruction" (MAD) with mutually assured survival.

"Medical care is impossible in any real sense...
because it is a complex activity that requires a
high degree of social organization."

Physicians Cannot Prepare for Nuclear Disaster

H. Jack Geiger

H. Jack Geiger is Arthur C. Logan professor of Community
Medicine and Director of the Program in Health, Medicine and
Society in the School of Biomedical Education of the City College
of New York. He is a founding member of the Physicians for Social
Responsibility, a national organization of physicians and supporters
committed to the education of the public and medical profession
on the medical hazards of the nuclear power and nuclear weapons
industries. In the following viewpoint, Dr. Geiger argues that
medical preparations for nuclear war are futile. Not only would few
physicians survive a nuclear attack, but these physicians would
have the impossible task of caring for hundreds of thousands of
injured and dying victims.

As you read, consider the following questions:

1. Why does the author believe that the Hiroshima and Nagasaki
   bombings cannot be used as precedents for a future nuclear
   attack?
2. The author argues that physicians are more likely than
   others to be killed in a nuclear holocaust. Why?

H. Jack Geiger, "The Illusion of Survival," from *The Final Epidemic: Physicians and
Scientists on Nuclear War*, edited by Ruth Adams and Susan Cullen, 1981. Reprinted by
permission of THE BULLETIN OF THE ATOMIC SCIENTISTS, a magazine of science and
world affairs. Copyright © 1981 by The Educational Foundation for Nuclear Science,
Chicago, IL 60637.

To attempt to measure and describe the consequences of a thermonuclear attack on a major American city is to confront a paradox.

On the one hand, the nature and magnitude of the effects of hypothetical—but eminently possible—nuclear attacks are entirely specifiable. The calculations are straightforward and only moderately complex. Indeed, over the past two decades, these consequences have been described in exquisite detail in hundreds of scientific journals, . . . books and government publications.

On the other hand, despite the specificity, these effects—the numbers of killed and injured, the destruction of the physical environment, the damage to the ecosphere—are unfathomable. In short, it is almost impossible fully to grasp the reality they represent, the implications they carry.

10 Million Killed

This is not merely because the numbers are so large as to be incomprehensible: close to 10 *million* people killed or seriously injured, for example, in consequence of a single 20-megaton explosion and the resulting firestorm on the New York metropolitan area. The difficulty occurs primarily because we are attempting to describe and understand an event that is without human precedent.

Hiroshima and Nagasaki do not serve as precedents for any probable nuclear war scenario. . . .

No Help from Outside

Hiroshima and Nagasaki were isolated, limited disasters. They could, in time, be saved and reconstructed with help from outside. Always, we think of an "outside"; this is our intuitive model of disasters, for our historical experience is confined to single-event phenomena of limited range, duration and effect—hurricanes, earthquakes, World War II bombings, even Hiroshima and Nagasaki—in which both short-term and longer-term relief efforts could be mounted.

In any full-scale contemporary nuclear exchange, *there will be no "outside" that we can rely upon.* We cannot safely assume that there will be unaffected major areas within reach of targeted cities that will have resources that can be mobilized effectively to help the stricken targets, or that are likely to regard even making the effort as a rational enterprise. In a population-targeted attack, every major population center may be effectively destroyed. . . .

There is no identifiable event in human history when a million people have been killed in one place at one moment. There is no previous situation in which there were 400,000 seriously injured human beings in one place. . . .

Physicians' offices and hospitals tend to be concentrated in central-city areas closest to ground zero. If anything, physicians will be killed and seriously injured at rates greater than those of the general population, and hospitals similarly have greater probabilities of destruction or severe damage. Of the approximately 4,000 physicians in San Francisco County, perhaps half would survive a one-megaton air burst; of the 4,647 hospital beds in the county, only a handful would remain. At 20 megatons, there would be only a few thousand physicians left in all of San Francisco, Alameda, Marin, San Mateo and Contra Costa Counties to try to care for 874,000 seriously wounded.

One carefully detailed study of an American city suggests that there would be 1,700 seriously injured "survivors" for every physician—and that includes physicians of all ages, types of training, states of health and location at the time of the attack. If, conservatively, we estimate only 1,000 seriously wounded patients per surviving physician, if we further assume that every physician sees each patient for only 10 minutes for diagnosis and treatment, and if each such physician worked 20 hours a day, it would be eight days before all the wounded were seen—once—by a doctor. Most of the wounded will die without medical care of any sort. Most will die without even the simple administration of drugs for the relief of pain.

A closer look at these calculations reveals that they are absurd—and the absurdities have implications that extend far beyond issues of medical care . . . .

John Trever, *The Albuquerque Journal.* Reprinted with permission.

It is important to examine medical care scenarios not merely as an element in the essentially hopeless task of response to a nuclear attack, but as a metaphor for *all* complex human—that is to say, social—activities in the post-attack period. *What becomes clear is that all such activities require an intact social fabric*—not merely the infrastructure of electric power, transportation, communications, shelter, water or food but the social enterprises, the complex human interactions and organizations supported by that infrastructure. That social fabric is ruptured, probably irreparably, by even a single nuclear weapon. Medical care is impossible in any real sense, not only because of the damage to the physical and biological environments, but most of all because it is a complex activity that requires a high degree of social organization.

The same is true of most other important human activities in complex urban societies. It follows that the only true meaning of "survival" is social, not biological. Simply to tally those who are still alive, or alive and uninjured, is to make a biological body-count that has little social meaning. The biological "survivors" in all probability have merely postponed their deaths—by days, weeks, months or at most a few years—from secondary attack-related causes. Life in the interim will bear no resemblance to life before a nuclear attack.

In the period from days to months after an attack, other problems of both social and medical significance will rapidly emerge. Without functioning transportation, even assuming that effective social organization continues on the "outside," no food will come into the stricken area; remaining undestroyed stocks will be depleted rapidly. Extreme water shortages will occur almost at once. The average citizen of a modern American city uses between 50 to 150 gallons of water a day; in the post-attack period, a quarter a day per survivor would be generous, and there will be no easy way to assure either potability or freedom from radioactive contamination.

Mass Infection a Certainty

Over the first two to four weeks after the attack, thousands of short-term survivors will die of radiation sickness, particularly of infection secondary to radiation-induced lowering of resistance. The problem of mass infection is particularly ugly. Even assuming that a firestorm conveniently incinerates 500,000 of the dead in a one-megaton attack, there will remain some 300,000 or more decomposing human corpses in the Bay Area. There will be no safe water supply or effective sanitation. The vectors of disease—flies, mosquitoes and other insects—will enjoy preferential survival and growth in the post-attack period because their radiation resistance is many times that of mammals. Most surviving humans will have reduced resistance to infection. It is hard to construct a scenario more likely to produce epidemic disease.

133

Finally, any *likely* population-targeted attack will assign many multi-megaton weapons to each major city, and therefore calculations based on a single one-megaton or 20-megaton strike are unrealistically conservative.

Nuclear War: #1 Health Threat

Physicians do not possess special knowledge of direct experience in atomic matters. They do, however, have unique expertise in areas relating to the medical consequences of nuclear war, to the possibilities of medical care in a post-attack period, to the non-involvement and denial by the intended victims, to the malfunctioning of technology and to the aberration of personality which may trigger a nuclear exchange. The physicians' analysis is precise, clinical and exorcises the mystifying verbiage, *Manichean* over-simplifications and sanitized statistics of the strategic experts. The physicians' movement is compelled by a growing conviction that nuclear war is the number one health threat and perhaps constitutes the final epidemic for which the only remedy is prevention.

International Physicians for Prevention of Nuclear War, *Last Aid*, 1982.

Other scenarios—the so-called "counterforce" exchanges aimed primarily at missile sites or various city-trading hypotheses—presumably would result in less *immediate* death and injury. But they pose medical and social problems of equal magnitude in the longer run, even if they do not almost automatically escalate into full-scale exchanges.

Evacuation Measures Provocative

Mass evacuation of cities in a nuclear crisis, the current favorite of civil defense enthusiasts, would in itself be seen as provocative by an adversary and therefore would increase risks. According to testimony before a Senate subcommittee by representatives of the Federal Emergency Management Agency, effective evacuation would require "only eight days" from warning time to completion.

It is, once again, a technique aimed at short-term biological survival, not social survival: to what would the dispersed urban residents return?

The danger of nuclear war is a public health problem of unprecedented magnitude. It is not, however, unprecedented in *type*. There are many other medical problems to which a coherent response is not possible and for which there are no cures. One medical (and social) strategy is still available in such cases: Prevention.

"Soviet leaders believe nuclear war can be won."

Soviet Civil Defense Plans Make Nuclear War Winnable

Leon Gouré

Dr. Leon Gouré is America's foremost authority on Soviet civil defense. Russian-born, Dr. Gouré has devoted many years of study to Soviet war policies and plans, in particular their civil defense activities. While a senior staff member for the Rand Corporation from 1951-1979, his speciality was Soviet civil defense and war survival strategies. He is presently the director of the Center for Soviet Studies at Science Application Incorporated (SAI), a private Washington research firm. He has published *Civil Defense in the Soviet Union*, and co-authored *Soviet Strategy for the Seventies: From Cold War to Peaceful Coexistence*. In the following viewpoint, Dr. Gouré expresses his opinion that the US is naive and suicidal in its lack of civil defense preparation for nuclear war. The Soviets' extensive civil defense planning is evidence that they plan to use their nuclear weapons and survive a counterattack by the US.

As you read, consider the following questions:

1. According to the author, how do the Soviets' projected post-nuclear war casualities compare to projected American casualties?
2. Does the author believe that the Soviets want a nuclear war to occur?

Leon Gouré, interviewed by Will Brownell, "Russia Is Bullish on Civil Defense," *Survive*, March 1982. Reprinted with permission.

Brownell: Why is it that the Soviets have the finest civil-defense system in the world, and the Americans have the weakest? I know that you go into great detail about this subject in your books.

Gouré: The Soviets have 100,000 full-time personnel under General Altunin, chief of U.S.S.R. civil defense and a deputy Minister of Defense, working to protect the people from nuclear war; America has less than one-sixth that number. They are spending from $20 to $40 per year per citizen for this kind of protection; we are spending—at the maximum—50 cents. They have a strategy that plans for their whole nation to survive a nuclear war. We have a lot of paper. If there were a nuclear war now, the Soviets are so well-protected, and America is so poorly protected, that we might suffer 120 million dead, compared to their 30 million casualties. And it could be worse, for the United States. It depends, of course, on what kind of conflict develops. A nuclear war can be fought many ways: Will they send their missiles against our military targets? Or military-defense support targets? Or industries? Or cities?

Brownell: Suppose the worst scenario: a surprise attack, a bolt from the blue, if you will—against our cities?

Gouré: If you involve cities, out of the blue, our casualties could total 165 million.

Brownell: Wouldn't that shatter the United States?

Gouré: Completely. With losses like that, the United States will lose 73 percent of its population. Figures get meaningless at that point. You have no society left of any kind, national or otherwise.

Brownell: And Soviet losses?

Gouré: A different matter; and it depends on how you calculate them. But an optimistic view of Soviet losses is about 17 million.

Brownell: Which is a minor percentage of their population?

Gouré: If they lose 20 million people, roughly, they have lost *eight* percent of their population. In the few figures they have published of projected losses, they estimate four to six percent. One school of thought believes that they may well lose fewer people than they lost in World War II. This compares with American losses in excess of 100 million.

Russian Surprise Attack

Brownell: That means they have less to lose in a nuclear war than we do. Can the Russians surprise us with a bolt from the blue?

Gouré: It all depends on how you think our civil-defense system will work; on how much warning we get; and other variables. The Soviets can accomplish a great deal through secrecy and conceal-ment, but nevertheless, they will have a problem not giving *any* advance warning by their initiation of civil-defense measures.

Brownell: How much time would the Soviets need to get ready, including their civilian population, for a nuclear war?

Gouré: It is generally believed that they can accomplish the bulk of their evacuation in about 48 to 72 hours, if they wanted to evacuate their cities. . . .

Evacuation Strategies

Brownell: Can you give more details on Soviet evacuation strategies?

Gouré: If the Soviets go into a dispersed position, we'll get nervous as hell. We'll be waiting for the attack, with our military on alert. You can't maximize your readiness to attack for very long. You know, you can't maximize fueling for all missiles constantly. The president of the United States, in response to Soviet evacuation, orders a U.S. evacuation, and our economy comes to a grinding halt. How long can we stay in that position? Meanwhile the Soviets are not only threatening, but continuing to work: Soviet industry will not be interrupted by a nuclear strike. Photographs of training exercises in Russia indicate that factories and other industrial plants have been designed to operate through an attack and are equipped with protective gas masks, food and other emergency supplies. And workers are drilled regularly so they can take necessary precautions and continue to work—in their masks if necessary.

Soviet Disinformation

What Americans would *like* to believe about Soviet civil defense is coincidentally just what the Soviets would like them to believe about it: that it is largely a confused paper program and that the blast shelters people talk about are not all that extensive—maybe for 10% of the urban population. And really, the story goes, Soviet shelter building cannot even keep up with population increases.

Comforting? Yes. Purposely so. A disarming use of reverse hyperbole.

What needs to be cranked in is the Soviet uncanny talent for and total dedication to deception and surprise. The "mutual suicide" line, cultivated only in the *West*, serves Soviet interests.

Journal of Civil Defense, April 1984.

Brownell: Speaking of Soviet photographs of civil-defense measures, I have seen your archives of hundreds of photographs, and they illustrate a frighteningly sophisticated degree of preparedness. But the one that most clearly emphasized that showed the measures the Soviets have developed to protect their livestock. They may have more cows survive than we have people. How long did it take the Soviets to develop this amazing civil-defense system?

Gouré: The Soviet view of civil defense is very straightforward.

It started essentially right after the Russian Revolution in 1917. You know their attitude: "We are always going to be in danger of war. Our objective is to ensure the survival of the First Socialist State. Wars can be protracted: we need production; we need workers, therefore, we need civil defense." Since 1924 they have had civil defense.

Brownell: What is the United States' position on civil defense?

Gouré: We started out in error in the early 1950s, played around with it, backed off in the 60s, partly due to cost and partly because of the American demand for absolute effectiveness. We felt that we had to save everyone or the system wasn't any good. We had other fantasies, too, including the romantic one that would have us believe that if America really decides to, we can lick anyone in any kind of conflict. . . .

A Winnable Nuclear War?

Brownell: Of course, there are a lot of people, including Americans, who assume that the Soviets are fairly decent people, who don't want war, and who think that a nuclear war is not winnable.

Gouré: That's a strange assumption. In a recent *Washington Post* article, an incensed writer wanted to know on what basis the Reagan administration could claim the Soviets believe in the feasibility of winning a nuclear war. I'm incensed that this writer—and other Americans—simply fail to read readily available information that documents this—information as recent as the January 1981 posture statement by Harold Brown, [Secretary of Defense under Carter], that said the Soviet leaders believe nuclear war can be won. For most, this is a new revelation. But it isn't a new concept; it goes way back.

Brownell: Unfortunately, if you quote Soviet leaders about winning a nuclear war—such as Brezhnev in *Pravda*—you are considered a war-monger in America.

Gouré: We have declassified the Soviet internal staff journal *Voyennaya mysl*, or *Military Thought*, which is really for internal consumption. It's called the VM Series in Russia. And it's very obvious that their objective is victory. And why shouldn't it be? If you, as a Russian, assume that war is likely or possible, and that the way to meet that problem is to be prepared for war, why are you fighting if not to win?

Brownell: But many Americans don't believe that.

Gouré: People either quote diplomats or say that war is just not thinkable: "The Russians can't mean it because everybody knows there is no nuclear-war survival. And if there is no survival, there can be no victory." When you point out the Soviets have a doctrine of survival, they say, "But it's not going to work." "Why won't it work?" you ask. "Because we all have these weapons that will destroy 200 Soviet cities, and they'll all die and that will be the end

138

of their civilization." Wait a minute. The Soviets lost 1700 cities in WWII and their civilization didn't end. Cities are not the important thing. People are. Talent, training, skills, knowledge: The Soviets will preserve these and rebuild the cities—maybe primitively at first, but rebuild they will. . . .

US and Soviet Similarities

Brownell: What similarities do you see between U.S. and Soviet plans?

Gouré: None. Soviet civil defense is binding on all governments. . . .

Brownell: Does the United States have a priority system for the order in which its citizens are evacuated?

Gouré: Absolutely not. You cannot say who should or should not survive. You would get tarred and feathered if you even established a priority system in which you determine that certain categories or skills deserve special protection because of their value to the nation. In the Soviet Union, the government can order all transportation organizations to be part of the civil-defense transportation corps. Simple as that. . . .

Soviet Civil Defense Works

Despite [their] extensive and intensive preparedness, Soviet leaders continue to tell the West that nuclear war is not survivable. This same line is fostered by various subversive groups in the United States.

The Soviets are protecting their population. They assume that any war, though it may begin with conventional weapons, may escalate to the use of nuclear devices. In-place shelters have been employed since 1973. The Soviets estimate that a surprise attack would result in 50-60% fatalities. This would be reduced to 5-8% if there were warning and if there were evacuation.

Max Klinghoffer, *Journal of Civil Defense,* August 1984.

Brownell: If we were in a conventional conflict with Russia, wouldn't we be tempted to use nuclear weapons, out of desperation?

Gouré: We might go nuclear out of weakness, and if we initiate a nuclear conflict, the effect is not the same for both parties. If one accepts Soviet superiority, the likelihood is that we will make the decision. But there's a catch: The Russians know that at a certain point, we must go nuclear. How long will they wait before we make the decision? They certainly won't wait for us to use nuclear weapons. They'll make the first strike.

"There [is little] basis for claiming that Soviet leaders. . .would risk war with the United States while counting on civil defense measures."

Soviet Civil Defense Is Inadequate and Meaningless

Fred M. Kaplan

Fred M. Kaplan writes regularly on defense for the *Boston Globe*, *The Bulletin of the Atomic Scientists*, and other publications. He is a graduate from Oberlin College in Ohio and has a Ph.D. in political science from the Massachusetts Institute of Technology (MIT) in Cambridge. The author of *Dubious Specter: A Second Look at the Soviet Threat* and *Wizards of Armageddon*, Mr. Kaplan is a well-respected writer on the liberal side of arms race issues. In the following viewpoint, Mr. Kaplan argues that Soviet civil defense plans exist primarily on paper and are used to pacify the Soviet people, not as plans to survive and prevail in a nuclear confrontation with the US.

As you read, consider the following questions:

1. Why are Soviet civil defense plans mandatory, according to the author?
2. What does the author think of Soviet measures to insure industrial recovery?

Fred M. Kaplan, "The Soviet Civil Defense Myth," *The Bulletin of the Atomic Scientists*, March 1978. Reprinted by permission of *The Bulletin of the Atomic Scientists*, a magazine of science and world affairs. Copyright © 1978 by the Educational Foundation for Nuclear Science, Chicago, IL 60637.

In the 1950s it was the "bomber gap," in early 1960s the "missile gap." Now there is much talk of "civil defense gap." . . .

The warnings envisage an alarming scenario: The Soviets, after evacuating their cities, force American leaders to give in to certain demands, threatening a nuclear strike otherwise; the United States would not be able, in a retaliatory strike, to destroy a significant portion of the Soviet population or economy. Another plot has the Soviets evacuating during a crisis, thereby gaining a political edge.

Soviet documents, as well as many U.S. analysts, portray a comprehensive, national Soviet civil defense program. Blast shelters have been provided for national leaders and essential workers, some of them in hardened areas near or at the industrial site. The rest of the population, it is said, can be sheltered in basements, tunnels, subways and existing structures; or they are to be evacuated far outside the city. The entire population, it is contended, has undergone compulsory civil defense training. The Communist Party supports the program, and the effort has been upgraded since 1973. . . .

Soviet Civil Defense Inadequate

The upshot of all this, . . . is that in the face of a retaliatory nuclear strike by the United States, all but 2 to 10 percent of the Soviet population could be protected as well as a significant portion of its industrial base—so that full recovery could be assured in two to four years. If these reports are correct, the implications for arms control are dismaying. Such a program would fuel the concern that the Soviets are trying to achieve "strategic superiority" and, as one observer concludes, would "substantially undermine the deterrent concept that has been the cornerstone of U.S. national security."

In all its phases, however—from the training program to the evacuation and sheltering, to the assumed nature of the U.S. attack, to the post-attack recovery estimates—the basic analysis, common to virtually all studies expressing concern over Soviet civil defense, suffers from unrealistic assumptions, leaps of faith, violations of logic and a superficial understanding of the dynamics of a national economy. It appears from the available evidence that the Soviet civil defense program would be inadequate in the face of a large-scale nuclear attack; that Soviet intentions are probably other than aggressive, and that the United States currently has more than sufficient capability to nullify whatever passive-defense measures may have been taken by the Soviet Union.

Training Programs

Compulsory civil defense training programs supposedly exist for all citizens in the Soviet Union—a combination of lectures, films, booklets, practical instruction and exercises. Leon Goure, director of Soviet studies at the University of Miami, notes with alarm that a 20-hour course is required for everybody, 70 to 90 hours of training for command-staff personnel, 36 to 44 hours for civil defense unit leaders, and 28 to 30 hours for members of civil defense formations drawn from factories. Children are taught techniques at school and play civil defense games at Pioneer Youth camps.

Much evidence suggests, however, that these programs are neither effective nor strongly emphasized. In 1975, the 35-hour training program was reduced to 29 hours. The study of nuclear weapons-effects and of decontamination techniques has been dropped from the compulsory course....

Soviet Faith in Civil Defense?

Several Soviet sources stress that the instilling of "deep faith" in the effectiveness of civil defense measures is "a vital function of the training program. Yet this seems to have failed. A standard Russian joke goes: "What do you do when you hear the alert? Put on a sheet and crawl to the cemetery—slowly. Why slowly? So you don't spread panic." The Russian phrase for "civil defense" is *grazhdanskaya oborona*. Taking the first two letters of each word, many Russians sardonically refer to civil defense as *grob*, meaning "coffin."

Soviet War Survival Impossible

Regarding the interpretation of Soviet motivations, a certain leap of faith is required to construe their non-military [civil] defenses as a sign that the Soviet leadership is embarking on a "war survival" strategy wherein Russia would emerge the relative victor from a nuclear exchange with the United States through an ability to recover more quickly. This interpretation overlooks the fact that, unlike the United States, the Soviet Union faces not one but several potentially hostile nuclear powers (NATO theater nuclear forces, China, France, Great Britain, and, in the future perhaps Iran, India, or Pakistan).

William H. Kincaid, *International Security*, Winter 77/78.

The impression of an ineffectual training program is reinforced by a statement of the Soviet civil defense chief, A. Altunin, in his latest annual report: "Our numerous [civil defense] activists can and should be trained." The implication is that they are not trained now....

Evacuation Plans

On paper the Soviet evacuation plan seems impressive at first glance. There are nine warning signals, each indicating different stages of a crisis and alerting the citizenry to particular forms of action. At the final alarm, ordering urban evacuation, the people are to take pre-specified motorcars, trains or buses to pre-specified shelters in rural areas. The rest of the population is to find shelter in the city or to start walking (in orderly columns of 500 to 1,000). They are then to build "expedient shelters," for which printed instructions exist. This entire procedure, according to Soviet documents, is to take 72 hours. . . .

On a strategic level, crisis evacuation is a highly risky step at which even the most adventurous aggressor would hesitate. Through national means of intelligence, massive movements of people would surely be detected. Soviet leaders must know that the United States could take countervailing action, possibly of a preemptive nature. At the very least, the United States could start dispersing heavy bombers and putting some on airborne alert, mobilizing more nuclear-missile submarines on-station, ordering a temporary missile launch-on-warning policy, perhaps second reinforcements to Western Europe and commence maneuvering exercises in the Mediterranean. The entire U.S. land-based ICBM force can be retargeted, in any configuration, in 10 hours. Such actions as these would sharply limit the efficacy of, say, Soviet first-strike threats. In any event, crisis evacuation would certainly escalate a crisis, probably far more than the Soviets would want it to go.

Overwhelming Obstacles

Aside from this, the technical and logistic obstacles are overwhelming. The Soviets have never staged an evacuation exercise in any major city nor, even in smaller towns, has an entire community been evacuated. Of the drills that have taken place, none were carried out simultaneously; all have used only one mode of transportation, and the drills had been in preparation long before the actual exercise. To start evacuating Moscow, Leningrad, Kiev—or any of the other 220 cities with populations of 100,000 or more—as a crucial aspect of a highly coordinated and risky offensive without a single rehearsal is an excessively demanding proposition. . . .

Shelter Programs

There are numerous problems with the shelter program as well. Very few existing shelters have any food stocks, only a few more have any water. In other words, people would have to bring at least two weeks' worth of food and water along with them. Given the grocery lines in Russia and the tendency not to stock up on items because of the expense, this becomes a serious problem. Even if the population could be adequately protected, many may starve.

If starvation isn't the cause of death, heat stroke may be the cause. The lynchpin of a shelter is its ventilation system, which filters the air and keeps the shelter from getting too hot, humid or cold. . . .

Moreover, in shelters housed in existing buildings, the power for the filtration system is connected to outside power plants. This means that if the plant is targeted, the filtration system is useless. Additionally, by Soviet estimate, a basement shelter is resistant only to blasts of 7 to 10 pounds per square inch. Even [T.K.] Jones [who reported at the Civil Defense Hearings in the US House Armed Services Committee] concedes that urban shelters "could not help much against a U.S. attack designed to destroy populations."

So that leaves the expedient shelters. One problem with these is how they could possibly be built. Leon Gouré says that materials used for their construction are "handy": timber, boards, sheetmetal, bricks, cinder blocks and shovels. Where these are located so they can be passed out to the tens of millions of people needing them is just one of the details with which Gouré and many others do not concern themselves. That the Soviet Union is basically an "apartment society" makes the requisite supply of shovels especially problematic.

Russians Are Not Stupid

The Russians are people that I would not trust to act in other than their own narrow national interest, so I am not naive. But they are not mad. They are not mad. They have suffered casualties, and their government feels responsible to their people to avoid those situations in the future. They are more sensitive to the impact of casualties on their people than we appear to be in some of our statements and analyses of fighting and winning nuclear wars which would extend over a period of months.

So they are not mad. They are aggressive; they are ideological; they need to be restrained and contained by the existence of our defensive forces. But they are not mad, and I see no evidence that they would accept the risks associated with a first strike against the United States.

Robert McNamara, *The Los Angeles Times*, April 4, 1982.

And *when* are the shelters to be built? The ground is frozen in Russia all winter. In the spring and summer, foodstocks are virtually depleted, as the planting season is about to begin. Autumn is the time of the *rasputitza*, when it rains nearly all the time and when everything is muddy. The Soviet civil defense handbook notes that it "is desirable to select as shelter sites dry, firm-soil sites that do not flood when it rains." For long periods of time in large parts of the Soviet Union such conditions do not hold. . . .

In short, only a small fraction of the population, whatever the season, would be sheltered at all—and most of them, inadequately. . . .

"One of the principal tasks of civil defense," claims that 1974 Soviet handbook, "is the conduct of measures aimed at increasing the...ability to continue production operations in wartime on a planned, normal basis, and to return quickly to projection upon sustaining minor or moderate damage or when supply is disrupted." Recommended measures include strengthening structures around vital machinery, shielding oil and chemical storage tanks, increasing the stock of spare parts, removing flammable materials from industrial sites, placing hoods, canopies, earth, water or sandbags over machinery.

There are some enterprises, notes the manual, that cannot be shut down even briefly, including chemical reactors, blast furnaces, boiler facilties, and open-hearth furnaces. "Personnel operating these facilities cannot leave their stations even if an air-raid signal sounds"; instead, individual or group shelters, with "remote-control consoles," are to be furnished for these workers. There is no sign that any of these recommended measures have actually been implemented anywhere. By the manual's own admission, a steel-reinforced industrial plant is disabled at 3 to 6 psi, and a bomb shelter receives damage at 17 psi. A 100-kiloton warhead hitting two miles from the site, in other words, could do disabling damage. As for possible strengthening devices, the Soviet handbook notes:

> It is impossible to make buildings less vulnerable to a shock wave without radical structural changes that involve considerable technical difficulties and cost....It is impossible to guarantee building survival in a damage area even by somewhat increasing the strength of individual structures and their components.

More important, many economic facilities cannot be protected at all, among them the Soviet Union's most crucial. These include oil refineries, power plants, chemical storage plants, steelmaking and petroleum plants, pharmaceutical producers, component assembly factories, major truck, tractor and rolling-stock manufacturers, repair and spare-part facilities as well as railheads and marshaling yards, major surface transshipment points and highway intersections, bridges and tunnels, airports and pipelines.

Nuclear Recovery

One of the most publicized claims in the Soviet civil defense controversy is the claim by Jones that "the USSR could recover" from a U.S. nuclear retaliatory attack "within no more than two to four years." There is no such claim in Soviet civil defense manuals. Nor does the assertion bear scrutiny. Leaders planning to do something that might provoke nuclear exchanges, and who want to recover only a few years afterwards, must know that they have a widely dispersed industrial base, that they could muster a quick rescue and repair effort, that they have sufficient spare parts and replacement capital, lasting food reserves, and adequate transportation for distribution....

Some claim that the Soviet Union has a year's supply of grain and other raw food sources, and that they are hardening grain silos as big as football fields. However, "primary food production and associated processing industries are geographically separated, especially in areas of recent agricultural development"—hardly a rational step for a civil defense-conscious government. Almost all of these processing plants are in the European part of the Soviet Union, most of them in large cities, which may not exist after an attack. Large modern dairy factories are in the largest cities.

Fallout would seriously affect farmland; in any event, Soviet agriculture, highly dependent on chemicals, could not be readily regenerated if any of the 25 chemical factories in the Soviet Union are blasted.

In short, there is little evidence that Soviet leaders have planned their economy with civil defense in mind. Nor—given the blatant inadequacies of Soviet civil defense programs (in all respects), the marked vulnerabilities of the Soviet economy, and the intrinsic limitation and uncertainties about civil defense generally—is there much basis for claiming that Soviet leaders, even in desperate straits, would risk war with the United States while counting on civil defense measures to limit the damage wreaked on the Russian Motherland.

Should Nuclear Education Be Taught in the Schools?

Whether or not nuclear war should be a topic in the schools is a hotly debated issue among educators, parents, and young people. Recently, in St. Paul, Minnesota, students at the College of St. Thomas were asked to vote on whether or not they would like nuclear education classes in their school. The students voted no. In other schools, students have asked to study this topic. This activity is designed to encourage discussion about the areas of nuclear education that are the most often debated.

Consider two opposing views on nuclear education:

Viewpoint I

It wasn't until my junior year of high school that I began to recognize and voice my feelings about nuclear war and the arms race. My high school provided a framework in which I could speak about my feelings and take initiative to educate myself on nuclear issues. Since this class began, I have seen other students and adults ignore the nuclear threat because they have not been given a chance to talk about it. I feel the school is the place where we, as students, are introduced to the nature of our world through classes in math, science and history. Yet, by not addressing important considerations about the nuclear age, educators are failing to prepare us for making important decisions on which our future depends.

Vanessa Kirch, 17, excerpted from *Social Education*, November/December 1983.

Viewpoint II

Exposing children to the pressure of trying to cope with the enormity of nuclear war will not mold them into the leaders of the next generation. It is more likely to cause crippling anxiety. Rather than preparing them to deal with problems effectively, and perhaps become the generation that will actually solve the questions of the nuclear age, these doomsday parents are raising their offspring to be anxious, maladjusted adults. More likely than not, these frightened children will stand out as a group for their lack of accomplishment as adults. They will have trouble dealing with their own personal lives, let alone confronting and overcoming major national and international problems.

Irene Mullan Petteys, excerpted from *Newsweek*, December 17, 1984.

Think about or discuss the following questions related to what you have read in this chapter.

1. Do you believe students should discuss the prospects of a nuclear war in school? Why or why not?

2. Some people believe that schools have a responsibility to teach and include current events in their curriculum as a way of preparing students to live and understand the world outside the schoolroom. This is one reason some people believe nuclear education courses should be included in the school curriculum. Do you believe schools have this responsibility? How does this affect your stand on nuclear education?

3. Have your fears increased or decreased as a result of discussing the nuclear issue? Why?

4. Should there be an age limit for nuclear education, so that younger children are not exposed to it?

5. Do you agree with the first quote above, that nuclear education is like math and other subjects? If not, how is it different?

6. Should parents, instead of schools, be the ones to provide nuclear education? Why or why not?

If you are doing this activity as part of a group, attempt to reach a consensus on each of the above questions. According to your analysis, *should nuclear education be in the schools?*

Periodical Bibliography

The following list of periodical articles deals with the subject matter of this chapter.

William M. Arkin	"Preparing for World War IV," *Bulletin of the Atomic Scientists*, May 1985.
Louis Rene Beres	"On the Road from Apocalypse," *Worldview*, May 1982.
Will Brownell	"Interview with Edward Teller," *Survive*, March/April, 1983.
	"Nuclear War: A Disarming Dilemma," *Survive*, November/December 1982.
Helen Caldicott	"Medical Consequences of Nuclear War," *New Catholic World*, November/December 1983.
Bruce Clayton	"Get Ready, Get Set, Go Where?" *Survive*, Winter 1981.
Brian Green	"The New Case for Civil Defense," *Backgrounder*, August 29, 1984. Available from The Heritage Foundation, 214 Massachusetts Ave. NE, Washington, DC 20002.
John Halford	"One Nation's Plan to Survive Nuclear War," *The Plain Truth*, November/December 1984.
James L. Holton	"In Defense of Civil Defense," *Society*, September/October 1983.
International Physicians for the Prevention of Nuclear War	"What We Can Do," *Bulletin of the Atomic Scientists*, June/July 1981.
George F. Kennan	"World War I, Then II, Then . . ." *New York Times*, November 11, 1984.
Larry Ledwick	"Evacuate," *Survive*, March/April 1983.
Lisa Peattie	"Normalizing the Unthinkable," *Bulletin of the Atomic Scientists*, March 1984.
Kennan Peck	"The Take-Charge Gang," *The Progressive*, May 1985.
Carl Sagan	"Nuclear War and Climatic Catastrophe: Some Policy Implications," *Foreign Affairs*, Winter 83/84.

Vernon Lee Schmid   "Dairy Farmers Prepare for Nuclear
                           Attack," *The Christian Century*, January 23,
                           1985.

Richard E. Sincere Jr.   "A Moral Argument for Civil Defense:
                           Advice to America's Catholic Bishops,"
                           Catholicism in Crisis, January 1983.

Survive   Special issue on nuclear war, March/April
                           1983.

Milton Terris   "Armageddon: The Civil Defense Fraud,"
                           The Journal of Public Health Policy, June
                           1982.

U.S. News &   "We Are Better Prepared for Tomorrow's
World Report   Disasters," March 19, 1984.

Allan M. Winkler   "A 40-year History of Civil Defense,"
                           Bulletin of the Atomic Scientists, June/July
                           1984.

4

Will Nuclear Arms Agreements Work?

Chapter Preface

Since the Soviets developed the atomic bomb in 1949, both the Soviet and American governments have made attempts at controlling nuclear arms. Arms control in the 1980s however, is forever complicated by several factors: the number of weapons each side has, the power of those weapons, verification of treaty compliance, and international politics. The leaders of the Soviet Union and the United States cannot even discuss meaningful arms control without teams of experts calculating the impact of each measure.

While the technical matters might be overcome with work, the political complications remain a perpetual problem for both the USSR and the US. Neither side wants to seem over-eager to reach an agreement for fear of appearing weak, and neither side wants to give any concession that it may regret later. In fact, numerous experts have claimed that the arms control agreements already achieved have failed to reduce and/or control nuclear weapons. Pro-arms controllers plead, on the other hand, that any agreements are better than none. The following debates center on the problematic features of arms control and whether or not these problems can be overcome.

"Arms control is not the answer to the perilous competition between the United States and the Soviet Union. . . . But without it, there are no answers."

Arms Control Can Work

Leslie H. Gelb

Leslie H. Gelb is a national security correspondent for *The New York Times*. He has also served as the director of the State Department's Bureau of Political Military Affairs under President Jimmy Carter. As a former chairman of the Carnegie Endowment Panel on Future US Security and Arms Control and a member of the International Strategic Studies' Council on Foreign Relations, Mr. Gelb has maintained an interest and an expertise in US national security. He is the author of *The Irony of Vietnam: The System Worked* and contributes numerous articles to magazines. In the following viewpoint, Mr. Gelb argues that it is not arms control that isn't working, but America's expectations of it that can't be fulfilled. By describing various treaties and arms control agreements that have been reached, he concludes that the world is safer today because of these stabilizing agreements.

As you read, consider the following questions:

1. What does the author believe is the primary purpose of arms control?
2. A common objection to arms control is that the Soviets cheat on treaties and agreements, making useful arms control impossible. How does the author refute this objection?

Leslie H. Gelb, "A Practical Way to Arms Control," *The New York Times Magazine*, June 15, 1983. Copyright © 1983 by The New York Times Company. Reprinted by permission.

Arms control is neither sin nor salvation. It is a way—along with diplomacy and military decisions—of managing Soviet-American competition. Without such negotiated mutual restraint, the competition would be far less controllable and both sides could acquire capabilities that just might make nuclear war more thinkable. It is not a way of solving our security problem. It is a way of preserving the Soviet-American "peace" that, with great good luck, has survived the last 40 years of tension and waste. To ask much more of a bargaining process between two powerful countries so mistrustful of each other is to condemn it to failure.

Our inability to appreciate arms control as a practical matter has contributed to flip-flops in American attitudes toward negotiating reductions in the superpowers' nuclear arsenals. And it has added to the clamor for arms control that has blown up into a political crisis for the Reagan Administration, a divisive problem for the Western alliance and a painful moral issue for many Americans. . . .

Attitudes and Arms Control

There has been the peculiarly American tendency to sharp swings between seeing little good in arms control and asking too much of it too soon. The main drawback to the agreements of the last decade was not that they did so little but that they took so long to do it. By taking many years to achieve marginal results, the accords became a convenient target for political forces in the United States with unreasonable expectations of arms control. What we need is a simplified process inoculated to a greater degree from political pressures. The idea is to try to take a small step, instead of a large strike—and, having done that, to take the next small step, and the next. However, to have a clearer appreciation of how doing less, rather than more, is apt to take us further in the long run, it would be helpful to go over the record.

Arms Control: Is It Hopeless?

The New Right regarded efforts at arms control as either hopeless (since the Soviet Union was not likely to give up its supposed nuclear superiority) or worse (since any treaty Moscow might agree to would lock the United States into its allegedly inferior position). In the rightists' view, the only way to bargain with Moscow and deter it from attacking us was by acquiring additional arms—even superiority.

The dominance of these extreme views in the last decade had a strong effect on the pattern for arms-control negotiations: extravagant demands for highly disproportionate cuts and restrictions on Soviet forces, followed by years of stalemate at the bargaining table, followed by mounting political pressure to compromise for fear of failure. It also determined the outcome of the talks. The treaties that accomplished most were completed between 1963 and 1972. Of the treaties completed after 1972, only SALT II was of comparable importance, and none were ratified by the Senate. . . .

Liberal Objections to Arms Control

The liberals had two objections: the treaties we had signed had been used to justify new arms commitments, and they had not resulted in any savings in military spending. In fact, many liberals had come to see arms control as a sham, a device to codify the arms race. . . .

Arms Control and Stability

Arms control negotiations and arms control agreements, for all their warts, have provided a degree of stability in relationships with our allies and with the Soviet Union. A totally unconstrained nuclear arms race with the Soviets in the last decade and a half would have generated an awful lot of pressures that to some degree we have ameliorated.

Lawrence Eagleburger, *Policy Review*, Winter 1985.

In the end, whatever their objections, liberals went along with the treaties as the lesser evil. Conservatives, however, dug in their heels. Their main arguments may be stated, and answered, as follows:

1. The Russians cheat on arms control pacts and gain important advantages.

A panel of conservative and liberal experts who studied the field of strategic-arms and test-ban treaties under the auspices of the Carnegie Endowment for International Peace concluded in its report last April that the record "does not support this claim." Nor has any Administration, including the present one, ever formally charged Moscow with violations. . . .

Even those who have charged Moscow with consistent cheating have rarely maintained that Soviet violations could not be caught. Virtually every top American official who has been involved with the matter during the last decade has expressed confidence publicly in the ability of our intelligence satellites, radar and listening posts to detect violations in time to prevent us from being placed at a significant disadvantage. . . .

Modifying Soviet Behavior

2. Arms-control treaties have not prevented Moscow from vastly increasing its nuclear forces, nor caused it to moderate its behavior.

Neither SALT I nor SALT II did much, if anything, to curtail the growth of the Soviet arsenal. American intelligence estimates were that the projected growth of Soviet forces would be greater without the treaties than under the treaty limits; conservative critics, on the other hand, charged that the limits were consistent with Moscow's plans. Neither estimate can be proven. But, by the same token—and provable on the record—the United States did not give up any of its own projected nuclear military growth.

As for the complaint that arms treaties have not inhibited Soviet behavior in the world, anyone who expected that result was guilty of star-gazing. The superpowers have deep conflicts of interest, which can have an impact on progress or deadlock in arms control and can be exacerbated by the development of new arms systems on either side, but which persist as policy objectives even when arms treaties are signed. Arms-control measures reflect far more than they shape the state of political relations. Arms treaties will have to be judged by how they help manage Soviet-American arms competition, not by expectations of political miracles.

3. Arms-control agreements have caused us to let down our guard and have brought about unilateral American disarmament.

Spending on conventional arms and the attendant military manpower declined somewhat after SALT I, and leveled off for several years thereafter, even as Moscow maintained its steady buildup in all categories. But this had little if anything to do with arms control. The primary reasons were the decreasing scale of American involvement in Vietnam and the demands of neglected domestic priorities, as the Nixon Administration stated at the time. Moreover, intended real increases were wiped out by runaway inflation, brought on principally by rising oil prices. As for outlays on strategic nuclear forces, these stayed pretty much constant—even allowing for inflation—and began rising, along with the entire defense budget, after 1976....

A Better Way

There must be a better way. And it can only be in the direction of more modest treaties, which do not take so long to complete that they become vulnerable to political shifts at home—of small steps, taken one at a time, with an agreed common purpose.

The process would have to begin with agreement on long-term objectives. The key ones would be these: restrictions on each side's ability to launch surprise attacks; an equal capability to maintain a survivable deterrent against any such attack; a phasing out of nuclear weapons that present attractive targets to the adversary; gradual reductions in the number of intercontinental and medium-range nuclear warheads and bombs; widening cooperation, including on-site inspection, to verify compliance. In effect, each stage, which would last for two or three years, would be aimed not at obtaining all possible advantage for your side but at assuring the other side the same degree of security you seek for yourself.

The first stage would deal with the medium-range forces in

Europe, as both sides now more or less agree. It could begin with a two-year agreement requiring Moscow to dismantle its older SS-4's and SS-5's, while Washington began deployments only of ground-launched cruise missiles. The Soviet Union did not hesitate to upgrade its capabilities substantially with the deployment of more than 450 SS-20's, and it is absolutely unreasonable for Moscow to reject some modernization of American missiles in Europe. The future integrity of NATO depends on some deployments, and Moscow knows this.

Persevere with Arms Control

Arms control has not been killed. Nor is it dying. The United States, from the President on down, must hang tough and persevere in its objectives if we are ever to fulfill the promise of arms control.

Kenneth L. Adelman, *The New York Times*, October 4, 1984.

Moscow would also be required to freeze its SS-20 total at its present level in both the European and Asian portions of the Soviet Union. In return, Washington would temporarily forgo the right to deploy the Pershing 2 ballistic missiles, which, unlike the relatively slow cruise missiles, could reach Soviet territory from European bases in about 12 minutes, and which, therefore, are of particular concern to the Soviet leaders. And each side would be limited to 300 medium-range bombers.

Negotiations, Second Stage

In stage two, the talks on medium-range weapons would merge with negotiations on intercontinental-range missiles and bombers, and the two sides would agree to reduce their over-all store of warheads and bombs—about 11,000 apiece—by about 25 percent. Each side would be free to decide where to put its permitted total. Thus, if the United States wanted more medium-range missiles in Europe, it would have to cut the number of its intercontinental weapons · · · ·

Initial steps could be taken to reduce the number of giant land-based missiles. Since this is the Russians' strongest suit by far, they will part with it only reluctantly and slowly. The Administration has a choice of retaining the MX and allowing the Russians to keep their heavy missiles, or cashing in the MX for reductions in Soviet heavies.

The most difficult problems would be left for stage three. The superpowers would seek agreement on a restructuring of their forces, retreating from the mutual threat of multiple warheads and leaving single-warhead missiles as the centerpiece for both. They would try to impose controls on ground- and sea-launched cruise

157

missiles. They would move toward a prohibition on development and testing of all new missiles.

Not before this last stage could one contemplate saving money or improving the overall political relationship between the super-powers. Until then, and even afterward, the main purpose would be to manage the competition in nuclear weapons. But, step by step, this kind of arms control would mean a progressive reduction of the risks of nuclear war.

Serious Obstacles

This approach is not without its own serious obstacles. We would have to learn to live for at least the next decade with Soviet advantages in land-based missiles, and to be satisfied with our superiority in submarine and bomber forces. After that, the expectation is that the two sides would develop more comparable arsenals across the board; but that is not easy to insure. The approach would also necessitate greater patience with arms control, and an American political leadership courageous enough to stand up to extremist demands.

But the alternative—inflated proposals with minimal chances of success that play into the hands of those who want to prove that "arms control does not work"—is likely to lead to an open-ended arms race. If that happens, if international restraints, such as they are, are allowed to erode, can we count on holding war at bay very much longer? Because deterrence has worked until now, can we be sure it will work in the future? While it stretches rationality to imagine a conscious decision to begin a nuclear conflict, we have every reason not to trust ourselves, let alone others.

Arms control is not the answer to the perilous competition between the United States and the Soviet Union and the security problems posed for both. But without it, there are no answers.

"Arms control. . . . does not serve our security, it does not save money, and it does not lessen the risk of war."

Arms Control Cannot Work

Seymour Weiss

Seymour Weiss is a retired US Ambassador who has also served as director of both the State Department's Office of Strategic Research and Intelligence and the Bureau of Politico-Military Affairs. He has been a private consultant on national security affairs and, with John Lehman, secretary of the Navy, has co-authored the book *Beyond the SALT II Failure*. In the following viewpoint, Mr. Weiss documents his case against arms control. By citing examples of treaties and agreements in which he feels that US security was compromised, he argues that arms control primarily serves Soviet objectives. Agreements therefore provide neither stability nor equality between the US and Soviet Union.

As you read, consider the following questions:

1. According to the author, have nuclear arms limitations agreements contributed to US security?
2. Does the author believe that nuclear arms agreements prevent nuclear war?
3. Is it better to "talk than fight," according to the author?

Seymour Weiss, "The Case Against Arms Control," *Commentary*, November 1984. Reprinted with the permission of the author.

In one sense the case against arms control is not difficult to make. One might simply ask just what evidence exists that recent nuclear-arms-limitations agreements with the USSR have actually contributed to U.S. security. Yet in spite of the fact that no such evidence can be found, emotional attachment to the hoped-for benefits, together with the presumption that arms control is politically attractive, has created what Albert Wohlstetter has sardonically described as the mad momentum of arms control. It is this emotional attachment that makes the task of rational assessment more difficult. There is an undeniable and understandable yearning among our people, reflected in Congress and certainly echoed by our allies, for a cessation of the tensions that have accompanied the years of confrontation with the USSR.

That yearning nevertheless sometimes takes forms which misperceive reality: the idea, for example, that arms control is necessary to stop the "arms race"; or that it helps to avoid wasteful military expenditures; or that it is essential to the prevention of nuclear war. Each of these pleas on behalf of arms control has been made (and no doubt will be made over and over again). But can these problems—the arms race, wasteful military expenditures, or the drift toward nuclear war—be attenuated or corrected by arms control?

To begin with the arms race: arms control cannot stop it for the simple reason that in no real sense has there been any such thing as an arms race. As Assistant Secretary of Defense Richard Perle stated in recent congressional testimony, the number of U.S. nuclear weapons has been "declining rapidly" for two decades. Thus the U.S. has over 8,000 fewer warheads and a fourth less megatonnage today than it had in the 1960s. This reduction in U.S. inventories has been the result of a modernization program, designed in part to put safer as well as more effective weapons in the U.S. inventory. It is not the product of agreements reached with the Soviet Union. . . .

No Arms Race for US

There has, in short, been no arms race so far as the United States is concerned; conversely, arms control has not prevented the Soviets from forging ahead in their military programs.

How about saving money? Have past agreements not saved otherwise needless expenditures for arms, and might not additional savings be achieved through arms control in the future? The answer is a clear "no" to the former and an "almost certainly not" to the latter. Take the jewel in the arms-control crown, the ABM Treaty of 1972. One argument advanced at the time this agreement was negotiated was that it would spare the nation a wasteful and massive expenditure for a ballistic-missile defense. Some estimated that such a system might cost as much as $10 billion; other estimates ran considerably higher. Moreover, by precluding

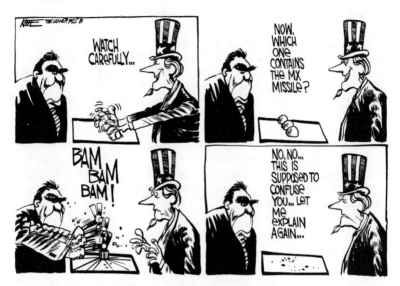

Michael Keefe for the Denver Post, reprinted with permission.

ballistic-missile defenses, each side would be saved the expenditure that would otherwise be required for offensive forces designed to overcome these defenses. The nation got an ABM treaty, but did it save itself the projected expenditures? It did not . . . .

Arms Control Does Not Save Money

In general, as most students of the subject will testify, savings have not resulted from arms-control agreements with the Soviets. Indeed, some have charged that arms control actually results in larger expenditures. For one thing, in order to gain the support of those directly responsible for providing for U.S. military security and who worry about the effect of arms control on the capacity for self-protection, other new and costly military programs must be promised. In addition, expensive new intelligence-monitoring systems must be developed. (It is arguable that certain military and intelligence programs might not have gained approval on their own merits without the pressures to provide for special safeguards generated by arms-control proposals.)

Finally, arms control, by constraining the kinds of systems we can have, as well as the numbers, increases the difficulty of providing for our security. Unless there is a commensurate reduction in the forces on the other side, the effect may be to raise the cost or endanger the security or both. The record clearly demonstrates that there has not been such a reduction.

The charge that the alternative to arms-control agreements is nuclear war would hardly warrant refutation were it not voiced at one time or another, directly or by implication, by a host of esteemed statesmen. On sober reflection, it is probable that so sweeping an assertion is not intended to be taken literally. Yet in the heat of political battle, when cherished policy objectives are being contested, extravagant statements do tend to be made.

In reality, the relationship between arms-control agreements and the avoidance of nuclear war is complex. Some even maintain that an inverse relationship exists—that arms-control agreements, by making it more difficult to provide for our security, may thereby have increased the ultimate danger of war. One need not go so far. Still, the positive relationship between recent agreements designed to limit nuclear arms and the prevention of nuclear war itself is anything but clear and direct. . . .

Why Believe in Agreements?

What is the basis for believing that the Soviets will ever agree to limit or reduce the very military power they require to maintain and advance their national objectives? What leads us to imagine that the Soviets might be willing to negotiate away their hard-won military advantages in an arms-control agreement? Why would the Soviets hand over at the negotiating table what they see no prospect of being forced to surrender in the ongoing political contest with the West, or—should it come to that—in a contest of arms? . . .

The Soviet Union will sign arms-control agreements with the West only if such agreements are consistent with its fundamental political objectives—that is, only if they contribute to the extension of Soviet power and influence, normally at the direct expense of the West.

Past agreements have been used by the Soviets to achieve this end in a variety of ways:

They have been designed to sow political discord between the U.S. and its allies, in the hope of promoting the dissolution of the postwar Western alliance. If an agreement can properly be seen as limiting U.S. power to support friendly states desirous of resisting the extension of Soviet power, it has served a vitally important Soviet objective. . . .

If an agreement can lull the U.S. into believing that arms control reduces—or even removes—the need for self-help military measures, this contributes to Soviet purposes. . . .

If an agreement disrupts the development of U.S. military technology while permitting the Soviets to close an important gap, it also serves Soviet purposes. . . .

If an arms-control agreement is clearly either unverifiable or unenforceable, it serves Soviet purposes. . . .

But if, in the broader sense, U.S. and Soviet political objectives are in radical conflict, what of those more narrowly defined interests that are presumed to emanate from successful arms-control negotiations—stability and equivalence?

Stability has generally been taken to apply to two issues: the so-called arms race and the management of crisis. As we have already seen, the arms race is largely an American illusion. American interest in and efforts at constraint are not shared by the Soviets. . . .

Even less do they appear to share U.S. concern with crisis stability. Years of effort to persuade the Soviets that fixed MIRVed ICBM's are inherently destabilizing have been unavailing. . . .

We have seen that fundamentally incompatible political objectives logically preclude arms-control arrangements which by U.S. standards are fair to both sides. Yet it now appears that even on narrower grounds involving arms-control objectives like stability and equivalence, there is little reason to project a commonality of interest. As George Kennan once said:

> There is no use trying to swing Russians into line by referring to common purposes to which we may both have done lip-service at one time or another. . . . For them it's all a game. And when we try to come at them with arguments based on such common professions, they become doubly wary.

Suppose, for the sake of argument, that the case made here against arms control is essentially correct. The indictment would be a powerful one. The only possible conclusion one could draw would be that contemporary nuclear arms-control agreements with the Soviet Union have been contrary to U.S. national interests.

Arms Control Illusions

[Arms control] illusions rest on the idea that by negotiating with the Soviet Union we can not only cut down the size of the arsenals on both sides but that we can also render them less threatening, thus increasing stability and reducing the risk of nuclear war. By now, this idea is so widely taken as intellectually and morally self-evident that anyone who questions it is treated with incredulity and outrage. Nevertheless, there is virtually no evidence to support the faith in arms control and a great deal of evidence that makes it seem altogether irrational.

Norman Podhoretz, *The New York Times*, January 24, 1985.

Even so, no issue as complex as this one is likely to lead to so simple and direct a conclusion. Might there be a consideration not yet addressed that would impart to the arms-control efforts of the last two decades something more than a passing redeeming value? May it not be that even if the agreements were "flawed" in some respects, *the process itself* was—and is—of great value? For whatever one may think of the substantive merit of any particular agreement, the process keeps U.S. and Soviet officials in direct contact, exchanging views on nuclear strategy, weapons capabilities, and the intentions of the two sides. Surely, in the nuclear age, nothing can be of greater importance than the continuing contact that the arms-control process provides. . . .

Talking or Fighting?

But still, is it not better to "talk than fight"? Consider the answer of Dean Acheson to this question:

> I have heard people who should know better . . . say happily, "As long as they are talking they are not fighting." Nothing could be more untrue; they are fighting. . . . To our minds international conferences and international negotiations are so completely means for ending conflict that we are blind to the fact that they may be and, in the hands of experts, are equally adapted to, continuing it. . . . "There is no alternative to negotiations with the Russians" is the constant theme of a well-known columnist and a prominent politician in this country. . . . This is, of course, silly. For if there is no alternative, and if the Russians will only negotiate, as is now the case, on their own terms, then there is no alternative to surrender. . . .

Nothing that has happened since has affected the truth of these words, and much that has happened since has strengthened the case against arms control. It does not serve our security, it does not save money, and it does not lessen the risk of war. Arms control is certainly politically popular, but it is just as certainly the repository of false and dangerous hopes.

"[America] is so overvigilant, by its structure and nature. . . that it is a miracle if agreements with us are ever reached at all."

America Hinders Arms Control

Jeremy J. Stone

Jeremy J. Stone is director of the Federation of American Scientists in Washington, a group of scientists and others who act on public issues where the opinions of scientists are relevant. The author of *Containing the Arms Race: Some Concrete Proposals* and *Strategic Persuasion*, Mr. Stone holds a Ph.D. from Stanford University and was a research associate on arms control and disarmament at the Harvard Center for International Affairs. In the following viewpoint, he argues that, contrary to popular belief, America is an overly-tough stringent competitor in arms control.

As you read, consider the following questions:

1. According to the author, why are arms control agreements difficult to achieve?
2. How does the author compare arms control agreements to the Olympics?
3. Why does the author believe that "it is a miracle if agreements are ever reached at all"?

Jeremy J. Stone, "In Bargaining, America's No Patsy," *The Los Angeles Times*, January 16, 1985. Reprinted with the permission of the author.

Nothing is more firmly entrenched in the minds of American citizens than that the Soviets are ferociously hard bargainers. By contrast, Americans deem themselves to be easy marks, softies, hopelessly addicted to compromise and dangerously committed to reaching even bad agreements.

In fact, a strong case can be made that it is America that is the more difficult bargaining partner. As a consequence, the United States, not the Soviet Union, usually gets the "better" bargain.

The reason is simple. The United States can ratify agreements only if two-thirds of the Senate will approve. And this requires the support of two political parties in constant rivalry with one another—often to show which is tougher in dealing with Bolshevism.

Politics and Arms Control

What else can explain the fact that the last three treaties solemnly approved and signed by our executive branch have never been ratified? Among them, the SALT II treaty was said by the Joint Chiefs of Staff to have only "nominal" effects on U.S. force planning. Nevertheless, a host of wholly political complaints killed the agreement, even though this "something for nothing" treaty did provide limits on the Soviet program if not on ours.

As a result of this kind of experience, negotiators on both sides know that, to be ratified, a treaty must look really favorable to the American public and to Congress—and this obviously influences the shape of the negotiations in our favor.

In fact, in the last 40 years the only two negotiations that produced important ratified treaties were both cases in which the United States sold the Soviet Union a dead horse. It was only because mothers were marching in the streets against strontium 90 in milk that above-ground nuclear testing was negotiated away in the atmospheric test ban. And it was only because 50 Senate votes opposed building the anti-ballistic missile that the United States negotiated the ABM treaty banning it. In both cases it was highly uncertain that this country could continue doing what was at issue anyway, even in the absence of a treaty. This was precisely why the treaties could be approved.

Where there is no similar public uprising, American Presidents simply do not have the political capital to secure the acceptance of even wholly fair treaties. They often need more.

US Positions Bizarre

U.S. negotiating positions have accordingly verged increasingly on the bizarre. In the case of intermediate-range missiles we offered to tear up plans to install Pershing and cruise missiles if the Soviets would dismantle missiles already in place. Yet, even when the threat of that posture began to get results, the Reagan Administration would not agree to substantial Soviet unilateral disarmament

166

of SS-20s in return for our building *up* to a missile equality in Europe that we had never had.

The Administration's present position has moved even further into superhard bargaining. For example, the "moderates" in the Administration are threatening to scrap the already signed and ratified ABM treaty of indefinite duration if the Soviet Union does not make cuts in already deployed offensive weapons. In short, they want further Soviet concessions as a price for our keeping to obligations that we have already undertaken through an earlier deal. This position gives new meaning to the word *chutzpah*.

Real Bargaining Impossible

And most of the Administration is taking a harder line. Its position is that the President's plans for a "Star Wars" defense brought the Soviets to the bargaining table, but that it should be non-negotiable. This school wants to spend the talks patiently explaining to the backward Russians that their position on anti-ballistic missiles is wholly wrong, even though it happens to be precisely the one that Americans spent 10 years talking them into with a view to securing their reluctant signature on the present ABM treaty.

Remaking Soviet Society

Q. Don't changes in position, like the one Kennan has undergone, attest to the vitality of the democratic society? You have been coming here for 25 years and have met many people who profoundly and publicly disagree with the government. Isn't there something exciting and valuable about that?

A. Let's say that's your way of doing business. We don't have to remake each other's society to avoid nuclear war. During the Cold War, you tried to force the Soviet Union to change its internal system, and only if we changed our internal system would you deal in peace with us. Detente meant trying to change both sides' international behavior, thereby creating security for both without going into the other's business. Live and let live. That's a good American slogan under which a lot of things could be done.

Robert Scheer interviews Henry Trofimenko, *Los Angles Times*, January 13, 1985.

As one observer suggests, the whole bargaining process is getting to be like the Olympics, with 600 American newsmen in Geneva asking who got the gold medals for making the fewer concessions.

The very publicity available in our free nation, and the political process of which we are so justly proud, tends to make real bargaining impossible.

The Soviet Union is not, by all reports, the world champion in tough negotiating; Middle Eastern nations can bargain harder, and so can Asian nations. But a nation like ours that is so complex as to be unpredictable, and so at odds with itself as to be unwilling to accept any bargains other than sweetheart deals, can be the worst.

Accordingly, it is not only the Soviets who have found us difficult. The British did also. During our negotiations with them in the 1920s over naval limits, at a most opportune time, Lord Lee of Fareham, first lord of the admiralty, felt constrained not to propose the naval conference that he wanted. Instead, he later explained, he gave an address that was "intended as an invitation for an invitation," because the invitation itself, he knew, had to come from America: "The American people would accept nothing that was not settled on American soil and at the suggestion of America."

Without any doubt, the United States and the Soviet Union both need to know more about the other if agreement is to be reached. But this analysis suggests that each may need to know more about itself as well.

In particular, Americans need not worry about being sold out at negotiations. The country is so overvigilant, by its structure and nature, and so prone to election-year hiatuses and political reversals of position, that it is a miracle if agreements with us are ever reached at all.

"For the Soviets, arms control agreements. . . . are simply another tool of Soviet policy designed to achieve military superiority over the West."

The USSR Hinders Arms Control

Michael F. Altfeld and Edwin F. Black

One of the most frequently cited obstacles to arms control is that the US cannot trust the Soviets. The authors of this viewpoint argue that an essential difference between the US and the Soviet Union is that the US seeks a meaningful arms reduction policy based on trustworthy behavior. The Soviets, on the other hand, use negotiated arms control as a way of achieving military superiority. Thus, attempting to agree on arms control with the Soviets is nothing more than an exercise in futility. Michael Altfeld, the author of part I, is a consultant for High Frontier, Inc., an organization that promotes the opening of space for military purposes by the US and its allies. The author of the second viewpoint, Edwin F. Black, is a retired brigadier general.

As you read, consider the following questions:

1. According to the author, why can't arms control agreements relieve East-West competition?
2. Why was the ABM treaty detrimental to the US, according to the author?

Michael F. Altfeld, "Arms Control Advances Soviet Goals," *The Washington Times*, August 28, 1984. Reprinted with the permission of the author. Edwin F. Black, "Arms Control in the Real World: Why this Holy Grail Eludes Us," *The Washington Times*, August 28, 1984. Reprinted with permission.

I

Arms control agreements do not in any way mitigate the basic hostility between values espoused by the West and those espoused by the Soviet Union. Such agreements, therefore, do not and cannot end strategic competition between us and the Soviets. Instead, they merely channel that competition away from some arenas and into others.

Because the United States and the Soviet Union are different countries with different resource endowments and political systems, they also have different strengths and weaknesses. The result is that a ruthless and intelligent government can use this channeling to move the competition away from arenas in which it is relatively weaker than its opponent and into those in which it is relatively stronger. There is a great deal of evidence that the Soviets already have done this once.

When the Soviets originally agreed to talks on an anti-ballistic-missile treaty, many U.S. analysts argued that this agreement implied final Soviet acceptance of Mutual Assured Destruction (MAD). (Some still do). It is interesting to note, however, that Soviet agreement to these talks occurred only after it became clear that the United States was going to build its own ABM and that it would be technically superior to anything which they could have fielded at the time.

Soviet Civil Defense

In and of itself, this juxtaposition of events was not necessarily suspicious or dangerous. However, almost immediately after the signing of the ABM treaty, the Soviets grossly increased their civil defense effort.

Now, civil defense is an arena of competition in which democracies such as the United States are naturally inferior in peacetime to totalitarian dictatorships such as the Soviet Union. Further, when our negotiators asked for talks on banning civil defenses, their Soviet counterparts adamantly refused. Thus, the Soviets, in signing the ABM treaty succeeded in moving the U.S.-Soviet competition away from a defensive arena in which they were relatively weaker than the United States (ABMs) and into a defensive arena in which they are relatively stronger (civil defense). The result has been a less-secure America.

For many analysts, the final confirmation that all this had been a conscious Soviet strategem came when the Soviets improved their technological base and began using loopholes in the treaty as well as outright violations to deploy a de facto ABM system. This system is based on "dual purpose" air defense such as the SA 5, 10 and 12, which are effective against both aircraft and ballistic missile warheads. The United States, meanwhile, adhered so closely to the ABM treaty that it redesigned, at great cost in time and money, such dual capability out of its own "Patriot" air-defense system.

Today, the Soviets are again asking for talks to ban competition in space, an arena in which they have a temporary advantage (by virtue of their ASAT system) but one in which we would far surpass them should we decide to do so. This time they probably plan no surprise for us as they did in 1972 with their civil defense program. Rather, they probably hope to keep us locked into a purely offensive strategy which they currently dominate. Meanwhile, the Soviets already have broken out of an offensive strategy by means of their efforts at civil defense and ballistic missile defense.

Arms Control and the Soviets

The American people must begin to realize that, for the Soviets, arms control agreements are neither sacred nor an end in themselves. Rather, they are simply another tool of Soviet policy designed to achieve military superiority over the West in general, and the United States in particular.

If we take the Soviets up on their offer to negotiate a treaty banning weapons in space, the outcome is predictable. We will, no doubt, five years hence, be debating with ourselves whether and how the Soviets have violated it, just as we are now debating Soviet violations of the ABM treaty. The only difference will be that, due

Steve Kelley, *San Diego Union*, reprinted with permission.

to the horrendous difficulties involved in verifying such an agreement, such discussion will be even less fruitful and more frustrating than it is now.

II

Let's not kid ourselves about arms control.

Meaningful nuclear disarmament is not possible in today's world. Neither the wishful thinking of supporters of a "nuclear freeze" nor further sacrifices on the altar of unilateral disarmament will alter this fact. The reasons are as clear and as brutal as the Berlin Wall:

1. The necessary preconditions for reductions in nuclear arsenals simply do not exist.

As long as deterrence based on mutual assured destruction (MAD) remains the guardian of peace, the arms race will continue. The superpowers have little choice. Under the MAD concept, the survival of their nations depends on their having a credible deterrent.

Credibility has both a physical and a psychological dimension. Physically it amounts to the capabilities of their respective strategic nuclear forces in being on the line. Psychologically it hinges on their perception of one another's willingness to use these forces when their "supreme interest"—their national survival—is threatened.

With the populations of the two countries pledged as undefended hostages to MAD, they have no alternative but to shape their defense policies on the "worst case" perception. This means they must continuously modernize and increase the offensive capabilities of their strategic forces.

No Common Objective

2. There is no common objective in arms control talks.

The U.S. seeks mutual reductions in both nuclear and conventional forces while maintaining an overall balance of military power.

The Soviets have a different objective: it is not disarmament. The record shows that since the early '70s, throughout SALT I, SALT II, and the more recent START and IMF talks, they have used the time spent in these negotiations to increase their military strength.

For them, these talks provide a forum, a focal point for mankind's hopes for peace, where they can exploit the world-wide media coverage to help create a perception of Russia's nuclear superiority.

Once this perception is accepted as reality, they will possess the ultimate weapon of coercive diplomacy, nuclear blackmail. They will then be able to shape the political destiny of the world.

3. There is not even a mutual understanding of the definition of peace.

For the United States, peace must start with the renunciation of armed aggression and the use of force in the settlement of international disputes.

The Soviet definition uses the same words, but in cynical "double-speak." Neither peace nor detente will prevent them from using every means available, including limited war, revolution, insurgency, and state-supported terrorism to achieve Lenin's goal: "the triumph of communism over capitalism."

No Code of Conduct

4. There is no agreed "code of conduct" for the superpowers.

The United States expects nations to act responsibly; to work to maintain conditions of non-violence and political stability; to encourage social change through the free expression of the views of the people.

The Soviet Union Must Be Flexible

Peace cannot be served by pseudo-arms control. We need reliable, reciprocal reductions. I call upon the Soviet Union today to reduce the tensions it has heaped on the world . . . and to show a firm commitment to peace by coming to the bargaining table with a new understanding of its obligations. I urge it to match our flexibility. If the Soviets sit down at the bargaining table seeking genuine arms reductions, there will be arms reductions. The governments of the West and their people will not be diverted by misinformation and threats. The time has come for the Soviet Union to show proof that it wants arms controls in reality, not just in rhetoric.

Ronald Reagan in a speech to the United Nations, September 26, 1983.

Again the Soviets disagree. They see such a code as just another capitalist trick to maintain the *status quo* and to justify the suppression of communist-led "peoples' national liberation movements."

Inherent in the concept of a code of conduct is the recognition that there exists a "linkage" between a nation's actions in world affairs and its reliability as a partner in any disarmament agreement. In arms control negotiations the Soviets refuse to recognize any such linkage.

5. Effective verification is no longer possible.

Modern technology makes it possible to design nuclear weapons of such small size (with high mobility, variable range, and a reload capability) that it is impossible to detect their cover deployment with the "national technical means" available today. Unless the Soviets become radically less paranoid about secrecy, internal security, and the sanctity of their borders, there simply is no way a system of reliable verification can be devised.

Where does this leave us? Back in the real world.

Meaningful nuclear disarmament is impossible under the ground rules of MAD. The Soviets have proven themselves very skillful in using arms control negotiations to slow down U.S. efforts to maintain nuclear parity.

History shows they have used the years spent in these talks to increase and modernize their strategic forces. Today the Soviets have not only achieved parity but are pressing ahead toward their goal of nuclear superiority.

Those who search so hard for some agreement on arms control have justified the Soviet build-up in strategic weapons on the grounds it was based on their traditional and understandable fears of attack or invasion by foreign powers. But this does not explain their present lunge toward nuclear superiority—an effort which seems unnecessary and places a heavy burden on the long-suffering Soviet people. Does the Politburo have some more sinister purpose in mind?

Political Game

It is time we recognized disarmament negotiations for what they really are: a game of political warfare waged at the highest level. It involves propaganda, disinformation, diplomacy, and mass demonstrations. Its targets are not cities or armies in the field, but parliaments, the media, peace movements, and opportunist politicians.

The Holy Grail of disarmament still eludes our grasp. Pursue it we will, as pursue it we must. But let us be clear what the name of the game is.

"The United States can tell whether or not the Soviets are cheating through 'verification,' using our sophisticated satellites and other detectors to catch any wrongdoing."

Arms Control Is Verifiable

The Union of Concerned Scientists

The Union of Concerned Scientists (UCS) is a Cambridge, Massachusetts-based, nonprofit organization of scientists, engineers, and other professionals concerned about the impact of advanced technology on society. In the following viewpoint, UCS explains that it is not necessary to trust the Russians in order to have effective arms control. Arms control agreements can maintain their effectiveness through sophisticated technology that can identify cheating.

As you read, consider the following questions:

1. According to the authors, "verification need not be perfect to be effective." Why?
2. How is most verification accomplished, according to the authors?
3. Why do the authors believe that risks involved in verification are less dangerous than to have no arms control agreements at all?

Union of Concerned Scientists, "Arms Control Verification: Briefing Paper," March 1985. Reprinted with permission.

Can we trust the Russians?

This question is often asked by people who are both worried about the arms race and afraid that the Soviets will cheat on any treaties which might be negotiated.

We Don't Have To

The simple answer is that "trust" doesn't really matter. The United States can tell whether or not the Soviets are cheating through "verification," using our sophisticated satellites and other detectors to catch any wrongdoing before it gets out of hand.

This article discusses the complex issues of verification and concludes that American know-how is up to the task of detecting cheating and that the US can, therefore, make treaties with the Soviets to limit the development and production of many weapons, especially the nuclear arms which so threaten our survival.

Verification of compliance with arms accords is a critical issue for the future of arms control. Before entering into an agreement, each side must be confident that it can detect cheating by the other. Verification ensures that a treaty serves its intended purpose, and bolsters confidence in future negotiations. Unfortunately, the need for perfect verification is often held up as an insurmountable obstacle to negotiating arms control agreements. In fact, the verification capabilities of the United States have been growing steadily and are now quite substantial.

Verification need not be perfect to be effective, because marginal changes in force levels are not of much military importance. The United States and the Soviet Union together have close to 20,000 strategic nuclear warheads; a few more will not alter the military balance. At issue is the Soviets' ability to undertake militarily significant activities without detection—"breaking out" of a negotiated agreement before the United States could respond. A good arms control agreement strikes a balance between what can be verified and what needs to be verified to fulfill the purposes of a treaty.

Weapons Tests and Verification

The testing of new weapons systems offers an ideal opportunity for verifiable arms control. Weapons tests are particularly important to control since new weapons cannot reliably be produced in quantity or deployed without first being tested; moreover, tests are relatively easy to detect. Thus test bans are both important and workable tools for arms control. In the past, several important opportunities have been lost: test bans could have prevented the development of the highly accurate multiple-warhead missiles that have increased fears of preemptive first strikes, as well as the cruise missiles now being deployed in large numbers.

Verification is a political process, not simply a matter of obtaining the most detailed technical information possible. Arms control agreements are often ambiguously worded, and in the face of such ambiguity each country tends to make unilateral interpretations and use them to judge the other's compliance. This process leaves a great deal of room for political posturing about "violations," and ascertaining compliance becomes a matter of political judgment as well as the routine technical monitoring of military activities. Similarly, the interpretation of incomplete information calls for judgment—political, military, and technical—as to whether observed activities comply with arms control agreements. . . .

Detecting Violations

The feasibility of verifying arms control agreements is tied to the likelihood that a *set* of activities, all related to developing or deploying a weapons system, could be undertaken without being detected. If there is an 80 percent chance that the United States can detect certain Soviet activities, the Soviets could in theory cheat on those activities 20 percent of the time. But if the development of a new *system* involves three separate activities, then the chance that the United States would fail to detect *any* of these is less than 1 percent (0.2 x 0.2 x 0.2 = 0.008).

Verification Can Be Worked Out

It's very hard to verify some things, and it's possible to verify others. By and large, we have to tailor the agreements so that they limit what you want to limit but in a way that can be verified.

Some people say you have to have on-site inspection. I think that's an impractical requirement. But there may be some intermediate procedures that could be worked out. We might have cooperative verification, where the side whose compliance is being verified does some things that makes it easier for the other to verify its actions. That way, you can have more ambitious agreements.

Harold Brown, *US News & World Report*, January 21, 1985.

Treaty provisions may complement each other and ease the verification task. If there were a ban on further testing, production, and deployment of nuclear weapons systems, a country contemplating cheating would have to take several steps in secret. For example, in order to develop a new submarine missile system, the Soviets would have to produce weapons-grade nuclear materials, test and produce warheads in quantity, test the delivery system and produce it in quantity, and deploy the system, all without detection—a formidable task.

Compliance must be verified in several areas: the testing, production, and deployment of ground- and sea-based delivery systems and of anti-satellite weapons; the testing of nuclear explosives; and the production of weapons-grade nuclear materials. The likelihood of observing a violation varies over time and with respect to individual weapons systems, largely based on the size and mobility of the system being monitored. Verification is facilitated by the fact that a critical element of the deployment process, testing, is readily observed.

Monitoring Delivery Systems

The United States is most confident of its ability to monitor *deployment* of ground- and sea-based delivery systems primarily using satellites, aircraft, and ships. There is high confidence in the ability to count fixed launchers for ICBMs and intermediate-range ballistic missiles (IRBMs), launchers for submarine-launched ballistic missiles (SLBMs), and launchers for multiple-warhead missiles, strategic bombers, and other primary nuclear missions aircraft. The United States has moderate-high confidence in its ability to count mobile systems such as nuclear-armed ships and submarines, nuclear artillery, and battlefield missile units. It is more difficult to count mobile launchers for ICBMs, IRBMs, or ground-launched cruise missiles (GLCMs). Large-scale deployment of cruise missiles could threaten chances for future quantitative limitations on nuclear weapons, because cruise missiles are small, easily transported, and may be fitted with nuclear or nonnuclear explosives in a way that is not easily distinguished.

The *testing* of delivery systems is monitored principally by technical intelligence sources such as imaging reconnaissance satellites, electronic reconnaissance satellites, ground-based monitoring posts, test observation radars, aircraft, and ships, as well as nontechnical intelligence sources such as spies, defectors, and foreign press. Through these means, we can determine with moderate-high to high confidence the number and weight of reentry vehicles being tested, the number of stages, the type of propellant, and the limits on operational ballistic missile flight tests. We are moderately confident of our ability to determine whether the length, diameter, throw-weight, and launch-weight of a new missile are more than 5 percent different from those dimensions of an older missile—that is, whether the United States considers the missile to be new or a modification of an older system.

Monitoring the *production* of missiles, bombers, and strategic nuclear submarines primarily uses imaging reconnaissance satellites and nontechnical intelligence collection methods. There is high confidence of monitoring the shutdown of shipyards or facilities for assembling weapons or making key components for nuclear weapons.

Space Tests Easily Verified

Anti-satellite (ASAT) systems are monitored by satellites, ground-based posts, test observation radars, aircraft and ships, and nontechnical intelligence sources. We have high confidence in monitoring the testing of the current Soviet ASAT interceptor, which uses a huge, easily observable booster rocket and has been monitored for 15 years. However, the production and deployment of smaller systems, such as the US ASAT interceptor carried under the wing of the F-15 fighter plane, would be much more difficult to monitor. It is true in general, however, that tests in space are easily verified.

Nuclear explosions are monitored principally by early warning satellites, nuclear explosion detection satellites, and ground-based seismic sensors. The United States has high confidence of detecting tests with a yield of greater than 5 kilotons, even without remote seismic stations. There is moderate-high confidence in the ability to detect "ambiguous" seismic events, but somewhat less confidence in the ability to determine whether they are nuclear explosions or earthquakes. The ability to detect nonseismic evidence of nuclear explosions (e.g., craters, radioactivity) and to monitor the activity and geography of potential test sites is also moderate-high.

Verification Can Be Effective

No compliance strategy can work effectively if signatories have lost interest in maintaining the viability of an agreement. A compliance strategy can work, however, when the Kremlin knows that the United States will respond in predictable ways to actions that undermine existing agreements, and when the political center feels that their President has a coherent approach to handling the ambiguities of treaty compliance.

Michael Krepon, *Strategic Stalemate*, 1984.

Ratification of the Threshold Test Ban Treaty (TTBT), already signed by both the United States and the Soviet Union, would improve our ability to assess the yield of nuclear weapons tests. In addition to limiting testing to designated sites, the TTBT also provides for an exchange of data, including the yield, time, depth, and geographic coordinates for two tests from each geophysically distinct test area. These data would allow further calibration of monitoring systems, by establishing the relationship between stated yields of tests at particular sites and seismic signals. President Reagan has refused to submit the TTBT to the Senate for ratification.

Restrictions on production of weapons-grade nuclear materials would be verified primarily by imaging reconnaissance satellites and nontechnical intelligence sources. Production of weapons-grade nuclear materials takes place in only a few well-known locations in each country. We have high confidence in our ability to monitor activities at these facilities, and it would be very difficult for a country to develop new facilities without detection by satellite.

179

Negotiating a treaty involves weighing the security risks of not having a treaty against the risks of undetected cheating. In considering whether to violate a treaty reached with the United States, the Soviets must weigh the potential gains of cheating against the costs of being caught—including the prospect of hostile relations—and the possibility that America would take advantage of its superior technical skill to accelerate its weapons programs.

Monitoring and verification must be viewed within the context of potential benefits and costs of arms control agreements. Those who demand 100 percent or "ironclad" verification are actually foes of arms control, because the risks of treaty violations are usually less than the risks of continuing with no arms control agreement. The world in which we live is one of uncertainty and risk, yet the United States has formidable, robust, and redundant monitoring and verification capabilities. In a perfect world, perfect verification would be possible. But in a perfect world, we would not need negotiated arms control agreements.

"We simply do not know how many missiles the Soviets have, or how many launchers, or where they are."

Arms Control
Is Not Verifiable

Samuel Cohen and Joseph Douglass Jr.

Samuel Cohen and Joseph Douglass Jr. are defense advisers to the Reason Foundation, a California-based think tank. In the following viewpoint, the authors maintain that arms control agreements —both past agreements and attempts toward new ones—are unverifiable. The US simply cannot tell how many weapons the Soviets have, or whether or not they are violating treaties. This makes arms control highly ineffective, and, indeed, damages rather than strengthens US national security.

As you read, consider the following questions:

1. What is the only area the authors say arms control violations are easily spotted?
2. Why is the verification of intercontinental missiles difficult, according to the authors?
3. According to the authors, does the US continue to forge arms control agreements?

Samuel Cohen and Joseph Douglass, Jr., "Into the Valley of Arms Control," *The Washington Times*, February 28, 1985. Reprinted with the permission of the authors.

In the arms control arena, there is one concept that most politicians and the entire public recognize and believe—the Soviets are not to be trusted, hence the need for any agreement to be verifiable. This belief is reinforced at every turn of the diplomatic turnstile, most recently, the succession of arms control treaties, almost every significant one of which the Soviets are now believed to have violated or circumvented. This finding was officially documented . . . in two presidential reports to Congress, and in a third sent to the Hill.

Implicit in the need for full verification is that this verification be based on U.S.-controlled factual intelligence, not on poorly founded assumptions or on what the Soviets tell us or openly parade for our benefit. But, just how good is our factual intelligence on Soviet nuclear capabilities?

The one area where we have had a reasonable chance of verifying Soviet compliance is atmospheric testing of nuclear weapons. In essence, the nuclear atmospheric test ban treaty of 1963 was based on our ability to detect most atmospheric tests. These tests can be detected because of a number of associated characteristics or signatures, such as radioactive debris, that are difficult, if not impossible, to reliably suppress or conceal. Even here, however, there are some troublesome questions, such as those raised following the apparent atmospheric test by some unknown country in the South Atlantic region several years ago.

Unfortunately, this is the only area where our ability to obtain good intelligence is, and is expected to remain, good. To claim that we have or will have continuing good intelligence across the board is naive, ill-informed, or deceitful.

Uncountable Nuclear Warheads

And, this is where the problem arises because, while we know little, the impression portrayed is that we know a lot, and this is not true. Take, for example, the case of nuclear warheads. The number and size of nuclear warheads is, perhaps, the ultimate arms control target. But, we have no concrete knowledge of how many and what kinds of nuclear warheads the Soviets have. We do not know their production schedules. Nor do we know how the Soviets design their warheads. This lack of knowledge of Soviet nuclear warheads has been clearly stated in official congressional testimony. Yet the impression is given that we discuss nuclear arms control with the Soviets on the basis of adequate knowledge of their nuclear warhead capabilities.

This same situation—the absence of reliable data, coupled with false impressions that we have detailed knowledge, also applies to the area of intercontinental missiles. The SALT I and SALT II agreements were intended to limit the size and number of intercontinental ballistic missiles on both sides.

Dana Summers, *The Orlando Sentinel*. Reprinted with permission.

They did succeed in limiting our side. But to suggest this also applies to the Soviet stockpile is contrary to the facts. We simply do not know how many missiles the Soviets have, or how many launchers, or where they are. All we can detect are obvious silos constructed in the open during good weather and not camouflaged.

Thousands of Concealed Missiles

The agreements were written in terms of launchers, which we interpreted to mean silos. However, we cannot look into silos to see whether or not they contain missiles. They may not. Indeed, most defense analysts believe there are thousands of Soviet missiles not in silos, concealed over millions of square miles in the U.S.S.R. We simply do not know whether the Soviet stockpile of ICBMs is 1,000 or 20,000, or where they are. Which raises the additional question of how we can safely negotiate an arms control treaty, let alone verify one.

Soviet nuclear submarines were once thought to be amenable to good intelligence-gathering. Submarines under construction supposedly could be observed, and this included the number of openings through which missiles could be launched.

However, major problems have developed. Submarines are now constructed under cover. The Soviets have also built massive underground submarine-berthing facilities. The arms control "counting rules" we have accepted do not allow for the possible missile reload of submarines. Such reload, however, is eminently

183

logical. The huge new Soviet submarines appear capable of carrying considerable extra missiles. How many, we do not know. Which again raises the question of how safely we can negotiate a treaty, in view of how inadequate our intelligence may be.

Arms Control as Pacifier

Similar problems abound in all areas of nuclear arms control, and chemical, biological, and conventional as well. Why, then, is there this continuing propensity to avoid reality, to focus on the need for new agreements rather than contend with the results of past agreements? Why the charade? . . .

Why politicians continue to push nuclear arms control has to be sheer politics. They must know by now that adequate intelligence to provide a basis for negotiation or to verify agreements is simply not in the cards. Yet, they continue to expound on the need to go forward with arms control efforts. Why?

One reason concerns the value of arms control as a placebo to allay fears of nuclear war. In recent years, there has been a growing fear of nuclear war, a fear at times bordering on hysteria. Espousing arms control and ignoring impediments, such as poor intelligence, shifts attention away from Soviet capabilities and doctrine, and dampens this hysteria. Raising hopes for avoiding nuclear war is far better politics than lowering them by bringing up alarming realities.

Agreements Are Good Business

Another reason, dominant in the government bureaucracy, is that arms control—any arms control—is by definition good. To suggest that it may be a dangerous process is bad for business and government careers. Bureaucracies do not have a record of letting reality put them out of business. The issue of how safe arms control may be is irrelevant to them. Good intelligence on the Soviets is unnecessary. After all, many arms controllers argue, the level of armaments is already so high that whether the Soviets have 500 or 5,000 nuclear missiles is irrelevant. Nothing else matters except to continue working harder and harder at arms control.

Ignorance of Soviet capabilities should not be allowed to get in the way. The fact that 25 years of arms control have produced nothing but disappointment and covered up a massive, across-the-board growth in all aspects of Soviet military capability is, from all apparent indications, totally—yes, totally—ignored.

Finally, there is the matter of detente, or, more accurately, doing business with the Soviets. Arms control and detente reinforce one another. Detente means increased trade, technology transfer, and banking transactions with Soviet bloc nations.

When it comes to doing business the American way, Soviet ideology and strategic goals are immaterial, even if they be our destruction. U.S. industrialists and financiers have shown precious

184

little concern over how Western trade, transfer, and financing facilitates the growth of Soviet military power.

National Security Affected

Arms control is seen to promote better business and hence there is little concern by this most influential group—the U.S. financial and business community—that arms control and detente may not promote better national security. There is not a more powerful and, by inference, astute group in this country than the financial and business community, which in the early 1970s recognized the danger of our Vietnam involvement and helped force it to a close. Why have not they recognized the danger of 25 years of unsuccessful nuclear arms control and the eroding U.S. nuclear deterrent and used their enormous leverage on the government to help force it to a close? Perhaps because it is not yet perceived as dangerous to their business. . . .

Soviet Secrecy and Arms Control

A knowledgeable Washington source said, "We simply don't know what goes on in Politburo meetings," so judging Soviet intentions is a guessing game.

Regrettably, this forces the United States into worst-case assumptions when dealing with Moscow on arms control or anything else. That surely is not in the Russian interest. By all indications, though, Moscow continues to perceive secrecy as one of the best things that it has going—and is not about to give it up.

Ernest Conine, *The Los Angeles Times*, December 3, 1984.

[Arms control] continues the self-deception process whereby we continue to mislead ourselves in the critical areas of national defense, and it is done at public expense.

a critical thinking skill

Distinguishing Between Fact and Opinion

This activity is designed to help develop the basic reading and thinking skill of distinguishing between fact and opinion. Consider the following statement as an example: "Many US presidents have attempted to establish arms control agreements with the Soviet Union." This statement is a fact with which few people would disagree. But consider a statement which attributes the lack of arms control to the failure of US presidents. "All US presidents have failed to achieve meaningful arms control agreements." Such a statement is clearly an expressed opinion. Many people frustrated by Soviet/American tensions might agree, but to Richard Nixon, or even Jimmy Carter, the statement is incorrect and an outright attack on their effectiveness as President.

When investigating controversial issues it is important to be able to distinguish between statements of fact and statements of opinion.

The following statements are taken from the viewpoints in this chapter. Consider each statement carefully. *Mark O for any statement you feel is an opinion or an interpretation of facts. Mark F for any statement you believe is a fact.*

If you are doing this activity as a member of a class or group, compare your answers with those of other class or group members. Be able to defend your answers. You may discover that others will come to different conclusions than you. Listening to the reasons others present for their answers may give you valuable insights in distinguishing between fact and opinion.

If you are reading this book alone, ask others if they agree with your answers. You too will find this interaction very valuable.

O = opinion
F = fact

186

1. The main drawback to the arms agreements in the past has been the amount of time they take to enforce.

2. Neither the US nor the USSR has wanted to make deep cuts in their nuclear arsenals.

3. The US could solve the arms control dilemma by cutting back on weapons unilaterally.

4. The idea that the Russians cheat on arms control pacts cannot be proven.

5. Arms spending has not been affected by arms control.

6. Only the Soviets benefit from arms control.

7. Arms control is a necessity.

8. No evidence exists to show that arms control has made the US more secure.

9. Arms control has not prevented the Soviets from forging ahead in their military programs.

10. Both superpowers continue to develop new weapons in spite of arms control.

11. If an arms control agreement is clearly either unverifiable or unenforceable, it serves Soviet purposes.

12. Arms control is politically popular, but it is a repository of false and dangerous hopes.

13. The US adheres more closely to treaties than do the Soviets.

14. Both the US and the USSR have committed violations of arms control treaties.

15. Because of the adversarial relationship between the US and the USSR, arms control may never work.

16. Sophisticated verification technology eliminates the need to trust the Russians on arms control agreements.

17. Arms control agreements cannot be verified because Russia is a closed and secret society.

18. Arms control is not good by definition.

Periodical Bibliography

The following list of periodical articles deals with the subject matter of this chapter.

Gordon Adams "Why There Is No Arms Control," *Dissent*, Spring 1985.

Kenneth L. Adelman "Arms Control: Where Do We Stand Now?" *Department of State Bulletin*, November 1984.

Tom Bethell "The Mugger's Deal in Geneva," *National Review*, March 8, 1985.

"The Costs of Arms Control," *The American Spectator*, December 1984.

Glenn C. Buchan "The Verification Spectrum," *Bulletin of the Atomic Scientists*, November 1983.

Kenneth W. Dam "Preserving Freedom and Security," *Department of State Bulletin*, August 1984.

Sidney Drell "In War Policy the Public Has a Vote: An Informed Constituency Will Shape Arms Control," *Los Angeles Times*, November 11, 1983.

Daniel O. Graham "Arms Control and National Security," *USA Today*, January 1985.

Harvard Nuclear Study Group "A Primer on Arms Control," *Current*, September 1983.

Arnold Horelick "US-Soviet Relations: The Return of Arms Control," *Foreign Affairs*, Vol. 63, No. 3, 1985.

Fred C. Ikle "Nuclear Strategy: Can There Be a Happy Ending?" *Foreign Affairs*, Spring 1985.

Henry Kissinger "A New Approach to Arms Control," *Time*, March 21, 1983.

Michael Krepon "Technology Won't Solve Verification Problems," *Bulletin of the Atomic Scientists*, February 1985.

Flora Lewis "From There To Here: Needed: a Study of Past Arms Talks," *New York Times*, January 15, 1985.

Thomas Longstreth "Report Aims to Sabotage Arms Control," *Bulletin of the Atomic Scientists*, January 1985.

Mary McLuhan and William J. Flynn — "To Get Rid of Nukes, Get Rid of War," *Los Angeles Times*, January 15, 1985.

Christopher E. Paine — "Arms Control Poker," *Inquiry*, June 1984.

Gerard C. Smith — "No Dead End for Arms Control," *Bulletin of the Atomic Scientists*, January 1985.

Stephen J. Solarz — "If the Arms Talks Are to Succeed," *New York Times*, January 21, 1985.

Edson W. Spencer — "A New Antinuclear Strategy," *Newsweek*, February 20, 1984.

John Tirman — "A Way to Break the Arms Deadlock," *The Nation*, February 16, 1985.

George F. Will — "Why Arms Control Is Harmful," *Newsweek*, June 18, 1984.

Alan Wolfe — "Nuclear Fundamentalism Reborn," *World Policy Journal*, Fall 1984.

Can Space Weapons Reduce the Risk of Nuclear War?

Chapter Preface

Star Wars, space weapons, the Strategic Defense Initiative (SDI), and High Frontier are all synonyms for a proposal by the Reagan administration for the establishment of a comprehensive and intensive research program aimed at eventually eliminating the threat posed by nuclear armed ballistic missiles. In essence, the program involves the concept of a multi-layered weapons system, including space-based hardware, designed to intercept and destroy ballistic missiles in flight. The controversy over the Strategic Defense Initiative centers on issues pertaining to nuclear strategy and arms control as well as technology.

SDI represents a fundamental challenge to the United States' current nuclear strategy, that of Mutually-Assured Destruction (MAD). This strategy maintains that the massive nuclear weapons possessed by both the US and the USSR are a deterrent to war: Since both the population centers of the Soviet Union and the West are left vulnerable to nuclear attack, neither side will use the weapons. SDI represents an entirely different set of ground rules. If perfected, the system would be purely defensive and would only be used to prevent a Soviet attack. Perfection is a long way off, however, and opponents of SDI worry over the Soviet reaction. They believe any counteroffensive from the Soviets would leave the world considerably more unstable than it now is under MAD.

These problems, and many others, have been responsible for Star Wars becoming one of the most controversial issues of the nuclear arms debate. The system's opponents believe the problems are justification enough for abandoning the idea. But many others see SDI as a sign of hope, of a way of eliminating the threatening and pessimistic MAD strategy. The authors in the following chapter are all anxious to reduce the threat of nuclear war, but disagree on the way to do it.

"Defense . . . undercuts . . . the immediate danger to peace posed by the very existence of nuclear weapons."

Space Weapons Can Eliminate the Risk of Nuclear War

Daniel O. Graham and Gregory Fossedal

Lieutenant General Daniel O. Graham has served as a deputy director of the Central Intelligence Agency and director for the Defense Intelligence Agency. He was a member of the staff of the American Security Council and a co-chairman of the Coalition for Peace Through Strength. He is currently director of High Frontier, Inc., an organization promoting space weapons. Gregory A. Fossedal has written for the *Wall Street Journal* and *Reader's Digest*. In 1981 he worked for the Reagan administration as a consultant to the White House Conference on Aging. In the following viewpoint, the authors argue that pursuing a program of space weapons can eliminate the danger that Soviet nuclear weapons pose for the US.

As you read, consider the following questions:

1. Some Americans, according to the authors, already believe America has adequate defense. Why do the authors believe that this is untrue?
2. What aspect of the nuclear weapons issue will both liberals and conservatives agree on, according to the authors?

Daniel O. Graham and Gregory A. Fossedal, *A Defense that Defends: Blocking Nuclear Attack*. Old Greenwich, Connecticut: Devin-Adair Publishing Company, 1983. Reprinted with permission.

A sudden flare-up of tensions in the Middle East . . . A breakdown in the tenuous stability of the Eastern bloc . . . An overnight coup and political turnaround in a Third World country . . .

America and the Soviet Union send in advisers to review the unfolding events. The two sides begin to lift vital equipment and supplies to local allies. Suddenly, local guerrillas launch an attack on a convoy of U.S. forces. The U.S. fires back, hitting not only the guerrillas but also several Soviet advisers. Direct shots are exchanged between American and Soviet troops . . . then, more shots.

From here, it is easy to extrapolate: The Soviets, fearing an American strike on their military bases in the area, launch a limited attack on American nuclear missiles. The Americans fire off part of the reserve before an anticipated Kremlin followup strike can occur. Moscow, Kiev, and Vladivostok are gone. Then New York, Chicago, San Diego, Paris, London, Oslo, Rome—the spark set off by initially small events ends in a fiery holocaust of nuclear destruction.

Every reasonable man and woman on the planet carries about with him some vision of this nightmare. One does not have to believe that the human race consists of paranoid nuclear scenarists to know that the threat of nuclear war has impressed itself deeply upon the human consciousness. . . .

America Has No Defense

Many Americans, knowing that we have our own stockpile of nuclear weapons, believe that we *have* a defense. And we do, of sorts: a defense that threatens to blow up millions of Russian people if their government decides first to blow up millions of Americans. Stop and think, though. What happens to all our offensive missiles if the Soviets decide to attack anyway? What happens if many of them are blown up in their own silos? What happens if, though they remain intact, an American president faces 150 million casualties and has recourse only to inflict the same punishment on millions of innocent Russians?

For two years, a growing number of Americans have demanded an alternative—a different approach to the threat of nuclear war. Some formed the nuclear freeze movement, urging that the U.S. and the Soviet Union simply stop producing weapons. But they seem to have little idea how to impose this solution on the Soviets, or of how a world frozen at current levels of destructiveness would be any safer.

There is, however, another choice, different from both the quixotic call to disarmament and the hardliners' demands for more and more offense. The world that spawned the technology to destroy millions of people has spawned the technology to save them, even if such weapons are used. In space there is the opportunity to shoot down intercontinental missiles as they arc toward American cities. In the air, there is the opportunity to seize on American techno-

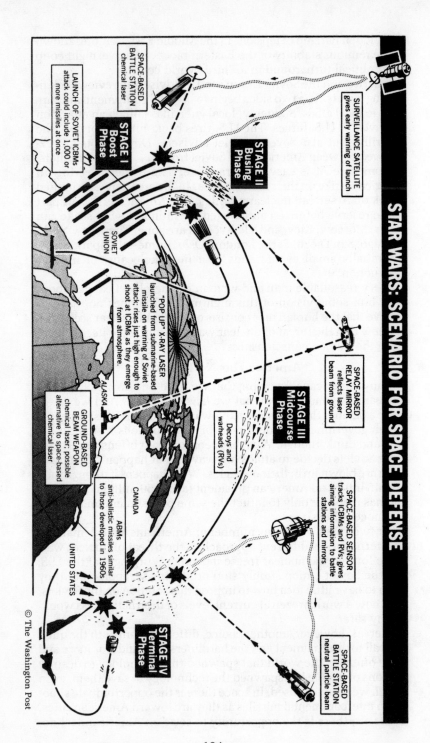

STAR WARS: SCENARIO FOR SPACE DEFENSE

SURVEILLANCE SATELLITE
gives early warning of launch

SPACE-BASED
BATTLE STATION
chemical laser

LAUNCH OF SOVIET ICBMs
attack could include 1,000 or
more missiles at once

STAGE I
Boost Phase

STAGE II
Busing Phase

SOVIET
UNION

"POP UP" X-RAY LASER
launched from submarine-based
missile on warning of Soviet
attack, rises just high enough to
shoot at ICBMs as they emerge
from atmosphere.

SPACE-BASED
RELAY MIRROR
reflects laser
beam from ground

ALASKA

GROUND-BASED
BEAM WEAPON
chemical laser; possible
alternative to space-based
chemical laser

STAGE III
Midcourse
Phase

Decoys and
warheads (RVs)

SPACE-BASED SENSOR
tracks ICBMs and RVs; gives
aiming information to battle
stations and mirrors

CANADA

ABMs
anti-ballistic missiles similar
to those developed in 1960s

UNITED STATES

STAGE IV
Terminal Phase

SPACE-BASED
BATTLE STATION
neutral particle beam

© The Washington Post

194

logical superiority to effectively screen out cities from a bomber attack. On the ground, there are new possibilities for inexpensive ABM measures and civil defense programs....

Escaping the Grip of Nuclear Weapons

Much of the significance of proposing a defense against nuclear weapons, though, lies in the fact that those weapons, even if they are never fired, touch the very essence of our culture. The thought of escaping from the grip of such weapons is enough to liberate the human spirit. Instead of enduring a never-ending stalemate with nuclear arsenals always waiting to go off, we find a way to make those arsenals as obsolete as the crossbow. Instead of threatening to blow up the Soviet Union if the Soviet Union blows us up first, we simply threaten to protect ourselves. The near-consensus is that whatever we find in the search for an alternative to the current strategy of Mutual Assured Destruction—MAD—the search is most assuredly worth conducting. Analysts as typically diverse as Meg Greenfield and William F. Buckley, Jr., *National Review* and the *New Republic, The Washington Post* and *The Washington Times*, have agreed on that point. The coming debate over strategy becomes all the more significant, moreover, when you take into account all the assumptions, policies, and careers linked in some way to the present MAD approach....

Doves and Hawks Think Alike

Both hawkish Pentagon generals and ardent nuclear freeze supporters will no doubt cringe at the suggestion that their approaches go hand in hand. Their respective agendas could hardly be more diametrically opposite: build more on the one hand, build no more, and perhaps get rid of what we now have, on the other. That does not mean, however, that the two approaches are not based on the same assumptions, or that the two groups, the traditional hawks and the traditional doves, do not share a common resistance to defense.

Both approaches, for example, make some similar assumptions about the character of Soviet leadership; that it is at least rational, and thus will refrain from risking some of its population by launching a nuclear attack on the U.S. The offensive buildup position assumes this because it assumes that the MAD doctrine will keep the peace, so long as we maintain sufficient offensive power of our own to absorb a Soviet attack and to strike back with awesome destructiveness of our own. The arms limitation position assumes that the Soviet leadership can eventually be wheedled and cajoled into seeing its true self-interest (as perceived by the West) and thus agree to arms limitations and, eventually, arms reductions.

A defense strategy, by contrast, says that we had better trust ourselves, and make peaceful preparations to limit the harm any country can inflict on us.

We might also note that, politically, both the offense-only strategy school and the arms control school grew out of, and now feed into the continuation of MAD strategy. MAD, after all, imposes a tremendous burden on both parties. For in a world where our defense depends on our ability to retaliate, a diminuation in that retaliatory power threatens our very survival. We have seen just such a reduction in recent years, as the Soviet Union constructed a missile force capable of knocking ours out of its silos with warheads to spare, and, arguably, built other systems capable of blunting much of our remaining bomber and submarine forces. And in a world with the potential for such ineffable destruction, the drive to eliminate such weapons becomes not just a cause, but a moral imperative.

Star Wars Won't Provoke Soviet Attack

Critics argue that a "perfect" strategic defense can never be devised, and that even if it could, it would threaten the "stability" of the balance of terror. They worry that the promise of free world self-defense would prompt the Soviets to launch a pre-emptive nuclear attack, out of fear that we, with our new nuclear shield, might be tempted to attack a less well-defended Soviet Union.

To assume that the Soviets will launch a suicidal nuclear attack is to assume that their leadership is both stupid and irrational. If the Soviets are in fact deterred from striking now, why will they be less deterred when America has a space-based defense? Of course, the Soviet leadership may be irrational. They might launch a first strike against America for any number of reasons—even today. But that argument is one of the best reasons for making a determined effort right now to defend ourselves. It is because the Soviet oligarchy may at some point become paranoid and irrational that we ought not to base our survival strategy on mutual terror and the premise that Soviet leaders think the way we do.

Lewis E. Lehrman, *Policy Review*, Winter 1985.

Defense, by contrast, undercuts both the need for future offensive buildups, at least to the degree now thought necessary, and the immediate danger to peace posed by the very existence of nuclear weapons.

This is not to ridicule either of the alternatives that have, until now, been offered to the American people. They are eminently rational, if we start from the assumption that defense is impossible. So, too, has the reaction of the American people, to the choices offered them, been sane and logical. Many observers in government, the media, and elsewhere—the policy elite—find great mystery in the shifts in public opinion on military matters, a particularly volatile process in the last few years....

A World Free of Nuclear Weapons

What the American people seem to be asking for is an alternative. And defense, in many ways, seems to provide one. If strategic defense has remained off the agenda by its implicit threat to both the disarmers and the rearmers, so defense, now on the agenda, offers a hope of a strategic consensus.

Defense offers the peace marcher one of his most cherished hopes: a world free of the threat of total nuclear annihilation. It offers the Pentagon general the fond dream of an America no longer subject to the blackmail of MAD. There are serious objections to a program of defense....But the intuitive reaction of most Americans is bound to be: Let's try it.

"There is literally no hope that Star Wars can make nuclear weapons obsolete."

Space Weapons Will Not Eliminate the Risk of Nuclear War

McGeorge Bundy, George F. Kennan, Robert S. McNamara and Gerard Smith

McGeorge Bundy was special assistant for national security affairs under Presidents Kennedy and Johnson and is currently professor of history at New York University. George F. Kennan was US ambassador to the Soviet Union in 1952 and to Yugoslavia in 1961. He is also the author of *Soviet American Relations*. Robert S. McNamara was secretary of defense from 1961 to 1968 and President of the World Bank from 1961-1981. Gerard Smith was chief of the US delegation to the SALT talks from 1969-1972 and is the author of *Doubletalk*. All four men have most recently been lecturing on the perils of nuclear weapons. In the following viewpoint, the authors argue that a Star Wars program will never work well enough to eliminate the risks of nuclear war.

As you read, consider the following questions:

1. What do the authors believe to be the two most overwhelming obstacles to a Star Wars program?
2. What type of missiles will Star Wars protect against, according to the authors? Why is this a significant limitation?

Sharing the gravest reservations about [the Strategic Defense Initiative], and believing that unless it is radically constrained . . . it will bring vast new costs and dangers to our country and to mankind, we think it urgent to offer an assessment of the nature and hazards of this initiative, to call for the closest vigilance by Congress and the public. . . . While we write only after obtaining the best technical advice we could find, our central concerns are political. We believe the initiative to be a classic case of good intentions that will have bad results because they do not respect reality.

An Unachievable System

What is centrally and fundamentally wrong with the objective is that it cannot be achieved. The overwhelming consensus of the nation's technical community is that in fact there is no prospect whatever that science and technology can, at any time in the next several decades, make nuclear weapons "impotent and obsolete." The program . . . offers no prospect for a leak-proof defense against strategic ballistic missiles alone, and it entirely excludes from its range any effort to limit the effectiveness of other systems—bomber aircraft, cruise missiles, and smuggled warheads.

The hopes are entirely understandable. There must be very few Americans who have never shared them. All four of us grew up in a world without nuclear weapons, and, we believe with passion that the world would be a much safer place without them. Americans should be constantly on the alert for any possibilities that can help to reduce the nuclear peril in which we all live, and it is entirely natural that a hope of safety should stir a warmly affirmative first response. But false hope, however strong and understandable, is a bad guide to action.

The notion that nuclear weapons, or even ballistic missiles alone, can be rendered impotent by science and technology is an illusion. It reflects not only technological hubris in the face of the very nature of nuclear weapons, but also a complete misreading of the relation between threat and response in the nuclear decisions of the superpowers.

Greatest Obstacle

The first and greatest obstacle is quite simply that these weapons are destructive to a degree that makes them entirely different from any other weapon in history . . . . [It has frequently been observed] that over the centuries every new weapon has produced some countervailing weapon, and up to Hiroshima that is right. But conventional weapons can be neutralized by a relatively low rate of kill, provided that the rate is sustained over time. The classic modern example is defense against non-nuclear bombing. If you lose one bomber in every ten sorties, your force will soon be destroyed. A pilot assigned to fly 30 missions will face a 95-percent prospect of

being shot down. A ten percent rate of kill is highly effective.

With nuclear weapons the calculation is totally different. . . . At today's levels of superpower deployment—about 10,000 strategic warheads on each side—even a 95-percent kill rate would be insufficient to save either society from disintegration in the event of general nuclear war. . . . In the words of the officer in charge of the program, Lieutenant General James Abrahamson, "a perfect defense is not a realistic thing." In response to searching questions from Senator Sam Nunn of Georgia, the senior technical official of the Defense Department, Under Secretary Richard DeLauer, made it plain that he could not foresee any level of defense that would make our own offensive systems unnecessary. . . .

The Soviet's Response

The terrible power of nuclear weapons has a second meaning that decisively undermines the possibility of an effective Star Wars defense of populations. Not only is their destructive power so great that only a kill rate closely approaching 100 percent can give protection, but precisely because the weapons are so terrible neither of the two superpowers can tolerate the notion of "impotence" in the face of the arsenal of the opponent. Thus any prospect of a significantly improved American defense is absolutely certain to stimulate the most energetic Soviet efforts to ensure the continued ability of Soviet warheads to get through. Ever since Hiroshima it has been a cardinal principle of Soviet policy that the Soviet Union must have a match for any American nuclear capability. It is fanciful in the extreme to suppose that the prospect of any new American deployment which could undermine the effectiveness of Soviet missile forces will not be met by a most determined and sustained response. . . .

But already important and enduring obstacles have been identified. Two are systemic and ineradicable. First, a Star Wars defense must work perfectly the very first time, since it can never be tested in advance as a full system. Second, it must be triggered almost instantly, because the crucial boost phase of Soviet missiles lasts less than five minutes from the moment of launch. In that five minutes (which new launch technology can probably reduce to about 60 seconds), there must be detection, decision, aim, attack and kill. It is hard to imagine a scheme further removed from the kind of tested reliability and clear presidential control that we have hitherto required of systems involving nuclear danger.

Attacking Enemy Satellites

There are other more general difficulties. Any remotely leak-proof defense against strategic missiles will require extensive deployments of many parts of the system in space, both for detection of any Soviet launch and, in most schemes, for transmission of the attack on the missile in its boost phase. Yet no one has been able to offer any hope that it will ever be easier and cheaper to deploy and defend large systems in space than for someone else to destroy them. The balance of technical judgment is that the advantage in any unconstrained contest in space will be with the side that aims to attack the other side's satellites. In and of itself this advantage constitutes a compelling argument against space-based defense.

Finally, . . . the program offers no promise of effective defense against anything but ballistic missiles. Even if we assume, against all the evidence, that a leak-proof defense could be achieved against these particular weapons, there would remain the difficulty of defense against cruise missiles, against bomber aircraft, and against the clandestine introduction of warheads. It is important to remember here that very small risks of these catastrophic events will be enough to force upon us the continuing need for our own deterrent weapons. We think it is interesting that among the strong supporters of the Star Wars scheme are some of the same people who were concerned about the danger of the strategic threat of the Soviet Backfire bomber only a few years ago. Is it likely that in the light of these other threats they will find even the best possible defense against missiles a reason for declaring our own nuclear weapons obsolete?

201

Inadvertent but persuasive proof of this failing has been given by the president's science adviser. Last February, in a speech in Washington, Mr. Keyworth recognized that the Soviet response to a truly successful Star Wars program would be to "shift their strategic resources to other weapons systems," and he made no effort to suggest that such a shift could be prevented or countered, saying: "*Let* the Soviets move to alternate weapons systems, to submarines, cruise missiles, advanced technology aircraft. Even the critics of the president's defense initiative agree that *those* weapons systems are far more stable deterrents than are ICBMs [land-based missiles]." Mr. Keyworth, in short, is willing to accept all these other means of warhead delivery, and he appears to be entirely unaware that by this acceptance he is conceding that even if Star Wars should succeed far beyond what any present technical consensus can allow us to believe, it would fail by the President's own standard.

America and the Soviets

The Star Wars proposal tries to create a unilateral advantage for the US, while ignoring the reality that the Soviets will respond in kind, and that the ensuing action-reaction syndrome will accelerate the arms race in ways that will make the world even more dangerous than it is today—dangerous beyond our present imagining.

We could see this more clearly if the situation were turned around. If it were the Soviets who were proposing to build a comprehensive Star Wars defense, could we treat it with equanimity or ignore it? Would we believe them if they told us it was a purely defensive action and not a threat to anyone?

Townsend Hoopes, *Committee for National Security Reports*, Winter 1985.

The inescapable reality is that there is literally no hope that Star Wars can make nuclear weapons obsolete. Perhaps the first and most important political task for those who wish to save the country from the expensive and dangerous pursuit of a mirage is to make this basic proposition clear. As long as the American people believe that Star Wars offers real hope of reaching the President's asserted goal, it will have a level of political support unrelated to reality. The American people, properly and sensibly, would like nothing better than to make nuclear weapons "impotent and obsolete," but the last thing they want or need is to pay an astronomic bill for a vastly intensified nuclear competition sold to them under a false label. Yet that is what Star Wars will bring us, as a closer look will show.

"Star Wars is a particularly good bargaining chip."

Space Weapons Should Be a Bargaining Chip

Charles Krauthammer

Charles Krauthammer is a senior editor for *The New Republic*, a liberal journal of opinion. He holds an M.D. in psychiatrics from Harvard and was Commonwealth Scholar in politics at Oxford University in London. A widely published author, Dr. Krauthammer's articles also appear regularly in *The Washington Post* and *Time* magazine. In the following viewpoint, Mr. Krauthammer argues that space weapon plans have made the Soviets perk up and take notice of the US. If US negotiators use space weapons as a bargaining chip, he believes they can successfully orchestrate a stabilizing arms control agreement.

As you read, consider the following questions:

1. What does the author believe holds more promise than space weapons?
2. Why have the Russians expressed an interest in ending development of space weapons, according to the author?
3. How can the US use the space weapons idea to its best advantage, according to the author?

Charles Krauthammer, ''Will Star Wars Kill Arms Control?'' *The New Republic*, January 21, 1985. Reprinted by permission of *The New Republic*, © 1985, The New Republic, Inc.

It is not difficult to make the case that [the] Star Wars plan aimed at making "nuclear weapons impotent and obsolete" is an illusion, and that the promise it holds out, of repealing deterrence, is a fraud. Deterrence can be abolished only by a leakproof population defense. . . . And even if such a miraculous ballistic missile defense were possible, the American people would remain vulnerable to nuclear retaliation—deterrence—by cruise missile or bomber.

A somewhat harder case to make is that even if Star Wars could work, arms control is better. Star Wars has great intuitive appeal. A "defensive transition" would make the world safer, it seems. perhaps, but not safer, not more stable, than an offensive transition by mutual agreement.

Consider two near-ideal scenarios. In scenario A, the dream of arms control advocates (like the Scowcroft Commission), both the United States and the Soviets have revised their offensive weaponry, banned multiple warhead missiles (known as MIRVs) and gone to a regime of single warhead (Midgetman) missiles. Neither has a defensive shield. In scenario B, the near ideal of strategic defense advocates, both the United States and Soviets have established elaborate, say 99 percent effective, defenses against ballistic missiles. They have also continued improving the quantity, accuracy, and MIRVing capacity of their offensive weapons. Which regime is more stable?

Stability: Two Examples

The strategic stability of regime A is based on the fact that both sides are deprived of any incentive ever to strike first. Since it takes roughly two warheads to destroy one enemy silo, an attacker must expend two of his missiles to destroy one of the enemy's. A first strike disarms the attacker. The aggressor ends up worse off than the aggressed. Moreover, in scenario A, the equilibrium is stable: to disrupt it, or, as the experts say, to break out, would require rebuilding a MIRVed missile force. And that would take years and hundreds of billions of dollars, and be easily observable.

Regime B also achieves equilibrium, but an unstable one. Regime B is based on a system of defensive shields that are extremely complicated and delicate. They are inherently subject to sudden breakdown, as we see, for example, in the far less sophisticated space shuttle program. A faulty valve or switch or computer could let down either shield. Furthermore, the shields are vulnerable to attack. In a crisis, if one side decides to strike first (remember: it has kept perfecting the offensive weapons to do so), it will surely begin by attacking the space-based defense, which itself is highly vulnerable to disruption or destruction. Thus under regime B breakdown or breakout can occur at any moment.

It seems to me, therefore, that arms control based on revision of offensive weaponry offers the hope of a less fragile nuclear balance than one based on exotic defenses.

Writing about Star Wars last year, I concluded that instead of a ruinous arms race in space that could never hope to achieve its objectives, a better alternative was arms control ("perhaps augmented by improved terminal defenses to protect missile bases and enhance deterrence," but more about that later). For all arms control advocates, however, the question is how to get there from here.

The US Needs Arms Control

There is a long list of standard things to say about "Star Wars": It's just another example of the American technical fascination with finding a "magic bullet"; the full-scale city-defense version won't work; even the economy version will cost a mint; the Soviets will just build more warheads to make sure enough get through, and so on. But stripped of all the persiflage of "declaratory policy," "Star Wars" is really another attempt to end-run arms control—an attempt to make ourselves safe, all by ourselves. . . .

If we're ever going to know safety again, the Soviets will have to be safe, too—and that means negotiated agreements, now, before we start spending serious money, and discover it feels too good to stop.

Thomas Powers, *The Los Angeles Times*, February 17, 1985.

In the intervening months the Soviets have provided a somewhat ironic answer to that question: Star Wars. Or more precisely, the threat of a certain kind of American strategic defense.

Ever since the President managed to turn his Star Wars idea into a $26 billion program, the Soviets have been positively desperate to stop it. So anxious are they, that they have returned to the Geneva talks which they had abandoned a year ago, without any of their conditions for returning having been met. Their principal objective, stated quite openly, is to stop the arms race in space. ("Militarization of space," they call it, as if the vast majority of their hundreds of Cosmos satellites are not military.) They are particularly anxious to stop American testing of anti-satellite (ASAT) weapons scheduled for this spring. Last summer they tried to make a moratorium on such testing a condition for a resumption of arms control talks in Vienna. They also insisted that these talks deal exclusively with space weapons. . . .

Kremlin behavior in the face of the possibility of American space weapons raises an important question. If Star Wars is as useless a system as it seems, why are the Russians so afraid?

Defending Weapons

One theory is that, like Americans who understandably would like to close their eyes and wish upon a star that American in-

205

genuity will somehow pop an impermeable astrodome over the United States, the Russians believe that American defensive technology will triumph, leaving the Soviet Union disarmed. I can't believe the Russians believe it. The Russians may be paranoid, but they're not stupid. They can read our technical journals as well as we can. And the overwhelming evidence from studies inside and outside the government is that a population defense, which must be perfect, is out of the question.

What scares the Kremlin is another prospect: an imperfect American strategic defense. It is possible, and it could perform an important function. It could defend weapons....

US First Strike Capability

That would have two major effects on the Soviets. In the strategic nuclear balance, the United States has clear advantages in submarines, in penetrating aircraft, and in cruise missiles. The one area where the Soviets have a countervailing advantage is land-based missiles. The SS-18s and -19s, heavy and MIRVed, are accurate enough to pose a serious threat to the American military targets. A partial American defense around such targets, even a leaky one, would, in effect and unilaterally, degrade this Soviet arsenal....

But that's not the worst of it. If coupled with a continuing American buildup of offensive weapons—particularly highly MIRVed, accurate missiles like the MX, and the D5 to be deployed on submarines in the next decade—it would have, from the Soviets' point of view, a second, even more alarming effect. It would give the United States a credible first strike capacity....

That is what is driving the Soviets to Geneva. Star Wars is a particularly good bargaining chip. Most bargaining chips work only when traded away. The MX, for example, does not solve American vulnerability to SS-18s. It simply creates a parallel (and, we hope, intolerable) vulnerability for the Soviets. An imperfect Star Wars works by thinning the Soviet SS-18 and -19 force whether they deal or not. It places the Soviets in the position where either they can see their offensive weapons degraded unilaterally, getting nothing in return, or they can reduce them bilaterally and get a reduction in American defensive (and perhaps offensive) deployments as well. It forces the Soviets, as it were, to negotiate on warning: use it (to deal) or lose it.

The warning has already concentrated Kremlin minds on the wisdom of dealing. Mikhail Gorbachev announced that the Soviets were prepared to negotiate deep reductions in offensive systems, once Star Wars was disposed of....

In arms control, ends (safety, parity, stability) are often obvious, and mutually, even sincerely, agreed upon. Means are the problem. Star Wars is a means. The Kremlin sees that point very well. The pity is that in the United States the most important advocates and the most important critics of strategic defense miss that point completely.

206

*"It is folly for us to place our security solely or
even primarily on arms control."*

Space Weapons Should Not Be a Bargaining Chip

Seymour Weiss and Leon Sloss

Seymour Weiss is a retired ambassador and former director of the
State Department's bureau of politico-military affairs. Leon Sloss,
a Washington consultant, is a retired director of the Arms Control
and Disarmament Agency. In this viewpoint, the authors develop
the argument that using space weapons as a bargaining chip would
be catering to the Soviets and would adversely affect US national
security.

As you read, consider the following questions:

1. What theory do most critics of space weapons support,
   according to the authors?
2. Do the authors believe that the Soviets have deployed
   defensive weapons systems?
3. According to the authors, how would deploying the space
   weapons system aid arms control?

Seymour Weiss and Leon Sloss, "Raging Against Star Wars," *The Washington Post National Weekly Edition,* January 21, 1985. © The Washington Post.

How is one to explain the passionate, sometimes almost frenetic, denunciation of the president's proposal for a defense against Soviet ballistic missiles? Even the label, "Star Wars," seems designed to denigrate, to conjure up a vision of Hollywood production, a matter for ridicule, not serious national debate. While the critics scoff, the public seems to appreciate the common-sense approach of seeking to defend ourselves. What, after all, is the sin of attempting to develop a defense against Soviet attack?

Let us acknowledge at the outset that there are aspects to the Strategic Defense Initiative (SDI) that warrant healthy skepticism. This research carries a costly price tag of $26 billion. However, by today's standards of $100 million bombers and $5 billion aircraft carriers, the SDI costs—which are to be spread over more than five years—are not unreasonable if the research effort produces results that will improve the nation's security and that of our allies. We think it can.

It is also a legitimate matter of concern that some of our allies are deeply opposed to SDI. As ones who have discussed the issue with some of our NATO partners, we are persuaded that there is much confusion and misunderstanding on their part. Past experience also suggests that these concerns may, in time, be allayed if our diplomacy is patient and skillful. Such would already appear to have been the case with Margaret Thatcher.

It is also true that the most extravagant expectations for SDI may never be fulfilled. It is not unreasonable to be skeptical about whether a perfect defense will ever be developed. The president's hope that SDI will help to make nuclear weapons disappear from the face of the earth is surely utopian. Still, these are not ignoble goals, and at this stage neither supporters nor critics of SDI can speak with confidence about what technology and diplomacy may accomplish decades hence.

Strategy and Arms Control

One must probe more deeply to comprehend the antagonism toward the SDI that has emerged from certain quarters. When one does, two underlying issues emerge. They have to do with nuclear strategy and arms control.

While declaring their confidence that SDI won't work, the critics, in fact, are fearful it will. At least they fear it will work well enough to call into question their preferred nuclear strategy. Most critics adhere to the school of mutual assured destruction (MAD). That emerged in the 1960s from the mind of Robert McNamara, who was then secretary of defense and is now one of the principal critics of strategic defense. His calculations convinced him that so long as milions of Russians and millions of Americans were at risk of nuclear attacks on the cities on each side, each would be deterred. In this view defenses were bad because they removed the hostages that assured deterrence. There was then, and there is now, much wrong with this thesis.

Not the least of the problems is that the Soviets never bought McNamara's strategy. They don't believe in city busting as the prime objective of nuclear strategy. Thus, it is not clear that such a threat is the one most likely to deter them. Indeed, the Soviets, despite McNamara's contrary prediction, spent massively to overcome America's lead in offensive weaponry, going well beyond any conceivable inventory justified soley in terms of the requirements for the MAD strategy. In time, many U.S. leaders came to the realization that MAD did not serve as well either, and U.S. strategy has, for more than a decade, under Democratic and Republican administrations alike, been moving away from this concept.

Since the Soviets did not believe in the MAD strategy, they refused to rely solely on offensive nuclear capabilities and in addition deployed impressive defenses. They have more than 10,000 ground-to-air defensive missiles and thousands of fighter aircraft to protect against our bombers. We have none of the former and pitifully few of the latter. They have deployed ballistic missile defense in the Moscow area that provides defense to their central government and party apparatus and to two-thirds of the heavily industrialized western U.S.S.R. They have an impressive civil defense system, which has concentrated on defending key government and industrial people. They have continued to harden and

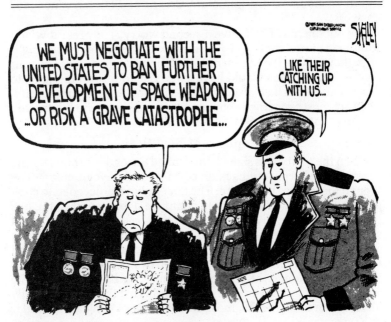

Steve Kelley, *San Diego Union*, reprinted with permission.

make mobile their ballistic missiles and command centers. As Defense Secretary Caspar Weinberger recently pointed out, they have spent more on strategic defense than on strategic offense since the signing of the ABM Treaty.

In fact, the Soviets built their forces to support the strategy they have held to consistently, based not on targeting U.S. cities but the U.S. military establishment. As a result, they are today capable in a first strike (and their doctrine has always emphasized the importance of surprise) of reducing the U.S. retaliatory force to a relatively small fraction of its nominal strength. Thus, we could be left with a force that, while having some countermilitary capability, was most suitable for attacking Soviet cities, even though our own cities had not yet been attacked by the Soviets—an unenviable choice for any president. Under the circumstances, we might find our strategy, having failed to deter, would leave him with unbelievably stark alternatives: suicide or surrender.

If Deterrence Fails?

Why is it not a good idea to seek alternatives that avoid such a stark choice? Is it not worth a considerable effort to see whether some degree of defense might help ensure deterrence? If deterrence could fail, why shouldn't we try to protect ourselves as best we can? Must we accept for all time a strategy based on the threat of killing millions of innocent people—a strategy Catholic bishops have rightly denounced as immoral? Critics of SDI have no good answers.

The opponents of SDI have a second worry. They fear it would complicate arms control negotiations with the Soviets. One might have thought that the barren results of the past two decades of arms control negotiations would have given rise to second thoughts to those who would have us rely so heavily on them for our security. They are most concerned about protecting the "jewel in the crown" of arms control, the ABM Treaty of 1972.

Unpleasant Realities

When the treaty was signed, the United States dismantled its one system and sharply cut back on research and development, even though these were permitted. The Soviets have proceeded to complete a nationwide radar net; to complete deployment of the one permitted system; to create a production base that would permit rapid expansion of conventional but advanced ABM capabilities; and to conduct extensive research in precisely those advanced technologies that would be encompassed by the SDI program. They have fully exploited the possibilities permitted by the treaty while we have not, and most observers are satisfied they have actually violated the treaty limits, most notably in deploying a large radar at Krasnoyarsk.

Apologists for the treaty hesitate to acknowledge these realities.

The Soviets, being realists, are unlikely to permit any arms control agreement to stand in the way of advancing Soviet interests, in most cases at the direct expense of the West. Indeed, the Soviets' recent initiative to draw the Reagan administration into new arms control discussions clearly appears to be based upon a desire to kill off SDI while leaving them as free a hand as possible to pursue their own ballistic missile defense and antisatellite efforts. Any objective review of arms control history will demonstrate this to be vintage Soviet arms control strategy.

Don't Give Up On Defense

The worst defense is none. That does not even protect against an accidental firing, and it invites political pressure or blackmail from the side that has a defense. . . .

Moscow wants to stop the research before it reduces the value of their offensive missiles. Unlike U.S. critics of the "star wars" defense plan, the Soviets obviously think it can work.

James Hackett, *The Washington Times*, February 13, 1985.

Still, critics of SDI hang fast to the belief that they can talk the Soviets into adopting a mutually suicidal strategy, while engaging in arms control efforts that, to succeed, would require the Soviets to abandon not merely some weaponry of which they may be fond, but their most fundamental political objectives. For Soviet exploitation of military power—the one thing the Soviets are good at developing—is not just some minor aberration in otherwise reasonable behavior. The Soviets develop that power because they require it for purposes of political intimidation and, should that fail, for actual employment, as they pursue their goal of a world pliant to Soviet views.

Arms Control Folly

Under these circumstances, it is folly for us to place our security solely or even primarily on arms control. The notion that the Soviets through arms control negotiations are likely to abandon hard-won military advantages over the West is about as naive as was the 1960s prediction that they would not even try to match our nuclear capabilities.

As we have suggested, the current defense debate is not just about the president's Strategic Defense Initiative. It is about more fundamental issues: How can we best prevent nuclear war? How ought we to deal with the Soviet Union in a continuing adversarial relationship? How do U.S. nuclear strategy and arms control concepts fit into and support nuclear war deterrence and prevent the expansion of Soviet influence?

No one side in our internal debates has a monopoly on wisdom, and one wishes the critics of the president's SDI program would cease acting as if they did. Would it not be reasonable to see whether this research effort can come up with capabilities that may promise the West a safer, more promising future than total reliance on the threat of mutual destruction?

Even though the research may be only partially successful, as Weinberger has recently suggested, if we can develop and deploy defensive systems with capabilities more modest than a perfect defense, might that not be very valuable in strengthening deterrence? Even if defenses initially provided protection of valuable military assets such as land-based ICBMs, bombers and command-and-control centers, might that not be preferable to proliferating generation after generation of new offensive weapons systems? Even if an imperfect defense could save "only" tens of millions of lives, is there not some merit in such a defense?

Finally, if we are successful in developing increasingly capable defenses against Soviet nuclear attack, might not this induce the Soviets to adopt a more forthcoming position on arms control? We cannot with confidence answer these questions positively. The prospects are not without merit, however, and it is to these issues that the 1985 defense debate should turn.

> *"With development and some additional research, we can now construct and deploy a two-layer...defense, which can be in place by the early 1990s."*

Space Weapons Are Technically Feasible

Zbigniew Brzezinski, Robert Jastrow,
and Max M. Kampelman

Zbigniew Brzezinski, professor of government at Columbia University and senior adviser at the Center for Strategic and International Studies at Georgetown University, was national security adviser to President Jimmy Carter. Robert Jastrow, a physicist and professor of earth sciences at Dartmouth, is the founder of the Goddard Institute for Space Studies. Max M. Kampelman, a Washington lawyer, has been named to head the US delegation to the new arms control talks with the Soviet Union. In the following viewpoint, the authors explain the technology involved in the space weapons project. They conclude that most of this technology is at hand, is relatively inexpensive, and is necessary to US security.

As you read, consider the following questions:

1. What kind of weaponry are Soviet forces primarily composed of, according to the authors?
2. Why do the authors think the critics' arguments against space weapons are baseless?

Zbigniew Brezezinski, Robert Jastrow and Max M. Kampelman, "Defense in Space Is Not 'Star Wars'," *The New York Times*, January 27, 1985. Copyright © 1985 by The New York Times Company. Reprinted by permission.

For many years, our search for security has been restricted to designing offensive weapons to deter aggression through fear of reprisals. We must not abandon nuclear deterrence until we are convinced that a better means is at hand. But we cannot deny that, for both the Soviet Union and the United States, the costs, insecurities and tensions surrounding this search for newer, more effective and more accurate nuclear missiles produce a profound unease that in itself undermines stability.

The conventional view is that stability in the nuclear age is based on two contradictory pursuits: the acquisition of increasingly efficient nuclear weapons and the negotiation of limits and reductions in such weapons. The United States is diligently pursuing both objectives, but the complexity of arriving at effectual arms-control agreements is becoming apparent as more precise and mobile weapons, with multiple warheads, appear on both sides. Unlike ours, moreover, many Soviet missile silos are reloadable, and thus the number of silos does not indicate the number of missiles, further complicating verification.

Soviet First Strike

We must never ignore the reality that the overwhelming majority of the Soviet strategic forces is composed of primarily first-strike weaponry. And given the large numbers of first-strike Soviet SS-17, -18 and -19 land-based missiles, no responsible American leader can make decisions about security needs without acknowledging that a Soviet first strike can become a practical option.

The Russians could strike us first by firing the reloadable portion of their nuclear arsenal at our missiles, the Strategic Air Command and nuclear submarine bases, and if the surviving American forces (essentially nuclear submarines) were to respond, the Russians could immediately counter by attacking our cities with missiles from nonreloadable silos and, a few hours later, with whatever of their first-strike reloadable weapons had survived our counterattack. They are set up for launching three salvos to our one.

To us, this catastrophic exchange is unthinkable. But, with the strong probability that the American response would be badly crippled at the outset by a Soviet strike, some Russian leader could someday well consider such a potential cost bearable in the light of the resulting "victory." Furthermore, such an analysis might well anticipate that an American President, knowing that a strike against our cities would inevitably follow our response to a Soviet first strike, might choose to avoid such a catastrophe by making important political concessions. No responsible American President can permit this country to have to live under such a threat, not to speak of the hypothetical danger of having to choose either annihilation or submission to nuclear blackmail. Hence the understandable and continual drive for more effective offensive missiles to provide greater deterrence.

The result is that weapons technology is shaping an increasingly precarious American-Soviet strategic relationship. For this reason, we urge serious consideration be given to whether some form of Strategic Defense Initiative (S.D.I.) might not be stabilizing, enhancing to deterrence and even helpful to arms control. . . .

Unexotic Technologies

A great deal has been written about the state of missile-defense technology. Some experts say the technology sought is unattainable, others that it is merely unattainable in this generation. Yet the promise of the Strategic Defense Initiative is real. Some of the technologies are mature and unexotic. Their deployment around the end of this decade would involve mainly engineering development. Technically, these vital defenses could be in place at this moment were it not for the constraints accepted by the United States in its adherence to the antiballistic missile treaty of 1972.

Technology Can Eliminate Nuclear Weapons

Today's emerging technologies support a reasonable hypothesis that non-nuclear defense options can provide a more stable strategic deterrent than the present reliance on offensive nuclear weapons. By holding forth the possibility of destroying warheads, not only in the last moments before impact but also by destroying both missiles and warheads during all phases of flight beginning with their launch, there is a real possibility that a non-nuclear defense against ballistic missiles could render a nuclear offense ineffective. At a minimum, this could further ensure that there is no rational basis for a first-strike option, and lessen the political and military tensions that arise from relying solely on deterrence through the threat of offensive nuclear forces.

There is also the possibility that prodigious defenses would render ballistic missiles so ineffective as to become, in the President's words, "impotent or obsolete."

Tom Marshall, *The Los Angeles Times*, February 21, 1985.

With development and some additional research, we can now construct and deploy a two-layer or double-screen defense, which can be in place by the early 1990s at a cost we estimate to be somewhere in the neighborhood of $60 billion. A conservative estimate of the effectiveness of each layer would be 70 percent. The combined effectiveness of the two layers would be over 90 percent: Less than one Soviet warhead in 10 would reach its target—more than sufficient to discourage Soviet leaders from any thought of achieving a successful first strike.

The first layer in the two-layer defense system—the "boost-phase" defense—would go into effect as a Soviet first-strike missile, or "booster," carrying multiple warheads rises above the atmosphere at the beginning of its trajectory. This boost-phase defense—based on interception and destruction by nonnuclear projectiles—would depend on satellites for the surveillance of the Soviet missile field and the tracking of missiles as they rise from their silos. These operations could only be carried out from space platforms orbiting over the Soviet Union. Because they are weightless in orbit, such platforms could be protected against attack by heavy armor, on-board weapons and maneuverability.

After the booster has burned out and fallen away, the warheads arc through space on their way to the United States. The second layer of the defense—the terminal defense—comes into play as the warheads descend. Interception would be at considerable altitude, above the atmosphere if possible. This second phase requires further engineering, already under way, because interception above the atmosphere makes it difficult to discriminate between real warheads and decoys. In the interim, interception can take place in the atmosphere, where differences in air drag separate warheads from decoys. In either event, destruction of the warheads would take place at sufficiently high altitudes, above 100,000 feet, so that there would be no ground damage from warheads designed to explode when approached by an intercepting missile.

Of the two layers in the defense, the boost phase is by far the most important. It would prevent the Russians from concentrating their warheads on such high-priority targets as the national-command authority (the chain of command, beginning with the President, for ordering a nuclear strike), key intercontinental-ballistic missile silos or the Trident submarine pens, because they could not predict which booster and which warheads would escape destruction and get through....

Technology At Hand

The likely technology for an early use of the boost-phase defense would use "smart" nonnuclear projectiles that home in on the target, using radar or heat waves, and destroy it on impact. The technology is close at hand and need not wait for the availability of the more devastating but less mature technologies of the laser, the neutral particle beam or the electromagnetic rail gun. The interceptor rocket for this early boost-phase defense could be derived from air-defense interceptors that will soon be available, or the technology of antisatellite missiles (ASAT) launched from F-15 aircraft. These rockets could weigh about 500 pounds, the nonnuclear supersonic projectiles about 10 pounds.

Interceptor rockets would be stored in pods on satellites and fired from space. The tracking information needed to aim the rockets would also be acquired from satellites orbiting over the Soviet missile fields. The so-called "space weapons" of strategic defense are indispensable for the crucial boost-phase defense. To eliminate

GREAT QUESTIONS OF OUR TIME #1

Reprinted by permission: Tribune Media Services.

them would destroy the usefulness of the defense.

We estimate that the cost of establishing such a boost-phase defense by the early 1990s would be roughly $45 billion. That price tag includes 100 satellites, each holding 150 interceptors—sufficient to counter a mass Soviet attack from all their 1,400 silos; plus four geosynchronous satellites and 10 low-altitude satellites dedicated to surveillance and tracking; plus the cost of facilities for ground-control communications and battle management.

The technology used for the terminal defense could be a small, nonnuclear homing interceptor with a heat-seeking sensor, which would be launched by a rocket weighing one to two tons and costing a few milion dollars each. Interception would take place above the atmosphere, if possible, to give wider "area" protection to the terrain below. These heat-seeking interceptors can be available for deployment in about five years if a decision is reached to follow that course. One concept for this technology was tested successfully last June by the Defense Department, when an intercepting missile zeroed in on an oncoming warhead at an altitude of 100 miles and destroyed it.

Technology Costs

The technology for a terminal defense within the atmosphere would be somewhat different, but would probably also depend on heat-seeking missiles. The cost of this terminal layer of defense would be about $15 billion and include $10 billion for 5,000 interceptors, plus $5 billion for 10 aircraft carrying instruments for tracking of the Soviet warheads.

The estimated $60 billion for this two-layer defense is a ball-park figure, of course. However, even with its uncertainties, it is surely an affordable outlay for protecting our country from a nuclear first strike. . . .

Two-Tiered Defense

We can begin a two-tiered strategic defense that would protect command structure as well as our missiles and silos and thus discourage any thoughts by the Soviet military that a first-strike effort would be effective. Some within the scientific community minimize the importance of this technical feasibility and emphasize instead the view that it is scientifically impossible today to provide a strategic defense that will protect our cities. Such a broad defense of populations is today not feasible, but it is prudent for our society to keep in mind the rising tide of technical and scientific advances so rapidly overwhelming the 20th century.

The "impossible" is a concept we should use with great hesitation. It is foolhardy to predict the timing of innovations. We are persuaded that the laws of physics do not in any way prevent the technical requirements of a defensive shield that would protect populations as well as weapons. A total shield should remain our ultimate objective, but there is every reason for us to explore transitional defenses, particularly because the one we have discussed would serve to deter the dangers of a first strike. Defenses against ballistic missiles can be effective without being "perfect," and the technology for this is nearly in hand.

Nothing's Impossible

Society must also not forget that ever since the beginning of the scientific age, the organized scientific community has not had a particularly good record of predicting developments that were not part of the common wisdom of the day. In 1926, for example, A. W. Bickerton, a British scientist, said it was scientifically impossible to send a rocket to the moon. In the weapons field, United States Adm. William D. Leahy told President Harry S. Truman in 1945: "That [atomic] bomb will never go off, and I speak as an expert in explosives." And Dr. Vannevar Bush, who directed the Government's World War II science effort, said after the war that he rejected the talk "about a 3,000-mile rocket shot from one continent to the other carrying an atomic bomb . . . and we can leave that out of our thinking." In the strategic area, as late as 1965, the capable Secretary of Defense Robert S. McNamara wrote: "There is no indication that the Soviets are seeking to develop a strategic force as large as our own." . . .

A three- or four-layer defense, using such advanced technologies as the laser now under investigation in the research phase of the Strategic Defense Initiative, may become a reality by the end of the century. If this research shows an advanced system to be practical, its deployment may well boost the efficiency of our defense to a level so close to perfection as to signal a final end to the era of nuclear ballistic missiles. A research program offering such enormous potential gains in our security must be pursued, in spite of the fact that a successful outcome cannot be assured at this juncture....

The aim of making nuclear weapons impotent and obsolete should be encouraged and not savaged.

"Technology fails, often. . . . Man has not even been able to devise a highly effective, 'leak proof,' air defense system against airplanes."

Space Weapons Are Not Technically Feasible

Fortney H. Stark

Fortney H. Stark is a democratic representative from California and a member of the Ways and Means Committee and the Arms Control and Foreign Policy Caucus. In the following viewpoint, Mr. Stark maintains that Star Wars technology will never be attainable.

As you read, consider the following questions:

1. How much will the space weapons system cost, according to the author?
2. What should be the goal of America's national security policy, according to the author?

Fortney H. Stark, "National Security or Pie in the Sky?" reprinted from *USA Today*, July 1984. Copyright 1984 by The Society for the Advancement of Education.

The American people should know that the President of the U.S. has decided to launch a full-scale arms race in space. He has done so in their name, and with their tax dollars. The FY 1985 budget request contains the first giant step down this perilous road. The President claims this road leads to greater security for our people, a defensive American military posture, and even the obsolesence of The Bomb itself.

A careful examination of the complex issue of space weapons has led me to conclude that the pursuit of a space-based missile defense capability could render us far, far less secure than we are today, result in the U.S. being perceived as more threatening than ever before, and greatly increase the number of thermonuclear weapons targeted on the U.S....

The President has presented a five-year space weapons plan entitled the "Strategic Defense Initiatives." The Pentagon estimates that this set of initiatives will cost a minimum of $24,271,000,000 during Fiscal Years 1985-1989—and this is just for research and development. This R&D, in the words of Secretary of Defense Caspar Weinberger's FY 1985 Report to Congress, "will support decisions in the early 1990s on whether to proceed with development of ballistic missile defenses and which systems appear most promising." If we are to spend over $24,000,000,000 to "support decisions" regarding eventual deployment of such a weapon system, it is a safe bet there will be irresistable pressures to proceed to deployment.

I can just picture the Pentagon and defense contractors saying, "But we have already spent over $24,000,000,000! You can't possibly want to throw that away by stopping now!" A $24,000,000,000 down payment will turn any "exploratory research project" into an economic and political snowball. Congress and the American people will be rolling uncontrollably down the road to deployment. Nobody knows what deployment would cost. Various estimates have ranged from $100,000,000,000 to $500,000,000,000. The unspeakable figure of one trillion dollars was mentioned by a Pentagon official at an Armed Services Committee hearing....

Rather, we must decide whether going ahead with the President's plan is in the best security interests of this country....

Is It Do-able?

The defensive measures involve a variety of existing and emerging technologies, including high-speed intercept missiles, high-energy lasers, charged particle beams, nuclear-pumped x-ray lasers, and the necessary tracking gear. The mission is to locate, track, and destroy thousands of Soviet ballistic missiles and their many thousands of nuclear warheads in flight. This must all be achieved in less than the maximum of 30 minutes it takes ICBMs to fly from Soviet silos to American targets.

"MR. PRESIDENT, I HAVE GOOD NEWS AND BAD NEWS. WE JUST SHOT DOWN AN INCOMING OBJECT...UNFORTUNATELY IT WAS HALLEY'S COMET!"

I am not a scientist, and thus will not even attempt an explanation of all the intricacies of what is necessary to successfully intercept and destroy these thousands of speeding objects in a very limited time frame. Nevertheless, some basic knowledge is essential, if only to illustrate the extent of the problem.

Given the short period of time allowed, a space-based ABM must be able to spot, track, and destroy its targets extremely rapidly. For this purpose, it is thought that some form of beam weapon would be best, as the beam will travel at the speed of light (186,000 miles per second). It is also thought that the best time to destroy enemy missiles would be soon after they lift off, in their "boost phase," as it is easier to destroy the relatively thin-skinned missile than it is to destroy the hardened, bullet-like warheads. In addition, the number of targets to track and destroy is much lower in the boost phase, as the multiple warheads have not yet separated from the missile.

Problems with the System

However, "boost phase" interception and destruction creates certain serious problems for beam weapons. In order to hit enemy missiles in boost phase, the beam weapons must be in position to do so. This means they must be permanently in orbit. Most proposed beam weapons, however, would require very large power sources which would be extremely expensive to place in orbit and maintain. For much of the boost phase, enemy missiles will be in the Earth's atmosphere, as they streak skyward. Beam weapons' effectiveness is weakened by penetration of the atmosphere, however. Thus, the already brief period of time available before the warheads separate from their boosters is cut even further, making targeting and "battle management" far more difficult.

The variety of Soviet nuclear weapon systems presents further problems for a potential space-based ABM system. For example, how will we deal with the much shorter flight times of Soviet submarine-launched ballistic missiles? Given the mobility of Soviet submarines, will it be possible to accurately pre-position our space-based ABM system to cover all possible attack routes? In addition, if our potential beam weapons can not destroy low-flying targets, such as bomber aircraft and cruise missiles, how will we prevent these weapons from hitting American targets?

Soviet Weapon Changes

The problems listed above are based solely on what would be necessary to destroy attacking Soviet nuclear weapons as they are today. One also must consider what possible countermeasures the Soviets would employ. Clearly, there are numerous ways in which to interfere with the operation of such a complex system. Perhaps the simplest one would be to orbit "space mines," explosive satellites, adjacent to many of our space-based ABM platforms. Various jamming and deception techniques could be used to baffle the system's tracking and targeting equipment. Changes could be made in Soviet missiles themselves which could reduce or eliminate their vulnerability to beam weapons. There is one additional countermeasure that is the most fearful of all, but I will get back to that one in a short while.

Let us look at the feasibility question in a more colloquial way. How often do various items break down or malfunction in your daily life? Do the "options" on your car work consistently? How about your household electrical appliances? The computer in your office? Your town or city's traffic signals? Now consider the numerous technical problems our current military equipment is subject to. What about our space program? We have real trouble even keeping the heat shield tiles on the Space Shuttle, and the last two efforts to launch satellites from the Shuttle failed.

Technology Often Fails

The point is, technology fails, often. Does anyone honestly believe that a system as complex as the proposed space-based ABM will function as planned in what might minimally be termed a hostile environment? Man has not even been able to devise a highly effective, "leak proof," air defense system against airplanes that are "merely" supersonic!

Further, what are the consequences of space-based ABM system malfunction? The Pentagon planners call these consequences "leakage." "Leakage" means nuclear weapons, hundreds, perhaps thousands, striking U.S. territory. How many hundreds of billions of dollars are we willing to spend on a sieve in the sky?

If the proposed system is incapable of stopping virtually all incoming weapons, it does not provide a defense of our people against surprise attack. "Star Wars" will still be war, albeit probably the last in human history.

The goal of our national security policy, our strategic nuclear policy, should be the absolute prevention of nuclear war. There is no meaningful "damage limitation." There is no way to "prevail," to "restore the peace on terms favorable to us and our allies." The most important question we must ask is, will the pursuit of the President's plan make nuclear war less likely?. . .

Technology Not a Good Solution

Technology often has a life of its own. Because a system *can* be built, it often *is* built—and more often than not with totally unforeseen consequences. Basing the primary defense of a nation—or a civilization—on such a "technological development" hardly seems a satisfactory long-term solution to the arms race.

The Christian Science Monitor, February 19, 1985.

There is no compelling reason to do this, nor is there a good reason to do so. There is a better course for future U.S. security.

It has been said that what we need is a technical solution (a space-based ABM) for a technical problem (the strategic balance, the nuclear threat, the "defense" of America). I disagree.

Preventing Nuclear War

The threat of nuclear war is a human dilemma. President Reagan claims to have a vision of the future which offers hope, but his vision is a high-tech, quick-fix fantasy. The way to defend America is to prevent nuclear war, and the way to do this is to sign and ratify arms control accords that are in the interest of both superpowers.

The U.S. should strongly reaffirm its commitment to the ABM treaty and hold Moscow to its commitments. As a hedge against potential Soviet breakout from the treaty, the U.S. should continue prudent basic research on the various technologies with potential ABM applications. This we have been doing since the ratification of the treaty. The President's program would go far beyond this level of research activity, however, and probably end up irrevocably committing us to deployment of some kind of space-based ABM system.

224

The U.S. should seek to negotiate a treaty prohibiting weapons of all kinds from space. Extension of the arms race into outer space is in the interest of neither country in the long run. The way to solve an arms race problem is not to expand its scope. Rather, it is to begin to clearly and verifiably prohibit certain activities.

Star Wars: A Disservice

The recent national debate over our country's arms control and security policies has been constructive and healthy. The President's space weapons plans should be included in that debate, and be carefully scrutinized before they are voted on. Much of the debate on both issues, however, has focused on the merits of technical proposals and weapon systems. This preoccupation with technical detail has obscured the most important factor in avoiding nuclear disaster: our mutual ability to resolve crises—differences in human ambitions, goals, and ideologies—which could result in nuclear disaster.

The U.S. should seek innovative means to reduce the risk of nuclear war by accident or miscalculation, such as the establishment of a joint crisis communications center to provide direct communication in a nuclear confrontation.

In my view, the President has done a disservice to all those Americans who justifiably fear that we are sliding toward nuclear war. He has held out an illusory hope that somehow, through the wonders of advanced American technology, we can turn the clock back and make The Bomb go away. Well, it just isn't so. Unfounded hope for the future is no substitute for positive action today. The most positive action the Congress can take alone is to reject the President's request for his "Star Wars" fantasy now, before it is too late.

a critical thinking skill

Distinguishing Bias from Reason

The subject of nuclear war often generates great emotional responses in people. When dealing with such a highly controversial subject, many will allow their feelings to dominate their powers of reason. Thus, one of the most important basic thinking skills is the ability to distinguish between opinions based upon emotion or bias and conclusions based upon a rational consideration of the facts.

Most of the following statements are taken from the viewpoints in this chapter. The rest are taken from other sources. Consider each statement carefully. *Mark R for any statement you believe is based on reason or a rational consideration of the facts. Mark B for any statement you believe is based on bias, prejudice, or emotion. Mark I for any statement you think is impossible to judge.*

If you are doing this activity as the member of a class or group, compare your answers with those of other class or group members. Be able to defend your answers. You may discover that others will come to different conclusions than you. Listening to the rationale others present for their answers may give you valuable insights in distinguishing between bias and reason.

If you are reading this book alone, ask others if they agree with your answers. You too will find this interaction very valuable.

R = *a statement based upon reason*
B = *a statement based on bias*
I = *a statement impossible to judge*

1. Every reasonable man or woman on the planet carries about with him or her some vision of the nuclear nightmare.

2. Our current defense is merely the threat of blowing up millions of Russian people if their government decides first to blow up millions of Americans.

3. Replacing mutually assured destruction with a defensive system would represent a vast improvement.

4. Americans should be constantly on the alert for possibilities that can help reduce the nuclear peril.

5. The technical community agrees that space weapons will not work.

6. Any weapons system the US designs is sure to be imitated by the Soviets.

7. There is no hope that space weapons can make nuclear weapons obsolete.

8. The Soviets' concern over the possible deployment of star wars weaponry is evidence that it would make a good arms control bargaining chip.

9. If Star Wars can work, then the cost of deploying it should not be a consideration.

10. An imperfect space weapons system could still be valuable.

11. Space weapons technology has not been completely developed, so the weapons are still a long way from being workable.

12. The scientific consensus may be wrong when they say star wars cannot work.

13. Star Wars could launch an arms race in space.

14. Technology often fails.

15. Even with star wars, nuclear war would be devastating.

16. The way to defend America is to prevent nuclear war through arms control.

17. The Bomb will not go away.

18. Throughout history, new weapons have replaced outmoded systems.

Periodical Bibliography

The following list of periodical articles deals with the subject matter of this chapter.

Harry Anderson	"Let's Make a Deal," *Newsweek*, January 28, 1985.
George W. Ball	"The War for Star Wars," *New York Review of Books*, April 11, 1985.
Hans Bethe	"Why Star Wars Is Dangerous and Won't Work," *New York Review of Books*, February 14, 1985.
William E. Burrows	"Skywalking with Reagan," *Harper's*, January 1984.
	"Ballistic Missile Defense: The Illusion of Security," *Foreign Affairs*, Spring 1984.
Peter Clausen	"SDI In Search of a Mission," *World Policy Journal*, Spring 1985.
Congressional Digest	"The Star Wars Controversy," March 1985.
Daniel Deudney	"Forging Missiles into Spaceships," *World Policy Journal*, Spring 1985.
Bernard T. Feld	"End Space Race Now," *Bulletin of the Atomic Scientists*, October 1984.
Charles L. Glaser	"Star Wars Bad Even If It Works," *Bulletin of the Atomic Scientists*, March 1985.
John G. Hubbell	"Reducing the Risk of Nuclear War," *Reader's Digest*, November 1984.
Robert Jastrow	"The War Against Star Wars," *Current*, March/April 1985.
Robert Kleiman	"Hostage to 'Star Wars,'" *New York Times*, February 5, 1985.
National Review	"Incentive Structures and the Evil Empire," March 8, 1985.
James E. Oberg	"Andropov's Orbiting Bombs: The Soviets' Outer-Space 'Peace' Strategy," *Reason*, December 1983.
Ronald Reagan	"The Case for Star Wars," *U.S. News & World Report*, January 14, 1985.
William F. Rickenbacker	"The War Against Star Wars," *National Review*, January 11, 1985.

Society	"The Human Uses of Outer Space," January/February 1984.
Evan Thomas	"Bigger Bucks for Smarter Bombs: Big Ifs for Star Wars," *Time*, March 4, 1985.
Lewis Thomas	"Scientific Frontiers and National Frontiers: A Look Ahead," *Foreign Affairs*, Spring 1984.
E.P. Thompson	"The Real Meaning of Star Wars," *Nation*, March 9, 1985.
Time	"Star Wars: Pro and Con," October 29, 1985.
Time	"Wild Card on the Table," January 21, 1985.
Bruce L. Valley	"The Ultimate Defense," *Vital Speeches of the Day*, March 1, 1985.

Organizations to Contact

The editors have compiled the following list of organizations which are concerned with the issues debated in this book. All of them have publications or information available for interested readers. The descriptions are derived from materials provided by the organizations themselves.

American Civil Defense Association
PO Box 1057
Starke, FL 32091
(904) 964-5397

The Association supports civil defense programs and conducts national civil defense seminars. They give the annual American Preparedness Award to those who promote an adequate defense. ACDA publishes the *Journal of Civil Defense, TACDA Alert*, and *Technical Reports*.

American Enterprise Institute for Policy Research
1150 Seventeenth St. NW
Washington, DC 20036
(202) 862-5800

The Institute, founded in 1943, is a conservative think tank that researches a number of issues including foreign policy and defense. Their publications include *Foreign Policy and Defense Review, Public Opinion*, and several books and studies.

American Friends Service Committee
Rocky Flats Project, 1660 Lafayette
Denver, CO 80218
(303) 832-4508

The Committee supports arms control and opposes the Star Wars program. Their resource catalog includes the books *Nuclear Illusion and Reality, The Freeze Economy*, and *The Arms Race and Arms Control*. It also includes films such as *Survival. . . Or Suicide* and *In The Nuclear Shadow: What Can the Children Tell Us?* The Committee has a speakers bureau.

Americanism Educational League
PO Box 5986
Buena Park, CA 90622
(714) 828-5040

The League conducts public education to promote the private enterprise system and protect citizens' freedom from internal and external threats. It has available booklets, tracts, newspaper articles, and editorials on Soviet/American relations.

Arms Control and Disarmament Agency (ACDA)
Office of Public Affairs
320 Twenty-first St. NW
Washington, DC 20451
(202) 632-8714

ACDA is a government agency which deals with arms control. Their publications include *US Objectives, Negotiating Efforts and Problems of Soviet Noncompliance, Documents on Disarmament,* and *World Military Expenditures and Arms Transfers.* Their annual report outlines the progress of arms negotiations over the past year.

Brookings Institution
1775 Massachusetts Ave. NW
Washington, DC 20036
(202) 797-6000

The Institution, founded in 1927, is a non-partisan research organization which researches and publishes information on economics, government, foreign policy, and nuclear weapons. It publishes *Brookings Review* quarterly, *Brookings Papers on Economic Activity* biannually, and an annual report.

Center for Defense Information
303 Capitol Gallery West
600 Maryland Ave. SW
Washington, DC 20024
(202) 484-9490

The Center is an organization of former military personnel, educators, and public officials who advocate a strong defense but oppose excessive defense spending. They publish *The Defense Monitor* ten times a year, a Nuclear War Prevention Kit, and the film *War Without Winners.*

Center for the Study of Foreign Affairs
SA-3, Room C-3, Department of State
Washington, DC 20520
(703) 235-8830

The Center works to coordinate and encourage foreign affairs research, to make such research more relevant to the Department of State, and to conduct studies on international democratic institutions. Write to the Center for a list of publications.

Center for War/Peace Studies
218 Eighteenth St. E
New York, NY 10003
(212) 475-0850

The Center does in-depth research on disarmament and the Lebanon conflict. Their publications include the newsletter *Global Report*, a series of Special Studies on peace issues, and "The Binding Triad," a brochure.

Christian Anti-Communism Crusade
PO Box 890, 227 E. Sixth St.
Long Beach, CA 90801
(213) 437-0941

The Crusade, founded in 1953, sponsors anti-subversive seminars in several cities to inform Americans of the dangers of communism. Their newsletter is a semimonthly publication. They also publish books and pamphlets.

Coalition for a New Foreign and Military Policy
120 Maryland Ave. NE
Washington, DC 20002
(202) 546-8400

The coalition of religious, labor, civic, peace, and public interest organizations advocates a demilitarized, humanitarian, and non-interventionist foreign policy. It lobbies for arms control and disarmament measures, for cutting military spending, and for transferring money for nuclear weapons programs to social service programs. The Coalition publishes a quarterly newsletter, *Coalition Close Up* as well as Action Alerts and Action Guides on lobbying issues.

Committee for National Security (CNS)
2000 P St. NW, Suite 515
Washington, DC 20036
(202) 833-3140

The Committee is a nonpartisan group which promotes debate on the nature of national security, how to best achieve it, and how to avoid military confrontation. CNS publishes *CNS Reports* and has a fact sheet series, position papers and a Common Questions and Answers series available to subscribers.

Committee on the Present Danger
905 Sixteenth St. NW
Washington, DC 20006
(202) 628-2409

The Committee is a conservative educational organization devoted to the peace, security, and liberty of the US. It has published several materials on national security, including "Deterring Aggression" and "Nuclear Arms." The Committee's publications are listed in *Alerting America: The Papers of the Committee on the Present Danger.*

Council for a Livable World
11 Beacon St.
Boston, MA 02108
(617) 742-9395

The Council favors arms control and disarmament and is a co-sponsor of the conference on the medical effects of nuclear war. They lobby Congress on arms control issues, have two political action committees, a hotline on arms control legislation, and an internship program. The Council publishes *Factsheets* every month and *Reports* bimonthly.

Council for the Defense of Freedom
1275 K St. NW, Suite 1160
Washington, DC 20005
(202) 789-4294

The Council is an educational organization which disseminates information on communism in order to combat it and protect national security. They support the Star Wars and civil defense programs. Their weekly newspaper is the *Washington Inquirer* and they publish a monthly *Bulletin*.

Department of Defense (DOD)
Office of Public Affairs, Public Correspondence Division
Room 2E 777
Washington, DC 20037
(202) 545-6700

DOD is responsible for defending the country and maintaining the armed forces and military arsenal. The Department plans for the development of conventional and nuclear weapons. Write for a list of publications on nuclear arms.

Educators for Social Responsibility (ESR)
23 Garden St.
Cambridge, MA 02138
(617) 492-1764

ESR believes children's fears and questions about nuclear war must be responded to sensitively and directly. They research and evaluate educational materials, sponsor conferences and development programs for teachers, and offer speakers, workshops, and consulting services. They have developed the *Perspectives* and *Dialogue* curricula. Their quarterly newsletter about nuclear education is *Forum*.

Emergency Planning Committee
13 Firstfield Rd.
Gaithersburg, MD 20878
(301) 948-0922

The Committee acts as a liaison between civil defense associations in the US and other countries and is an arm of the International Association of Chiefs of Police. They prepare recommendations for coordinating police and civil defense efforts in disasters.

Fellowship of Reconciliation (FOR)
PO Box 271
Nyack, NY 10960
(914) 358-4601

FOR is a pacifist organization of people from several religions who promote arms control efforts. FOR has a US-USSR Reconciliation Program and publishes pamphlets, books, and the monthly *Fellowship*.

Foundation for Economic Education
30 S. Broadway
Irvington-on-Hudson, NY 10533
(914) 591-7230

The Foundation sponsors research on free market theory and limited government. They support the Star Wars program. Their publications are the monthly *Freeman*, and several pamphlets and papers including "Communism and Capitalism" and "Space Exploration and Development."

Heritage Foundation
214 Massachusetts Ave. NE
Washington, DC 20002
(202) 546-4400

The Foundation is a research institute "dedicated to limited government, individual and economic freedom and a strong national defense." It supports civil defense, meaningful arms control, and the proposed Star Wars program. Heritage publishes research in various formats on national defense, including the monthly *National Security Record* and the quarterly *Policy Review*, in addition to several papers and studies.

High Frontier
1010 Vermont Ave. NW, Suite 1000
Washington, DC 20005
(202) 737-4979

High Frontier advocates using space for commercial and defensive military purposes as a way to protect Americans and their property. They have published the book and brochure, *High Frontier: A New National Strategy.*

Institute for Defense and Disarmament Studies
2001 Beacon St.
Brookline, MA 02146
(617) 734-4216

The Institute advocates confining the military to defensive purposes as a way to move toward disarmament. They compile information on worldwide military forces and policies. Their annual publications are the *American Peace Directory* and the survey *World Military Forces.* They also publish a monthly looseleaf reference journal, *Arms Control Reporter*, and several studies on freezing nuclear weapons and disarmament.

Institute for Policy Studies (IPS)
1901 Q St. NW
Washington, DC 20009
(202) 234-9382

IPS is a center for research, education, and social intervention which sponsors analysis of US policy and proposes alternative strategies. The Institute has several books available including *Nuclear Arms and Disarmament, Dubious Specter: A Skeptical Look at the Soviet Nuclear Threat*, and *US/USSR Exchange on Disarmament.* They also have books on third world development and human rights.

Institute for Space and Security Studies (ISSS)
7720 Mary Cassatt Dr.
Potomac, MD 20854
(301) 983-1484

ISSS believes the Star Wars space defense system is a waste of money and would encourage rather than prevent nuclear war. They publish news releases and issue papers to teach the public and Congress about space weapons.

International Physicians for the Prevention of Nuclear War (IPPNW)
225 Longwood Ave.
Boston, MA 02115
(617) 738-9404

IPPNW, an international organization of physicians who work to focus attention on the medical consequences of nuclear war, consider civil defense unrealistic and dangerous. They distribute *Last Aid: The Medical Dimensions of Nuclear War*. IPPNW publications include the semiannual *Newsletter* and annual *Congress Proceedings*.

National Coordinating Council on Emergency Management
3126 Beltline Blvd., Suite 101
Columbia, SC 29204
(803) 765-9286

The Council is a coordinating body of local, state, and federal civil defense agencies that develops comprehensive disaster relief programs. They publish a monthly *Bulletin* and the quarterly *Emergency Management Review*.

National Emergency Management Association (NEMA)
110 E. Adams St.
Springfield, IL 62706
(217) 782-2700

NEMA conducts specialized civil defense education programs on a state level. They are affiliated with the National Governor's Association. NEMA has a speakers bureau and publishes a quarterly newsletter.

Physicians for Social Responsibility (PSR)
639 Massachusetts Ave.
Cambridge, MA 02139
(617) 491-2754

PSR works to halt and reverse the arms race in the belief that nuclear war cannot be survived, limited, or won. They hold symposia and publish materials on the medical effects of nuclear weapons and nuclear war. PSR maintains a resource center and publishes a quarterly newsletter.

Policy Studies Organization
University of Illinois at Urbana-Champaign
361 Lincoln Hall, 706 S. Wright St.
Urbana, IL 61801
(217) 359-8541

The Organization promotes the application of political and social sciences to important policy problems. It publishes the quarterly *Policy Studies Journal*, the *Policy Studies Review*, and directories.

Rockford Institute
934 N. Main St.
Rockford, IL 61103
(815) 964-5053

The Rockford Institute is a conservative research center which studies capitalism and liberty. It publishes three periodicals, *Chronicles of Culture*, *The Rockford Papers*, and *Persuasion at Work*. The Institute has also published occasional papers on nuclear freeze and antinuclear activism in the United States.

SANE, Committee for a Sane Nuclear Policy
711 G St. SE
Washington, DC 20003
(202) 546-7100

SANE opposes excessive military spending and favors nuclear disarmament. Their activities include lobbying, grassroots organizing, and public education. They publish a monthly newsletter, *SANE World*, and have a slide show, *The Race Nobody Wins*.

Union of Concerned Scientists
26 Church St.
Cambridge, MA 02238
(617) 547-5552

The Union researches the impact of advanced technology on society and advocates peace through arms control. They have several publications on nuclear weapons available, including two reports and videotapes on space weapons. They also have briefing manuals, *A Collection of Materials on Nuclear Weapons and Arms Control* and *No-First-Use Study*, in addition to the *Choices: A Unit on Conflict and Nuclear War* curriculum. The UCS has a fact sheet on MX missiles and "The Arms Control Debate" brochure. Write for a complete listing of their publications.

Annotated Book Bibliography

Ruth Adams and Susan Cullen, eds.	*The Final Epidemic: Physicians and Scientists On Nuclear War.* Chicago: The Educational Foundation for Nuclear Science, 1981. Doctors and scientists express the horrors and complications that a nuclear war would represent.
Robert C. Aldridge	*First Strike!: The Pentagon's Strategy for Nuclear War.* Boston: South End Press, 1983. Expands on the premise that the US plans to initiate a nuclear war.
Ian Bellany	*The Verification of Arms Control Agreements.* London: Cass, 1984. Examines the growing number of gray areas in arms control verification and the problems created by politics and treaty compliance.
Ben Bova	*Assured Survival: Putting the Star Wars Defense in Perspective.* Boston: Houghton Mifflin Company, 1984. Promotes the idea that through the star wars defense program, a world without the horror of nuclear war is within our grasp.
Helen Caldicott	*Missile Envy.* New York: William Morrow & Company, Inc., 1984. An eloquent plea for arms control.
Helen Caldicott	*Nuclear Madness: What You Can Do!* New York: Bantam Books, 1980. Graphic depictions of the bombs dropped on Hiroshima and Nagasaki make a convincing case for the idea that nuclear war cannot be survived.
Eric Chivian, Susanna Chivian, Robert Jay Lifton, and John E. Mack, eds.	*Last Aid: The Medical Dimensions of Nuclear War.* San Francisco: W.H. Freeman & Company, 1982. Collection of essays by physicians on the medical atrocities posed by a nuclear war; haunting photos.
Bruce Clayton	*Thinking About Survival.* Boulder, CO: Paladin Press, 1984. A collection of essays by this well-known survivalist provides a unique perspective on the issue of nuclear war.

Committee on the Atmospheric Effects of Nuclear Explosions	*The Effects on the Atmosphere of a Major Nuclear Exchange.* Washington, DC: National Academy Press, 1985. Report compiled at the request of the Defense Department to analyze effects of a nuclear war. The study confirmed the Sagan report of a nuclear winter.
Ann Marie Cunningham and Mariana Fitzpatrick	*Weapons for the Apocalypse.* New York: Warner Books, 1983. A gripping exposé of the nuclear weapons industry. Includes an interesting chapter on nuclear weapons accidents.
Defense Intelligence Agency	*Soviet Military Space Doctrine.* Pamphlet available from the Defense Intelligence Agency, Washington, DC, 20301-6111. Documents Soviet plans to militarize space and emphasizes that the US needs a comparable space military defense.
Joseph D. Douglass, Jr. and Amoretta M. Hoeber	*Soviet Strategy for Nuclear War.* Stanford, CA: A Hoover Institution Publication, 1979. The book dissects Soviet government policies and pronouncements and concludes that the US has much to fear from a surprise Soviet first strike.
Freeman Dyson	*Weapons and Hope.* New York: Harper and Row, 1984. A unique approach to understanding weapons technology. Documents with historical examples that new weapons are developed in the hope that they will bring peace.
Paul R. Ehrlich, Carl Sagan, et al., eds.	*The Cold and the Dark.* New York: W.W. Norton & Company, 1984. A collection of essays on nuclear winter.
Lawrence Freedman	*The Evolution of Nuclear Strategy.* New York: The International Institute for Strategic Studies, 1983. Analyzes nuclear strategy from a historical perspective, including the concept of fighting a limited nuclear war.
Joseph Gerson, ed.	*The Deadly Connection: Nuclear War & US Intervention.* Pamphlet available from the American Friends Service Committee, 2161 Massachusetts Ave., Cambridge, MA, 02160. A collection of essays by prominent people emphasizing how US intervention in other countries could begin a nuclear war with the Soviet Union.

Peter Goodwin	*Nuclear War: The Facts on Our Survival.* New York: The Rutledge Press, 1981. Excellent overview on the effects of nuclear weapons. Helpful glossary and bibliography included.
David O. Graham and Gregory A. Fossedal	*A Defense That Defends: Blocking Nuclear Attack.* Old Greenwich, CT: Devin-Adair Publishers, 1983. The man behind the star wars concept shows how star wars can be implemented with existing technology.
Ground Zero	*Nuclear War: What's in it for You?* New York: Pocket Books, 1982. A tongue-in-cheek book of the ABCs of nuclear war.
Mark A. Harwell	*Nuclear Winter: The Human and Environmental Consequences of Nuclear War.* New York: Springer-Verlag, 1984. A rather technical yet informative study of the effects of a nuclear winter.
Gregg Herken	*Counsels of War.* New York: Alfred A. Knopf, 1984. Documents nuclear strategy since 1945 and gives the overwhelming feeling that policy is generated by chance and emotion.
Thomas Karas	*The New High Ground.* New York: Simon & Schuster, 1983. An overview of the proposed star wars system.
Cresson H. Kearney	*Nuclear War Survival Skills.* Coos Bay, OR: Nuclear War Survival Research Bureau, 1982. A survival manual *par excellence*: Everything you wanted to know about surviving a nuclear war, from building your own shelter to US maps showing where the fallout would be.
George F. Kennan	*The Nuclear Delusion: Soviet-American Relations in the Atomic Age.* New York: Pantheon Books, 1982. This collection of essays spanning a 40-year period is an interesting commentary on Soviet-American tensions and the possibility of nuclear war.
Roman Kolkowicz and Nick Joock, eds.	*Arms Control and International Security.* Boulder, CO: Westview Press, 1984. A wide variety of articles on the necessity of arms control.

Jennifer Leaning	*Civil Defense in the Nuclear Age*. Pamphlet available from Physicians for Social Responsibility, 639 Massachusetts Ave., Cambridge, MA, 02139. Interesting critique of the nation's civil defense plan. Good bibliography of pro/con civil defense articles.
Ernest W. Lefever, ed.	*The Apocalyptic Premise: Nuclear Arms Debated*. Washington, DC: Ethics and Public Policy Center, 1982. One of the best books available on nuclear arms because of its diversity of opinion. Thirty-one essays by statesmen, scholars, religious leaders, and others provide pros and cons on a variety of nuclear arms issues.
Edward Myers	*The Chosen Few: Surviving the Nuclear Holocaust*. South Bend, IN: And Books, 1982. A fascinating examination of the nation's survivalists. Chronicals their view that nuclear war is imminent and makes survival preparation essential.
T.F. Nieman	*Better Read Than Dead*. Boulder, CO: Paladin Press, 1981. An in-depth look at nuclear war survival.
Patrick O'Heffernan, Amery B. Lovins, and L. Hunter Lovins	*The First Nuclear World War*. New York: William Morrow and Company, 1983. Starts with the premise that a nuclear war is most likely to begin somewhere in the third world, and presents ideas as to how to prevent it.
Bernard J. O'Keefe	*Nuclear Hostages*. Boston: Houghton Mifflin Company, 1983. An excellent history of our nation's fascination with nuclear weapons.
Office of Technology Assessment	*The Effects of Nuclear War*. Washington, DC: Government Printing Office, 1979. Original government report on the effects of nuclear war. Interesting for its unusual view that simple steps can prevent casualties.
Jeannie Peterson, ed.	*The Aftermath: The Human and Ecological Consequences of Nuclear War*. New York: Pantheon Books, 1983. A variety of scientific and medical opinions document the horrors of nuclear war. Interspersed with shocking photographs of Hiroshima and Nagasaki.

Physicians for Social Responsibility	*Civil Defense in the 80's: Key Aspects of the Debate on Civil Defense.* Cambridge, MA: Physicians for Social Responsibility, 1983. An amazing collection of articles on both sides of the civil defense issue.
Richard Pipes	*Survival Is Not Enough.* New York: Simon & Schuster, 1984. Presents the view that the Soviet Union is out for world domination. Thus, the US needs to keep a constant military vigil to make sure the Soviets never reach nuclear superiority and threaten the US with annihilation.
Richard Pipes	*U.S.-Soviet Relations in the Era of Detente.* Boulder, CO: Westview Press, 1981. Collection of essays discussing the very real possibility that the Russians will begin a nuclear war.
James Pournelle	*There Will Be War.* New York: Tom Doherty Associates, 1983. Interesting collection of fiction that emphasizes nuclear war themes.
Peter Pringle and William Arkin	*The Secret US Plan for Nuclear War.* New York: W.W. Norton, 1983. Fascinating expose of the nation's contingency plans for nuclear war and their history.
Robert Scheer	*With Enough Shovels: Reagan, Bush, and Nuclear War.* New York: Random House, 1982. Chronicles embarrassing statements made by top US officials on the survivability of a nuclear war. The book has been severely criticized for quoting out of context, but nevertheless provides for amusing reading.
Richard F. Starr	*Arms Control: Myth versus Reality.* Stanford: Hoover Press, 1984. A collection of articles focusing on past, present, and future arms control questions by some of the leading experts in the field.
Strobe Talbott	*Deadly Gambits.* New York: Alfred A. Knopf, 1984. An exposé of the Reagan administration and its arms control policies, and the way in which they take us to the brink of nuclear war.
L.B. Taylor	*Space: Battleground of the Future?* New York: Franklin Watts, 1983. An overview of the issue of space weapons. Technical, ethical, and political implications are discussed.

Union of Concerned
Scientists

The Fallacy of Star Wars. New York: Vintage
Books, 1984. This well-written analysis of
the star wars program vehemently
declares it a disaster. Good diagrams.

James Woolsey, ed.

Nuclear Arms: Ethics, Strategy, Politics. San
Francisco: ICS Press, 1984. A variety of
perspectives on arms control, high frontier,
and ethical issues of the arms race.

Edward Zuckerman

*The Day After World War III: The US
Government's Plans for Surviving a Nuclear
War*. New York: Viking Press, 1984.
Examines federal emergency planning
measures designed to maintain government
integrity following a nuclear attack.

Index

attitude toward national
  defense, 90-91
doomsday predictions of, 89,
  125-126
harmfulness of, 91, 100
importance of, 97
misguided nature of, 88-89
seriousness of, 35, 38
Soviet influence in, 174
Physicians for Social
  Responsibility, 75, 92, 99, 128,
  130, 236
Pipes, Richard, 22, 26
Podhoretz, Norman, 163
Powers, Thomas, 205
proliferation
  and disarmament, 35-37
  as cause of nuclear war, 34-38
  US responsibility for, 37
  ways to stop, 37-38
psychic numbing, 82-83

radiation, 66-72, 74-79
  American attitude toward, 94
  dangers of
    cancer, 93-94, 102
    contamination, 104-105, 133
    environmental, 118-120
    genetic, 93-94
    sickness from, 95, 114, 133
  fallout from, 113, 118
  penetration of, 114
Reagan, Ronald, 173

Sagan, Carl, 80, 97-98
  TTAPS report, 81-85
    fallacies of, 87-91
    lack of data for, 90
    motives of, 88-89
SALT treaties, 98, 155-156, 166,
  172, 182
Scheer, Robert, 167
Schell, Jonathan, 78, 91, 117
Schlafly, Phyllis, 114
Schlesinger, James, 20
Sincere, Richard B., 127
Sloss, Leon, 207
Smith, Gerard, 198
Sokolovskii, V.D., 24
Soviet Union
  American trade with, 184-185
  and arms negotiations, 162

and space weapons, 202,
  205-206, 211
benefits from disarmament, 88
civil defense of, 135-146
defensive weapons of, 209
enemies of, 142
fears of invasion, 174
history of, 48-49
internal affairs, American
  interference in, 167
leadership of
  sanity of, 144
US assumptions about, 195
nuclear strategy of, 209-210
nuclear superiority of, 174
secrecy of, 185
strategic intentions of, 49-50
weapons of
  US knowledge about, 182
  and concealing, 183
  submarines, 183-184
space shuttle, 223
space weapons, 190-225
  and eliminating nuclear war
    impossibility of, 198-202
    possibility of, 192-197
  and national defense, 193-196
  and peace movement, 195, 197
  and Pentagon generals, 195, 197
  arms control more effective
    than, 204-205, 224
  as defense
    of people, 195, 200, 204, 206,
      210, 212
    of weapons, 206, 212, 218
  as giving US first-strike
    advantage, 206
  as stabilizing, 215
  effectiveness of, 215-219
  impact on arms negotiations,
    203-206, 212
  monitoring of, 178-179
  NATO reaction to, 208
  negotiations on, 167, 171
  opposition to, 208, 210
  potential of, 207-212, 215,
    218-219, 225
  problems of
    accelerating arms race, 167,
      202
    cost, 202, 205, 208, 217-218,
      221

248